A Leader and a Laggard

Advanced countries in all parts of the world are concerned with the geographical unevenness of their development. Canada's preoccupation is with the Atlantic provinces, and for years government departments and agencies have tried to improve the region's economy. However, the evidence suggests that the economic gap between the Atlantic provinces and the rest of Canada has remained remarkably constant.

This persistent gap has no shortage of explanations: lack of resources, the cost of transportation, insufficient markets, and a poor supply of skilled labour are problems often mentioned. This study investigates how far these and other factors account for slow industrial development.

The author compares two regions of Canada: Quebec and Ontario, which together are considered the industrial leader; and Nova Scotia, the industrial laggard. He compares the costs of inputs for an average manufacturing firm in Nova Scotia from 1946 to 1962 with what those costs would have been had the firm been located in the Quebec-Ontario region. The analysis includes relative wage rates, labour productivity, the costs of materials, energy, and fuel, rates of interest and investment, transportation charges, levels of local taxation, and the supply of business enterprise. Canadian official statistics form the main basis of the comparisons, but where these are inadequate, information derived from three special studies carried out by the author is used.

Dr George then explores the implications of the study's findings for public policy. He examines the relative cost and effectiveness of tax concessions, capital grants, industrial estates, transportation subsidies, and other remedial measures often advocated.

Although the book uses a case study approach involving just two regions, it is relevant to the general theory of the location of industry, to regional economic policies, and to industrial development. It is essential reading for politicians and public servants who shape regional policies; for industrial promotion managers of municipalities; for businessmen choosing sites of new enterprises, and the consultants who advise them; for academics concerned with the theoretical aspects of the location of industry; and for anyone interested in industrial development.

ROY E. GEORGE was born in England and received a PH D from the University of London. He has been teaching since 1960 and is at present Professor of Commerce, Dalhousie University.

T0335247

University of Toronto Press

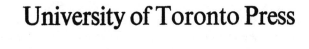

A Leader and a Laggard

Manufacturing Industry in Nova Scotia, Quebec and Ontario

Roy E. George

ATLANTIC PROVINCES STUDIES

A series of studies, edited by John F. Graham, sponsored by the Social Science Research Council of Canada, and published with financial assistance from the Canada Council.

1 Fiscal Adjustment and Economic Development: A Case Study of Nova Scotia. BY JOHN F. GRAHAM

2 A Leader and a Laggard: Manufacturing Industry in Nova Scotia, Quebec and Ontario. BY ROY E. GEORGE

© University of Toronto Press 1970

Reprinted in paperback 2017

University of Toronto Press, Toronto and Buffalo

ISBN 978-0-8020-1695-9 (cloth)

ISBN 978-1-4875 9895-2 (paper)

Preface

All the advanced countries of the world are nowadays concerned with the geographical unevenness of their development. The United States is disturbed about Appalachia, Britain worries over Scotland, Italy frets over Sardinia. All try in one way or another to steer economic activity from their more prosperous to their less prosperous areas.

Canada's main preoccupation is with the Atlantic provinces, which comprise Newfoundland, Prince Edward Island, Nova Scotia, and New Brunswick. Various government departments and agencies have for years been engaged in programmes designed to improve the situation in that region. To date there is little evidence that they have achieved very much, unless one believes that the situation would have deteriorated further without their efforts. Perhaps their lack of success has been because the locational disadvantages are greater than was realized and the various programmes have consequently been inadequate; or perhaps the programmes have been big enough but have been badly designed. No one seems to know for certain. Economic science, which should underpin such programmes and explain their successes and failures, is unequal to its task. The theory of the location of industry is not in a very satisfactory state and empirical evidence is scanty and inconclusive. Economists will have to do a lot more work before they will be able to guide with certainty the hand of the politician as he tries to steer new activity into regions which seem in most need of it.

This study is intended as a contribution to the store of knowledge on this subject. It takes the form of a comparison of two regions of Canada which have demonstrated very different rates of growth. We shall not range over the whole of economic activity in the two regions, but shall, for reasons to be discussed in chapter 1, confine our attention to manufacturing industry.

The choice of Ontario for the role of the leader will not come as any great surprise since it is industrially the most highly developed province of Canada, producing half of Canada's output of manufactured goods. It is true that it is a vast heterogeneous area comprising all types of terrain ranging from wilderness to the richest agricultural land in Canada; habitation patterns vary from boisterous cities to sleepy rural communities; and economic conditions are such that affluence and grinding poverty exist side by side. And, for this reason, one might have preferred to select a particular part of Ontario as the basis of comparison. However, every area which might have been taken is heterogeneous and there is no criterion to help one decide where to stop once one starts chopping up a province. Also, and of supreme importance, sub-provincial statistics in Canada are inadequate, and thus the extent to which economic research can be concentrated on districts of a province is restricted.

The decision to lump Quebec in with Ontario requires more justification. Though they have a common history of economic development – from furs to lumber to agriculture to mining to manufacturing – the two, when combined, make up a truly enormous and varied area. Quebec is a poorer province than Ontario; indeed, Gaspésie, near the eastern fringe of Quebec, gives the economic planners as much cause for concern as do the Atlantic provinces. And Quebec is less highly industrialized than Ontario. However, there were two main reasons for considering them as one unit. First, Canada's great belt of industry stretches from Windsor in southwestern Ontario to Quebec City; to have divided it merely because of a political boundary seemed unjustifiable. And, secondly, certain important statistical information for the combined region is not available for the individual provinces. The Board of Transport Commissioners' *Waybill Analysis* presents figures only for a zone which coincides fairly closely with Quebec and Ontario combined; and one of the special studies (the Multiplant Firm Study) upon which my analysis will have to rely to fill gaps in official statistics could not provide separate information for each province because of the small number of firms qualified for inclusion in that study.

The laggard area with which the Quebec-Ontario region will be compared is Nova Scotia. This is not because it is the best example of an industrially backward area in Canada (it leads the other three Atlantic provinces in manufacturing output per capita), but mainly for historical reasons.[1] Though relatively small, it was, only a century or

1 A subsidiary reason, but of considerable practical importance, was that I lived in Nova Scotia and found research in the province easier than it would have been elsewhere.

so ago, as prosperous a region as any in the country which is now Canada and could boast of many healthy little manufacturing industries. But while Quebec-Ontario developed into the industrial core of Canada, Nova Scotia's manufacturing sector became less and less significant. Not that we shall try to explain why this happened. Others have sought to do so;[2] but even if they have really discovered the truth, their explanations do not necessarily tell us why Nova Scotia's industrial development continues to lag. Conditions have changed so much during the last century (in particular, the types of commodities produced, the speed of communication, the cost of transportation, and the sources of power) that there is no reason to assume that the factors which were important in 1850 remain the determinants of industrial location today.

We shall confine our attention to the post–Second World War period until 1962. During this period, Nova Scotia did not manage even to hold on to its already lowly position, despite the continuous efforts of governments to revive it.

For this there is no shortage of explanations. Some observers stress the absence of a pool of skilled labour, the low productivity of workers, the shortage of good-calibre executives, the high cost of getting materials into and products out of such an isolated region, the lack of enterprise of the local population, and so on; but other observers will accept none of this, claiming rather that labour is plentiful, intelligent, industrious, and low-priced, that the splendid local educational facilities turn out men of the stuff from which first-class executives can be made, that transportation costs are nowadays of relatively little importance to many industries, that the long list of Nova Scotians who have reached the top in Canadian business and public life shows that any lack of business enterprise is due to a shortage of opportunities rather than to the absence of an adventurous streak, and so on. In the chapters that follow we shall be testing these and other assertions against the available evidence.

Acknowledgments conventionally occupy a part of every preface. However, I have relied so heavily on the help of so many people that my

2 For instance, R. E. Caves and R. H. Holton, *The Canadian Economy: Prospect and Retrospect* (Cambridge, Mass., 1959), explain it in terms of the types of primary industry for which the two regions were naturally suited. The larger, more fertile areas in Quebec and Ontario provided raw materials on which the millers, the leather tanners, the meat curers, the distillers, and others could thrive. The fruit and fish of Nova Scotia provided few opportunities for further processing and only lumber offered material which might have formed a basis for manufacturing.

thanks to them are intended in no way to be mere formalities. Without them, I should have had to struggle along much more slowly than I did, I should have had to make do with much less adequate information than I had, and I should have fallen into even more errors than I have. Hundreds of executives in Nova Scotia, Quebec, and Ontario took time out from their busy schedules to answer questions about their firms' policies and costs. Professor John F. Graham, a colleague of mine at Dalhousie University, was a constant source of encouragement in his capacity as general editor of the Atlantic Provinces Studies series, and together with three other of my colleagues, Professors A. Milton Moore, Norman H. Morse, and Alasdair M. Sinclair, read drafts and helped me to avoid many errors. The staff of Dalhousie's computer centre processed a considerable volume of data for me. Miss B. J. McGinn, Mr J. W. Graham, and Mr B. S. Lesser acted as research assistants. Miss Zilpha Linkletter of the Nova Scotia Department of Trade and Industry gave me the benefit of her great store of knowledge of the economic structure of the province. Mr Craig Dickson of the Maritimes Transportation Commission helped with information on transportation matters. My wife and two young daughters bore with admirable restraint my absence from the family while the book was in preparation, and undertook some of the arithmetic chores and proofreading. Mr Gerald Hallowell edited the manuscript for the book with expertise, insight, and good humour. To all of them, and to those others whom I cannot name personally, I offer my most grateful thanks.

I acknowledge permission from l'Institut de Science économique appliquée to use material from my article "Coûts de production dans les localisations distinctes : comparaison entre la Nouvelle-Ecosse, l'Ontario et le Québec"; and from the Department of Industry for permission to use the contents of a report I prepared in 1967.

This book has been published with the help of a grant from the Social Science Research Council of Canada, using funds provided by the Canada Council.

Dalhousie University   R. E. G.

Halifax, Nova Scotia

December 1969

Contents

Tables

Part One
Introduction

1 The Background

SIZE AND POSITION

Even Canadians often lose sight of the vastness of their country. The Quebec-Ontario region occupies just about one million square miles – an area nearly as big as Britain, Scandinavia, the Common Market countries, Spain, and Portugal, all put together. It extends from the Lake of the Woods in the west to the Strait of Belle Isle in the east, and from the tip of the Niagara Peninsula in the south to Cape Wolstenholme at the head of Hudson Bay. Montreal, its largest city and biggest port, is a thousand miles from the Atlantic.

By comparison, Nova Scotia is tiny. It is a little strip of land about 370 miles long and between sixty and a hundred miles wide running roughly southwest to northeast and covering a mere twenty-one thousand square miles (about 40 per cent of the size of England). The peninsula is joined to the province of New Brunswick by the Isthmus of Chignecto and juts out into the Atlantic only twenty-five hundred miles from Britain, which puts it nearer to Europe than to Canada's own west coast. Until Newfoundland joined Confederation in 1949, Nova Scotia had the geographical distinction of being Canada's most easterly province. It consists principally of two parts: the smaller, Cape Breton Island, lies to the northeast and is separated from the rest of the province (the "mainland" as Cape Bretoners call it) by the Strait of Canso. The two parts have been joined since 1955 by the world's deepest causeway.

CLIMATE

Extending from about 57°w to 95°w and from 42°N to 63°N, Quebec and Ontario encompass very different climatic regions. The St Lawrence and Great Lakes region, by far the most economically important, has warm summers (the June average is about 75°F) which are sometimes accompanied by sweltering humidity brought in by moist air from the south, and fairly cold winters (the January average is about 20°F); its spring seasons are very short but the autumns are usually long and pleasant; about forty inches of precipitation are evenly distributed throughout the year – most of it as rain, though some parts (the Laurentians behind Quebec City are the best example) receive one hundred inches or more of snow. In the western part approaching the border with Manitoba, the climate becomes mid-continental and more extreme. The north around Hudson Bay is subarctic, with long winters reaching a monthly average of about −15° F and short summers which have a monthly average of around 45°F; precipitation in this region is only about fifteen inches, the major part falling in the summer.

As one would expect, Nova Scotia, being under the influence of the sea, has a more equitable climate than Quebec and Ontario. Average temperatures for January and July are about 25°F and 65°F, the range widening somewhat as one goes northwest. Considering it has much the same latitude as Mediterranean France, these temperatures are rather low. For this Nova Scotians can thank the winds which blow from the cold interior of the continent in the winter and from the cool ocean in the summer, and the influence of the Labrador Current which sweeps down the coast forcing the Gulf Stream out into the ocean. The meeting of these two currents results in considerable amounts of fog at some times of the year, because the winds pick up moisture as they blow over the warm Gulf Stream and then are cooled as they pass over the Labrador Current. Indeed, by Quebec-Ontario standards, Nova Scotia has a generally moist climate, receiving precipitation of about fifty-five inches, evenly distributed throughout the year, about one-fifth of it falling as snow.

LAND SURFACE

The Quebec-Ontario region falls into four distinct parts. Gaspésie and the eastern part of the Eastern Townships belong to the Appalachian zone. This is the hilliest part of the region, Mt Jacques Cartier in the Gaspé Peninsula rising to a little over four thousand feet, but it does contain some quite good arable land. Adjoining this to the west are the sloping lowlands of the St Lawrence and Great Lakes area. They are very fertile and suitable for intensive agriculture, particularly in the Niagara Peninsula. They support livestock and crops like fruit, vegetables, tobacco, and fodder. Around the southwestern side of Hudson Bay there is a plain of poorly drained clay, most of which is unsuitable for agriculture because of both its soil and its climate. The remaining 80 per cent of the region consists of the Canadian Shield – a vast rolling plateau which approaches three thousand feet in only one or two isolated places and consists almost entirely of rock and poor soil.

Nova Scotia belongs to the Appalachian region and is rather similar in terrain to the Gaspé area of Quebec. A backbone of hills of complicated pattern runs almost its whole length, reaching a height of about 1,750 feet in Cape Breton. The soil in the Annapolis Valley is quite good by any standard, and around Truro there is good grazing; but nowhere are there large stretches of good agricultural land like those found in the Niagara Peninsula. Over much of the province, the land surface is badly drained, stony, and acid.

NATURAL RESOURCES

The Quebec-Ontario region is rich in natural resources. Animal wildlife was the main attraction to early European settlers, but exploitation was so thorough that trapping is now of very minor importance. In his second stage of exploitation of natural resources, man cleared the great stands of hardwood which used to cover southern Ontario. However, vast reserves of forest still remain in the rest of the region. Some are mixed forests which include hemlock, maple, and cedar but most nowadays comprise mainly softwood such as white and red pine, spruce, aspen, and birch. The Canadian Shield gave man his third source of natural wealth. It is a great storehouse of mineral resources containing large known reserves of almost every important mineral except coal and tin, and no doubt it still holds undiscovered treasure. It supplies most of the world's nickel and is a major source of gold, silver, copper, zinc, iron, platinum, and uranium. Deposits of copper are also worked in Gaspé, and the Sherbrooke area supplies 35 per cent of the world's output of asbestos. Even the absence of coal from the list has not proved serious since the region contains enormous reserves of water power and hydro-electricity is generally available. Finally, the lakes and rivers yield appreciable supplies of fish – whitefish, trout, herring, and pickerel – though the Gaspé is the only part of the region which relies on fishing to any great extent.

Nova Scotia is comparatively poor in natural resources. Its wildlife has never been commercially important; it has some minerals – coal, gypsum, salt, and barytes – but all are of the low-value variety; its forests, which cover 80 per cent of the province, yield modest supplies of lumber and enough pulpwood to support a sizable pulp industry, but they are modest compared with the vast reserves of the Quebec-Ontario region. Only in three respects can Nova Scotia challenge Quebec-Ontario's overwhelming superiority in natural assets. First, it has easy access to plentiful stores of sea products. The great continental shelf of some seventy thousand square miles, which extends from the south of Newfoundland to the southwest of Nova Scotia, is one of the world's major fishing grounds. Cod, haddock, redfish, plaice, sole, and halibut are the principal deep-sea yield, while lobsters, scallops, clams, and oysters are the most important inshore catch. Second, it can boast of several excellent deep-water ports which, unlike the principal ones in Quebec-Ontario, are ice-free the year round. The chief port, Halifax, has a truly magnificent harbour which could probably handle the largest ships which are afloat or now under construction. And, third, there is the natural beauty, which must be considered a commercial asset since it is important for tourism and as a lure for industry. On one side of the province is the ruggedness of the Atlantic coast, made more attractive by the picturesque fishing villages which occupy many of its bays; on the other are the pleasant valleys of the Bay of Fundy and the Northumberland Strait. The area between is mainly lakes and woods. The scars of urban agglomeration are few and small. These characteristics, together with a climate which is equitable by North American standards and a smallness which puts a great variety of landscape within a few hours' drive, make it a pleasant place in which to work and vacation.

SETTLEMENT AND PRE-CONFEDERATION
DEVELOPMENT

Jacques Cartier claimed Gaspé for France in 1543 but the first permanent settlement in Quebec[1] had to await the early years of the seventeenth century when Champlain founded what was to become Quebec

___

1 Quebec was an ill-defined region even into the nineteenth century. At one time it included a good slice of the United States, but in 1763 its boundary was pushed back to the 45th parallel. It formally became the province of Quebec in that year, but was in fact limited mainly to the height of land north of the St Lawrence River except during the periods when it also took in what is now Ontario. Bit by bit, its northern boundary has been extended to the Hudson Strait.

City. After 1663 the French government made a determined effort to attract immigrants, but with limited success; by 1763 its population was still only about sixty-five thousand. Ontario[2] was visited by Hudson and Brûlé in 1610 and 1613 respectively, but was still a fur trader's wilderness in 1763. After the British conquest, the flow of immigrants to the two provinces quickened: settlers were brought in as a convenient return cargo for boats which took lumber to Europe, and United Empire Loyalists moved into southern Ontario followed by United States citizens enticed into the same area by offers of generous land grants. By Confederation, about a century later, the population of the Quebec-Ontario region had reached about two and a half millions.

To a region as vast as Quebec-Ontario, even though its population was concentrated in the St Lawrence valley, transportation was important to development. The river and the Great Lakes formed the principal means of getting people and goods from one place to another. They became much more effective after the canal building period between about 1797 and 1850 when canals were constructed at Sault Ste Marie (linking Lakes Huron and Superior), at Welland (linking Lakes Erie and Ontario), and at Montreal (to skirt the Lachine rapids). But the winter freeze-up made the development of roads necessary; the first road joining Montreal and Quebec was completed in 1735 and was the beginning of a gradual expansion. Railways also started to play their part: the first line ran from La Prairie to St-Jean, and the opening of the Grand Trunk from Toronto to Montreal in 1856 was an important milestone in transportation development.

Cast out on the extreme east coast with a small population and rather difficult terrain, Nova Scotia[3] was much less well-served. The deep channels and bays gouged out of its southeastern coastline by glacial action and the beating of the Atlantic, the rocky terrain, and the dependence of its people mainly upon activities connected with the sea, all combined to keep Nova Scotia a series of poorly connected coastal

2 Ontario was an unnamed and mainly unknown territory until the latter part of the eighteenth century. In 1774 it was made part of an enlarged Quebec and seventeen years later received a separate status and the name "Upper Canada." In 1840 it was again united with Quebec, only gaining its present status and name after Confederation in 1867.

3 The name "Nova Scotia" was applied to various combinations of areas in the early days. Up to 1763 it included what is now mainland Nova Scotia, New Brunswick, and Prince Edward Island. In that year, by the Treaty of Paris, Cape Breton was ceded by the French and was joined to Nova Scotia. In 1769 Prince Edward Island broke away and was followed in 1784 by New Brunswick and Cape Breton, but in 1820 Cape Breton returned and the present Nova Scotia was formed. To avoid confusion, the provincial title will be used to refer to the area which is now so named.

settlements until well into the nineteenth century. Even in 1800 roads leading from Halifax petered out after a few miles. In the early part of the nineteenth century roads were built mainly by statute labour, and regular, if uncomfortable, stagecoach runs became available between Halifax, Windsor, Annapolis, Truro, and Pictou. And Nova Scotia got a small share of the rail boom of the 1850s when a line connecting Halifax, Windsor, and Truro was completed in 1858.

The pre-Confederation economy of Quebec-Ontario was (as indeed it still is to a considerable extent) based upon its natural resources. Furs, the original resource which had attracted men to the region, gave way to products of the forest and of the land. The cancellation of the British tariff on lumber in 1795 laid the foundation for an international trade in square lumber. Manufacturing also developed in a modest way, mainly to serve local needs, but the first Canadian pulp mill, which had been built at St André d'Argenteuil in 1803, was a sign of things to come.

Nova Scotians still look backwards with nostalgia to the glory that was theirs before Confederation. Like Quebec and Ontario, the Nova Scotian economy was resource-based, fish and lumber being the most important. Fish were exported to the West Indies and other parts of North America. Lumber, too, was exported, but gradually it came to support a boat-building industry which supplied not only the colony's own mercantile fleet (in the mid-nineteenth century the Maritime provinces were fourth most important in the international carrying trade, measured in terms of registered tonnage) but also those of Britain and other overseas countries. However, ominous clouds started to gather in the 1830s and 1840s. The world's first railway building boom collapsed and with it the demand for lumber for ties, the United States raised its lumber tariff, Britain allowed the United States to enter the West Indies trade and a few years later adopted general free trade, thus destroying Nova Scotia's traditionally favoured position in intra-British empire commerce. The overseas trade, upon which Nova Scotia had relied so heavily, was thus being threatened, and up to that time there was very little commercial contact with the other Canadian colonies. The future looked unpromising. But in fact the years immediately before and after Confederation turned out to be the most prosperous in Nova Scotian history and became known as the "golden years." The general world prosperity, the Crimean and American Civil wars, another world railway building boom, and the 1854 Reciprocity Treaty in raw materials with the United States, all seem to have played their parts.

CONFEDERATION TO THE END OF THE

SECOND WORLD WAR

Confederation was a milestone in the political and economic development of both regions. Though one of the founding members, Nova Scotia did not enter without misgivings. Supporters of the move towards union hoped that it would give Nova Scotia the hinterland that it needed for further development and would allow it to become the industrial heart of the new Canada. However, it was not very long before the doubters seemed to have been proven right by events. The importance and prosperity of the Quebec-Ontario region grew rapidly while Nova Scotia started slipping into relative oblivion. The west was settled, but Quebec and Ontario, not Nova Scotia, developed into the main industrial region. The centre of power, political and economic, shifted westward. Immigration into Nova Scotia, which had reached considerable proportions during the first half of the nineteenth century, dried up. Later waves leap-frogged over into the central provinces and the west. From housing 10 per cent of Canada's population in 1861, Nova Scotia could claim only 5 per cent at the outbreak of the Second World War. With the opening of the west, Quebec-Ontario lost some of its dominance in respect to population, but its share of the Canadian total was still 62 per cent at the end of that same period.

Nova Scotia did get a transportation link with the rest of Canada. The Intercolonial Railway was extended through New Brunswick down to Halifax, a branch line being built into northern Cape Breton. Another line from Montreal was joined with a line running between Halifax and Yarmouth by a ferry linking Digby and Saint John, New Brunswick. Also, within the province a few local lines were built, bringing Nova Scotia's rail mileage to about thirteen hundred miles. But this was all small-time compared with the approximately fourteen thousand miles of first main track which were built in Quebec-Ontario during the railway booms of the 1850s, the 1870–90s, and the early 1900s. This construction created a network with focus on Montreal and Toronto which provided east-west links by three trans-provincial lines, northwards into the shield, and southwards to connect with the American system. And whereas new railways provided the outlets for Quebec-Ontario's manufactures and primary products, they seemed to do Nova Scotia little good since they tended to carry food in from the west rather than to open up a market for the manufactures of the Nova Scotians.

Not unnaturally, many Nova Scotians blamed Confederation for everything. The National Policy, inaugurated in 1879 to bind the new nation together by building the trans-continental railway, settling the west, and erecting a tariff wall against the world outside, inevitably obstructed the outward-looking trading pattern of Nova Scotia's "golden years." They also blamed the failure of the Canadian government to renew the Reciprocity Treaty with the United States after its expiry in 1866. But it was really technological change which was undermining the traditional position of Nova Scotia. The strength of its wood, wind, and water economy was being weakened by the coming of steel ships driven by steam engines. No longer were its lumber resources and its skill in building wooden ships the assets they had previously been. Then, as railways cheapened and speeded up land transportation, the obstacles to the development of central and western Canada were removed. Finally, the coming of the new factory technology, itself stimulated by the improvements in communications, established new conditions in which the location of economic activity would be decided.

Even that seemingly unequalled gift of nature, Halifax harbour, lost much of its attraction as the building of locks and canals allowed ocean-going vessels to penetrate deeper and deeper into the country's interior, and as much of the cargo destined for central Canada was attracted by the superior facilities of the east coast ports of the United States. In 1870, some 11 per cent (by value) of all Canadian trade was handled by Nova Scotian ports; by 1939 this proportion had dwindled to a little over 4 per cent.

These forces had been operating before Confederation but they were hidden by the favourable world conditions during the previous decade or so. When the chronic world depression of the 1870s arrived, the mask was removed and Nova Scotia's true situation became apparent. Its agriculture, which had really never developed beyond the stage required to supply its own domestic needs for fruit, livestock, poultry, and dairy products, was exposed to the pressure of the agricultural regions farther west. Only Nova Scotia's apples, grown mainly in the Annapolis Valley, proved a match for inland competition. By contrast, Quebec-Ontario's agriculture did well. In particular, the Niagara Peninsula developed into a most prosperous commercial market garden.

Fisheries continued to be Nova Scotia's prime staple. But problems were arising even here. Competition from Britain, Norway, and Iceland cut into traditional markets, and the coming of refrigerated transportation made it possible for meat producers to oust fish from many formerly reliable markets. Again, as Nova Scotia suffered, so Quebec-

Ontario benefited from these developments. Since the fishing industry of Quebec-Ontario had never been of importance, the problems of that industry were of no great moment; and as a big livestock producer the region benefited from the transportation improvements.

In lumbering it was the same sort of story. The opening up of the great forests of Quebec-Ontario by roads and railways allowed the timber industry of that region to develop into one of the world's most important producers. At the same time as increased supplies from Quebec-Ontario entered world markets, demand was falling off because of the end of the railway building booms and the invasion of steel. Thus one of Nova Scotia's main supports was undermined. In 1914, to make matters worse, the Panama Canal started letting west coast timber through in enormous quantities to traditional Nova Scotian markets. Relief, and then only partial, had to await the development of the pulp industry. From this development Quebec-Ontario drew even greater benefit.

Nova Scotia's mineral wealth in the form of coal at one time promised to become the prop of a highly developed industrial area as well as a valuable export. It is true that the coal industry did have some good periods. The Canadian tariff in 1879 made it easier for Nova Scotian coal to compete in central Canada with American coal, and the growth of the iron and steel industry at Sydney in the latter part of the nineteenth century was a godsend. But the American market fell away in the late nineteenth century partly because of competition from its own producers and partly because of the favourable treatment afforded American coal firms by the American railways with which they were often financially linked. Then steel ran into trouble of its own after the First World War and competition from American coal imported into central Canada necessitated freight subventions on Nova Scotian coal beginning in 1928. As far as other minerals were concerned, Nova Scotia's endowments were meagre compared with the bounty bestowed on Quebec and Ontario. While coal, salt, gypsum, and barytes represented the limits of its known resources, the Canadian Shield was discovered to be a great treasure chest and finds of large reserves of metallic minerals of almost every kind rapidly followed each other. The region became a major supplier of many of the world's valuable minerals.

Though Quebec-Ontario continued to rely heavily upon the production of raw materials as its main source of wealth, it also became Canada's centre of manufacturing, a position upon which the challenges of the other provinces made little impression. In almost every major industrial group it reigned supreme. The achievements in manufacturing by Nova Scotia were puny by comparison. While it had been isolated from the rest of Canada, it had operated many very capable though small-scale manufacturing operations to fill local needs and to service the large merchant fleet that operated from Halifax and other local ports; but the technological developments already noted led to many of these small establishments being squeezed out, and with a few exceptions no new industries arose to replace them. These exceptions were nearly all primary manufacturing activities which grew up to exploit local raw materials. The iron and steel complex was established in the late nineteenth century based upon Cape Breton coal and ore and limestone brought in by boat from Newfoundland; but secondary manufacturing never developed around it and it shared the same misery of the inter-war period with most other such heavy industries. Fish processing thrived and eventually became the second largest employer among Nova Scotia's manufacturing industries. Timber production continued but fell upon hard times because of the depletion of reserves and a decline in demand. Small lumber milling shops continued to exist in the province to supply local needs for construction. Ship building and repairing partially changed over from wood to steel but was never more than a shadow of its former greatness in the days of wooden sailing ships. Most of the rest of Nova Scotia's manufacturing was concerned with supplying local markets for goods which could not be brought in from elsewhere in Canada sufficiently cheaply – dairy products, bread, butter, and the like. A few firms did succeed in carving out markets in central and western Canada – a knitwear manufacturer, a confectioner, and a spice firm were perhaps the best examples. And, in the interwar period, a pulp and paper industry did develop in the province.

POST–SECOND WORLD WAR DEVELOPMENT

Because of its geographical position, Nova Scotia comes into its own in wartime. Great strides were made during the Second World War towards closing the economic gap with the central provinces. Ship building, for instance, expanded by 2,000 per cent. Manufacturing industry was deliberately steered towards it by government action designed to ensure geographical dispersion of production and to take advantage of surplus resources wherever they existed. But the first few postwar years saw a reversion to the original situation. While all provinces of Canada enjoyed generally prosperous conditions, Nova Scotia's development proceeded at a rate slower than that of the Quebec-Ontario region.

TABLE 1 / 1

Personal income per capita in Nova Scotia, actual and as
percentage of Quebec-Ontario, 1946–62 (selected years)

| Year | Actual (dollars) | Percentage of Quebec-Ontario | |
		With transfer payments	Without transfer payments[a]
1946	678	86	82
1951	776	68	65
1956	971	70	67
1961	1,197	73	70
1962	1,252	73	69

SOURCE: Derived from Tables B/1, B/4, and B/5.

a Had tax equalization grants, Atlantic Provinces Adjustment Grants, and stabilization payments also been eliminated, the figures in this column would have been even lower. For instance, 1962 would have been about 67 per cent.

Table 1/1 shows the relationship between personal incomes in Nova Scotia and the two central provinces during the postwar period.[4] The slump in Nova Scotia's relative position up to 1951 was most pronounced. This year was the trough but the little recoveries which appeared from time to time during the next eleven years never quite lifted the Nova Scotian percentage as high as 75 per cent. But for transfer payments, it would not have climbed above 70 per cent.

Even this lowly position seems only to have been maintained because of exceptionally large non-civilian activity. Halifax metropolitan area is the naval station for Atlantic Command and also garrisons substantial army and airforce units. Defence payrolls in the year 1962–3 came to 10 per cent of Nova Scotia's personal income[5] and, though the size of the garrisons did increase during the 1950s, the percentage for the earlier postwar years was probably not much smaller. Taking account of other defence expenditures and the effects of the income

4 Personal income is of course an imperfect measure of welfare. As the Royal Commission on Canada's Economic Prospects observed in its *Final Report* (Ottawa, 1957) "many people in the Atlantic region would not exchange on any terms their more peaceful way of life and the comparative ease and quiet that goes with it for the noise and bustle and the tenseness which one associates with living in large metropolitan areas like Montreal, Toronto, and Vancouver" (p. 403). But it is the best measure we have.

5 Atlantic Provinces Economic Council, *Defence Expenditures and the Economy of the Atlantic Provinces* (Fredericton, 1965), p. 12.

multiplier,[6] it seems that defence expenditure may directly and indirectly have accounted for over a quarter of Nova Scotia's personal income.

Technical developments have continued to reduce the importance of Halifax and other Nova Scotian ports as they have increased the attractiveness of Quebec-Ontario ports. The opening of the St Lawrence Seaway has given large vessels access to the farthest corners of the Great Lakes system, and the use of ice-breakers has kept open the St Lawrence ports during what was formerly their closed season. In addition, the other by-pass to central Canada via the east coast ports of the United States continues to prove attractive to many shippers, its superior facilities and shorter haul to the main centres of population apparently outweighing any additional cost, even when there is a loss of tariff preferences.

Quebec-Ontario's roads now form a highly developed network over the populated areas. The great highway 401 runs from Windsor directly through Ontario's industrial belt and links up with major Quebec roads to provide the sort of facilities ideal for high-speed trucks. Another thirty thousand miles of paved highways and rural roads, some giving entry into the mines and forests of the northland, complete the network, all of which is linked to eastern and western Canada and the United States.

Though the more populous parts of Nova Scotia are connected by paved roads which are good enough to allow reasonably quick movement of persons and goods from one part of the province to another, its road system is still rather primitive compared with the highways of southern Ontario and Quebec and would be inadequate for a more highly developed road transport system. Quite good roads now connect the province with Quebec, Ontario, and the west, but they follow circuitous routes through northern New Brunswick or southwards via the United States.

New railway construction since the 1920s in Quebec-Ontario has been limited mainly to that needed to provide access to the northlands, but the region still has a well-developed railway system made up of fifteen thousand miles of track covering the region. Nova Scotia's thirteen hundred miles of track still provide the principal means of transportation for goods within the province and with the rest of Canada

6 G. Rosenbluth, "Problems of Regional, Industrial, and Occupational Mobility in Relation to Disarmament," in Canadian Political Science Association Conference on Statistics, 1964, *Papers on Regional Statistical Studies*, ed. S. Ostry and T. K. Rymes (Toronto, 1966), demonstrates that the employment multiplier relating employment on defence operations and total employment is approximately two in the larger Canadian metropolitan areas. It seems reasonable to suppose that the income multiplier is not very different.

and the United States; but the service offered by the railways is slow and infrequent compared with what is available in the Quebec-Ontario region.

Aircraft have transformed travel in the vast region of central Canada and there are now some three thousand landing areas in Ontario alone. Air Canada operates between the principal towns, and other regional carriers fly fairly frequent services into the less populated areas. Montreal and Toronto rank as two of the world's busiest airports with frequent departures to other parts of Canada and direct flights to north and central America and Europe.

Near Halifax there is an airport capable of handling any aircraft now in general service, and smaller airports at Sydney and Yarmouth are also used for Air Canada's scheduled routes. From Halifax, Air Canada provides four flights each day to Sydney (but compare the twenty-five-odd flights each day between Quebec-Ontario's two principal cities), one a day to Yarmouth, eleven to other Atlantic provinces, about sixteen a day to Quebec and Ontario cities, four a day to Boston or New York, and five a week in summer direct to Europe (but compare the forty-odd Air Canada flights per week in summer to Europe from Montreal or Toronto). Air Canada's short-distance services are supplemented by a regional carrier, but foreign airlines which just about double international flights from central Canada do not stop over in Halifax.

Quebec-Ontario also enjoys to an increasing extent the advantages of pipeline connections with western Canada and the United States; but Nova Scotia, having no large concentrations of population and being separated from the present eastern terminals of the pipelines by hundreds of miles of sparsely populated and difficult country, seems unlikely to enjoy this form of transportation for many years.

Nova Scotian agriculture has maintained its generally uninspiring record. Some sections of it, the apple industry of the Annapolis Valley and the cattle farming of the Truro area for instance, have remained fairly prosperous. But much of the rest is subsistence farming, often carried on part-time by people who also do fishing or some other sort of work. Compared with the intensive commercial agriculture in southern Ontario and some other parts of the St Lawrence and Great Lakes region, it is grossly inefficient, but so long as it is based on its present part-time subsistence system it seems unlikely that much improvement will be achieved. Were it not for the lavish subsidies paid by governments, most of the farms would not continue at all. As it is, Nova Scotia's agriculture still gives employment of a kind to about 5 per cent of the labour force compared with over 7 per cent in the Quebec-Ontario region (see Table 1/2).

TABLE 1 / 2

Distribution of Nova Scotia and Quebec-Ontario labour forces,
by industrial sectors, 1961 (percentages)

	Nova Scotia	Quebec-Ontario
Agriculture	5.1	7.2
Forestry	1.8	1.4
Fishing and trapping	3.2	0.1
Mines, quarries, and oil wells	4.3	1.6
Manufacturing	14.4	26.7
Construction	6.6	6.7
Transportation, communications, and other utilities	10.5	8.6
Trade	15.5	14.9
Finance, insurance, and real estate	2.4	3.9
Community, business, and personal services'industries	19.0	19.7
Public administration and defence	15.5	6.7
Unspecified and undefined	1.7	2.5

SOURCE: Derived from Table B/6.

Table 1/2 also shows the relative importance of other sectors of the economies of the two regions. Fishing has held its own in Nova Scotia during the postwar period, remaining a much more important industry to that province than to the Quebec-Ontario region. The demand for fish in the United States has generally been good and generous subsidies have been made to encourage capital investment in more efficient boats and equipment. Forestry has been active owing to the demand for pulpwood to feed the expanding pulp and paper industry. The Nova Scotian forests yield good pulpwood, and with reasonably good management should do so indefinitely. They are, however, on a small scale compared with the enormous reserves of Quebec and Ontario.

Quebec-Ontario has continued to enjoy its riches and to discover that it has even more than it thought. Even Gaspésie, the Cinderella of the region, struck copper in 1952. By contrast, in Nova Scotia's mining sector upon which almost 4.5 per cent of the labour force of Nova Scotia relied, the plight of coal, its previously most important mineral, was pitiful by 1962. Enormous subsidies have been poured in by governments, but the industry has still continued to contract. It is a high-cost operation compared with its American counterpart and the tendency in Canada, as elsewhere, to switch to alternative forms of energy has reduced coal to a subsidiary position. There seems little doubt that within a few years the industry will be finished.[7] The other mineral

7 Towards the end of 1966 a report, *The Cape Breton Coal Problem* (Ottawa, 1966), prepared for the federal government by J. R. Donald, recommended

producing industries have been prosperous. Eighty per cent of Canada's production of gypsum is mined in Nova Scotia, mostly for export as rock to the United States. Salt mining also continues to expand. And barytes mining has gone on making its modest contribution. However, none of these secondary minerals is sufficiently valuable to make a great deal of difference to the economy of the province.

As is to be expected in highly developed economies (and even Nova Scotia must be so classified in spite of everything that has been said or will be said), the service sectors have continued to expand in both regions. Personal services, government administration, education, and the like have all grown. Nova Scotia, taking advantage of its unusual beauty, its pleasant climate, its excellent facilities for hunting, shooting, and fishing, its relics of the past, and its less hectic living pace manages to entice increasing numbers of New Yorkers, Torontonians, and Montrealers out of their steaming urban agglomerations at summer vacation time; and so its tourist industry thrives, aided by the energetic road-paving which has made some of the most attractive areas easily accessible by car. This is one of the few fields in which Nova Scotia in recent years can claim to have done something to close the gap with Quebec-Ontario, though central Canada can offer enough attractions to draw many visitors. Finally, the continuing importance of defence activity has already been remarked upon.

In manufacturing industry, which is to be our primary concern, the contrast between the two regions has remained during the postwar period. Value-added by manufacture in Nova Scotia did rise from $71.7 million in 1946 to $179.9 million in 1962 (see Table B/27), which represents about a 40 per cent increase in real terms.[8] This was, however, a slow rate compared with that achieved in Quebec-Ontario. The relative position of Nova Scotia deteriorated particularly rapidly between 1946 and 1951. In 1946, the value-added in Quebec-Ontario was thirty-nine times as great as Nova Scotia's; by 1951 it had grown to forty-seven times. And the trend continued until, by the end of our period, the multiple had reached fifty-three.

the phasing out of Nova Scotia's coal industry over a period of fifteen years. Though not publicly acknowledging the inevitable death of the industry within any specified period, the federal government has set up a Cape Breton Development Corporation charged among other things to oversee any changes which will become necessary.

8 Dominion Bureau of Statistics (DBS), *Prices and Price Indexes, Dec. 1960* and *Feb. 1963*, catalogue number 62-002, gives the price index of fully and chiefly manufactured goods produced in Canada as 138 in 1946 and 249 in 1962 (1935–9 = 100). Though national indexes may sometimes yield misleading results when applied to regional activities, they should be adequate to give a general picture of the growth of Nova Scotia's real manufacturing output.

TABLE 1 / 3

Value-added by manufacturing industry, actual, per capita, and per establishment, Nova Scotia as percentage of Quebec-Ontario, 1946–62 (selected years)

	Actual	Per capita	Per establishment
1946	2.58	32.7	41.0
1951	2.11	28.4	35.7
1956	2.06	29.8	37.2
1961	1.90	29.6	38.5
1962	1.88	29.4	38.2

SOURCE: Derived from Tables B/1, B/8, and B/27.

Measured in terms of value-added per capita, the deterioration in Nova Scotia's relative position was not very great. Again, the worst period was 1946 to 1951, but after that the fall was arrested and the situation even showed a very slight improvement. However, stability at less than one-third of the level of Quebec-Ontario is hardly a happy achievement; and even this was only possible because of the relatively slow increase in Nova Scotia's population, which was itself a symptom of a relatively poor economic situation. Table 1/3 also indicates that Nova Scotian manufacturing establishments, on the average, shrank in size relative to those of Quebec-Ontario. Again, most of the change took place soon after the war and from 1951 there were some signs of a slow movement back.

Table 1/4 gives a picture of the structure of manufacturing in the two regions at the end of our period.[9] As would be expected because of its size, Nova Scotia's manufacturing was much less diversified than was that of Quebec-Ontario. In particular, its heavy dependence on fish processing and iron and steel mills was very marked.[10] On the other hand, the pattern of industry is not so very different, half of each list overlapping with the other and the common industries appearing very roughly in the same order. However, three of Nova Scotia's most important ones are absent from Quebec-Ontario's list. They are fish products (which are mostly destined for export to central Canada and the United States), saw mills (which feed the pulp and paper industry and provide lumber for the home construction industry and export), and ship building and repair (much of which relies on defence con-

9 The census year 1961 is used so that information may be available for those Nova Scotian industries the data for which are omitted from DBS publications based upon censuses of manufactures.
10 Employment in Nova Scotia's iron and steel mill fell during the mid-1960s to about two-thirds of its 1961 level.

TABLE 1 / 4

*Principal manufacturing industries of Nova Scotia
and Quebec-Ontario, 1961*

Nova Scotia	Percentage of manufacturing labour force
Fish products	15.5
Iron and steel mills	11.5
Saw mills	7.4
Ship building and repairing	6.5
Pulp and paper mills	4.5
Dairy products	4.5
Printing and publishing	3.8
Aircraft and parts	3.5
Bakery products	3.2
Other food processors (confectionery, sugar refineries, and miscellaneous)	2.9
Sash and door and planing mills	2.7
Beverage manufacturing	2.8
Knitting mills (other than hosiery mills)	2.5
Petroleum refining	1.6
Total	72.7

Quebec-Ontario	
Pulp and paper	4.6
Bakery products	3.0
Iron and steel mills	2.9
Truck bodies and trailers	2.8
Printing and publishing	2.7
Men's clothing	2.6
Women's clothing	2.6
Dairy products	2.4
Commercial printing	2.4
Aircraft and parts	2.3
Miscellaneous machinery and equipment	2.3
Communications equipment	2.1
Beverages	2.0
Shoe factories	1.9
Total	36.6

SOURCE: Derived from Tables B/7 and B/11.

tracts). Three other Nova Scotian industries missing from the Quebec-Ontario list are knitting mills (which produce mainly for the Canadian market), other food processors (mainly sugar refineries, confectioners, and spice makers producing for export to other provinces), and petroleum refiners who process imported oil for the needs of the Atlantic provinces. The Quebec-Ontario industries not found on the Nova Scotia list are the clothing industries (men's clothing, women's clothing, and shoes), certain capital goods industries (miscellaneous machinery and equipment and communications equipment, serving mainly industry in the region), commercial printing (also serving local industry), and truck bodies and trailers (for the Canadian market).

The retardation of Nova Scotia relative to the Quebec-Ontario region made it an unattractive province for new Canadians. Between 1946 and 1962, as Table 1/5 shows, Nova Scotia received immigrants in numbers which would have served to increase its mid-1946 population by 5.6 per cent; but immigration into the Quebec-Ontario region during the same period was 20.2 per cent of its mid-1946 population. Even when they did come to Nova Scotia, many immigrants seem to have used it merely as a jumping-off board; for, although about 18,900[11] were destined for that province between the two censuses, only 11,738 of them were living there in mid-1961.[12]

TABLE 1 / 5

Immigrants from abroad as percentages of mid-year populations, Nova Scotia and Quebec-Ontario, 1946–62 (selected years)

	Nova Scotia	Quebec-Ontario
1946	.76	.51
1951	.32	1.74
1956	.24	1.22
1961	.12	.46
1962	.13	.48
1946–62ᵃ	5.58	20.23

SOURCE: Derived from Tables B/1 and B/3.

a All immigrants, 1946–62, as percentage of 1946 mid-year population.

Even Nova Scotians born in the province apparently drifted away in considerable numbers. Net emigration between the two censuses was almost 34,000 persons.[13] Allowing for the arrival from abroad between 1951 and 1961 of the approximately 11,700 immigrants who were still there in 1961, it seems that about 46,000 more Nova Scotians left the province in that period than other persons arrived from elsewhere in Canada.[14]

11 Adding the immigration for 1952–60 and half of that for 1951 and 1961 (to correspond roughly to the mid-year censuses) produces a total of 18,931 (see Table B/3).
12 DBS, *Census of Canada, 1961*, vol. I, part 3, no. 11 (92–562).
13 DBS, *Canada Year Book, 1962*, p. 163.
14 Some of those leaving the province may have been pre-1951 immigrants. In 1951, 28,680 pre-1951 immigrants were living in the province (DBS, *Census of Canada, 1951*, vol. II, pp. 41–5) while in 1961 only 22,430 remained (DBS, *Census of Canada, 1961*, vol. I, part 3, no. 11), but some of this 6,250 loss must have been because of deaths.

As is normally the case, emigration tended to draw off the younger people. Table 1/6 indicates the large depletion between 1951 and 1961 of those who were in the 5–24 age groups at the start of that period. The 10–19 age group of 1951 particularly suffered, its 110,000 having shrunk to 93,000 by 1961. It was to a large extent this loss of the young people, just when they reached the age to enter the working force, that caused the Nova Scotian population to be rather older than that of the Quebec-Ontario region and also perhaps deprived it of the most enterprising and energetic element of its population. It was left to support greater proportions of young people below twenty, and of elderly people over sixty-five.

As a result of this migration, Nova Scotia's population had by 1966 grown to only three-quarters of a million – a mere 4 per cent of the Canadian total compared with the twelve and a half million people living in Quebec-Ontario (about two-thirds of Canada's inhabitants). Though a relatively tiny population, Nova Scotia's density of about thirty-six per square mile is the highest of all Canadian provinces excepting Prince Edward Island (compare Quebec-Ontario's density of fifteen and a half per square mile, though like many averages this is misleading since it includes the vast northern wilderness with a density of one per square mile and the southern part of Ontario with one hundred per square mile). Nova Scotians are predominantly from British

TABLE 1 / 6

*Population in various age groups, Nova Scotia and
Quebec-Ontario, 1951 and 1961*

	Nova Scotia		Quebec-Ontario	
Age	1951	1961	1951	1961
		(percentages)		
0–4	12.8	12.4	12.2	12.3
5–9	10.7	11.5	10.0	11.3
10–14	9.0	10.9	7.9	10.1
15–19	8.0	8.7	7.6	7.9
20–24	7.2	6.7	8.0	6.6
25–29	7.3	6.0	8.3	6.8
30–34	7.2	5.9	7.5	7.2
35–39	7.0	6.1	7.1	7.2
40–44	5.9	6.0	6.3	6.1
45–49	4.7	5.6	5.5	5.5
50–54	4.3	4.7	4.9	4.8
55–59	3.9	3.7	4.0	3.9
60–64	3.3	3.2	3.5	3.2
65–69	3.0	2.9	2.9	2.6
70 and over	5.5	5.7	4.4	4.5

SOURCE: Derived from Table B/2.

stock, a characteristic also true (though to a lesser degree) of Ontario, while Quebeckers are mainly from French forebears. The concentration of immigration into central Canada, particularly to Ontario, has produced a more cosmopolitan society there, though Nova Scotia still has a few areas where the populace traces its origin back to early non-British immigrants.

One population characteristic is shared by both regions: both are urbanized, only about 7 per cent of each being rural farm dwellers. Four and a half million (over a third) of Quebec-Ontario's twelve and a half millions live in the Montreal and Toronto metropolitan areas; 40 per cent of Nova Scotia's people dwell in the Halifax and Sydney metropolitan areas.

THE PROSPECTS

What hopes are there that Nova Scotia's relatively dismal position can be improved in the future? It can scarcely hope to move into a more prosperous era based upon agriculture – its soil and climate simply could not support a large-scale prosperous agricultural sector. There is no sign that it can look for salvation to its fishing industry – due to overfishing of Canada's traditional Atlantic fishing grounds, the time required to land a ton of fish from them is increasing, and inshore fishing is suffering from a shortage of lobsters, its most valuable catch; so the number of Nova Scotians who make a living at fishing is declining and the industry has only been kept from rapid contraction by generous government subsidies of one sort or another. About the potential of Nova Scotia's forest industries opinions seem to differ, but even the most optimistic estimates do not suggest that the province will be able to rely upon those industries for the future prosperity it is seeking.[15] As far as extractive industries are concerned, coal mining is being steadily run down and proven reserves of other mineral resources are of the low-value varieties; so, unless there is a major discovery of oil (for which drilling is at present in operation) or of some other mineral the existence of which has not been established, the province's extractive industry seems destined for further decline. Tourism should expand, though the Nova Scotian summers are too short to allow it ever to be the major prop of the economy. Government spending on defence and administration seems likely to decline with the changing role of the armed services; and other sectors of the economy cannot very well expand greatly on their own. The only sector left is manufacturing. Even

15 See, for instance, the Atlantic Development Board's *Forestry in the Atlantic Provinces* (Ottawa, 1968), pp. 2–1 to 2–35.

here the recent history has not been reassuring.[16] But this seems to be the only field worth exploring since manufacturing firms are almost certainly more footloose than are firms in most other industrial sectors. One cannot steer oil mining firms to a region which has no oil reserves; the agricultural industry cannot very well be induced to go somewhere where the soil and climatic conditions are all against farming; lumbering has to stay where the trees are; and many service industries have to go where the consumers of the services live. But manufacturing can fairly easily be carried out anywhere. Costs may be somewhat higher in certain locations if materials are expensive to bring in, or the finished product is expensive to transport to the market; but in many industries these considerations seem to be of little importance.

That Nova Scotia's hope lies in its manufacturing sector does not make it unusual. Indeed, there is a commonly held belief that manufacturing provides the only base which can support any nation's continuous growth.[17] It is true that there seems no reason why this should inevitably be so and there are indeed many exceptions. (New Zealand and Denmark, for instance, grew prosperous on commercial agriculture, minerals formed the basis for the wealth of South Africa and Kuwait, and Canada itself relies very heavily on its resource industries.) But even those countries whose early development was based upon other industries are now more and more coming to look to their manufacturing sectors to act as the engines of future growth.

For these reasons, we shall from this point onward be concentrating our attention upon manufacturing industry. In Part Two we shall be comparing the cost structures of manufacturing industry in Nova Scotia and Quebec-Ontario during the seventeen-year period from 1946 to 1962 in order to try to determine why the industry in these two regions developed at different rates, and the extent to which these different rates of development may be expected to continue in the future.

16 Nova Scotia's primary iron and steel industry, its largest industry measured in terms of value of output, came near to closure in 1967. Only the willingness of the government of Nova Scotia to take it over and manage it on a subsidized basis led to its being reprieved, at least for the time being.
17 E. M. Hoover, The Location of Economic Activity (New York, 1948), for instance, asserts that manufacturing industry and mining afford the only means of achieving continuous progress.

Part Two
Cost Comparisons

2 The Method

THEORETICAL BASIS

Students of industrial location suffer the disadvantage that economic theory, which should underpin their research, is in an unsatisfactory state. The least-cost theory in the Weberian tradition and the market area theory based largely upon Losch's work are still not properly married despite the matchmaking efforts of Greenhut, Isard, and others.[1] Each is reasonably adequate within the assumptions upon which it relies. The least-cost theory is at home with a given and even distribution of demand over the region considered and pure competition in the product markets; the market area theory can handle problems so long as costs of production, except for the cost-reducing effects of agglomeration, are given. But neither can quite deal with realistic situations. In the analysis we are about to attempt, we are fortunate, however, that we can avoid involving ourselves in the theoretical conflicts. By constructing a model which does not violate reality too much, we can utilize the least-cost approach. We shall initially assume that the only market for manufactured goods produced in Nova Scotia, Quebec, and Ontario is in the region comprising the last two provinces.

It is true that Nova Scotian manufacturers are well-placed to supply the Atlantic provinces market; but about two-thirds of Canadian effective demand is in Quebec and Ontario, most of the rest is scattered in isolated pockets to the west, and a mere 5 per cent is in the Atlantic provinces. It is also true that there is the export market, and a look at

1 See C. J. Friedrich, *Alfred Weber's Theory of Location of Industries* (Chicago, 1929); A. Losch, *The Economics of Location* (New Haven, Conn., 1954); M. L. Greenhut, *Plant Location in Theory and Practise* (Chapel Hill, NC, 1956); W. Isard, *Location and Space Economy* (Cambridge, Mass., 1956).

the map might encourage one to expect that Nova Scotia's position hundreds of miles nearer Europe than the main ports of Quebec and Ontario would make overseas markets a favourable target for Nova Scotian manufacturers. But again the situation is not as favourable as it might seem. During the season the St Lawrence is open, exporters from Halifax have to pay the same rates for trans-Atlantic shipping space as do Toronto and Montreal exporters, in addition to having to suffer from a less frequent and reliable service. And during the closed season, which ice-breakers and reinforced ships have in any case nowadays almost eliminated, United States east coast ports offer convenient and reasonably cheap outlets for central Canadian goods destined for overseas.

While some firms, therefore, may live and prosper off Atlantic provinces markets (one bakery serving chiefly the Nova Scotian market has grown to be as large as most bakeries in Quebec and Ontario), and there are opportunities for export (Nova Scotian fish products already go mainly to the United States), it seems self-evident that if Nova Scotian manufacturing is to develop until it is the same size per capita as its Quebec-Ontario counterpart, it must be able to compete in the central Canadian markets. The whole Atlantic provinces region, plus traditional overseas markets, would not be sufficient to support a Nova Scotian manufacturing sector with production units big enough to take advantage of quite elementary economies of scale. The comparative cost of supplying the central Canadian market from Nova Scotia and from Quebec-Ontario seems therefore to be the appropriate measure. Since the market is given and we know that the amount of Nova Scotian manufactures sold in that market will be too small to affect significantly the level of prices, we are left with a model which the least-cost theory is designed to handle. When the model has served its purpose, we shall relax its assumptions to take recognition of the existence of the Atlantic provinces market.

To define our purpose a little more precisely, let us imagine that a manufacturer new to Canada has the choice of building his plant in an average location in Nova Scotia or on an average site in Quebec-Ontario, and that this plant is typical of manufacturing plants in general in respect of the types and proportions of inputs. We shall then compute the cost of producing in these two average locations and of supplying the single market from them. The technique will be to assess the relative cost in the two locations of a unit of each factor[2] and then, by using

2　In other circumstances, the cost of factors per unit of output would be a more appropriate measure. For our present purposes, however, where we are pricing out identical units of factors making appropriate adjustments for any quality

weights according to the importance of each factor in the costs of a typical Nova Scotian manufacturing plant,[3] calculate the relative overall costs of the plant in each location.

This may sound somewhat rarefied, but in fact firms intending to sell in any given market normally have a plant of particular type in mind and the only decision is where to site it. Of course, no individual firm will be average in every respect, but over a period of some years the firms which have to make location decisions will combine factors in average proportions and the sites available to them will be average of the sites usually available in the two regions. Pursuing the analysis as we have described will therefore indicate, on average, the relative cost of manufacturing in the two provinces and marketing the output in the Quebec-Ontario region. If we find that the average cost of operating in Nova Scotia was significantly higher than operating in Quebec-Ontario, the relative backwardness of Nova Scotia's manufacturing industry will be explainable in conventional cost terms. If, however, it turns out that Nova Scotia was not at a significant cost disadvantage, we shall have to look elsewhere for the explanation.

AGGREGATION

From some points of view it is a pity that the analysis will have to be carried out on an aggregate basis and all measurements will be of manufacturing industry as a single unit. If examination of the individual industrial groups[4] had been possible, then differences between Quebec-Ontario and Nova Scotia would have been explained by the contributions that those groups made to the result. This would have shown the spokes that held the wheel to a certain shape. However, it is the shape of a wheel which determines its behaviour as it rolls; so an examination of the various components of manufacturing industry still has to end with a summation if any generalizations are to be reached.

---

differences, and assuming that factor inputs are in the same proportions, the result is the same. At one stage (when we consider the cost of labour) we shall revert for a moment to the measure of input per unit of output to deal with a point about quality.

3 Since the typical proportions of factor inputs vary slightly from one region to another, we shall be working on the proportions in which a typical firm in Nova Scotia combines them. The difference which would have arisen had we instead based our calculations on the proportions used in Quebec-Ontario will be referred to later.

4 The word "disaggregation" now seems well established in the jargon to mean what six words were required to imply here. It is, however, one of the uglier words concocted by economists, apparently being a synonym for "unaddingup." It will therefore be "disadopted" in this text!

In any event, aggregation can never be avoided in practice. If one is interested in the economic activities of Nova Scotia, one may split them up into individual industries of which one is manufacturing – our present concern and about 15 per cent of the whole in terms of its contribution to gross provincial product. To proceed with further division into (say) the twenty groups used by the Dominion Bureau of Statistics (DBS), leaves one still with very heterogeneous units. For instance, the group "chemical and chemical products industries" includes establishments ranging from those employing thousands engaged in the production of industrial chemicals to two-man backyard enterprises turning out briquets. Indeed, in the dividing up of establishments into these twenty groups, a little fibreglass boat-builder is put in the "transportation equipment industries" along with a large foundry producing two-ton iron wheels for trains, while other foundries go in with ferrous metal products. The composition of any industrial group in one province might well be completely unlike the same industrial group in another province and comparisons between them become more misleading than comparisons of manufacturing industry as a whole, particularly if either province is small. Further splitting up produces the same effect in an even more exaggerated form until one reaches the ultimate when each group contains only one establishment. Since no two plants are the same and some are different in every way, we have still not achieved a logically defensible basis for analysis. One might even make the contrary argument that, since plants differ so much from each other, aggregation is necessary so that some of these differences may be cancelled out or their differences may be diluted in the mixture; and that the greater the degree of aggregation, the more valid the comparisons.

The degree of aggregation or splitting up which is appropriate in any study depends, of course, upon the purpose in mind. R. J. and P. Wonnacott were interested in the effects upon individual industries of the elimination of US-Canadian tariffs and therefore were obviously right to examine each of the twenty groups used in official statistics of the two countries[5] (though it might well be argued that there was no logical reason to stop at the twenty groups, which they did in most of their analysis, since each of these twenty is still very heterogenous).

However, whatever stand one takes on the desirability of examining manufacturing as a single unit or studying individual sub-groups, practical issues decided the matter in the present study. Because of the smallness of Nova Scotia, official statistics have to conceal details for

5 *Free Trade between the United States and Canada: The Potential Economic Effects* (Cambridge, Mass., 1967).

some industrial groups; indeed, several of the leading industries which account for 30 per cent of all manufacturing output in the province are lumped together in DBS manufacturing statistics as "groups for which data cannot be shown." Also, official statistics make no attempt to give some important information (electricity purchased and capital investment, for instance) for Nova Scotia on an industrial group basis. In some cases they are completely silent on some important facets of firms' activities (the importance of capital and product transportation in firms' cost structures, for instance), so the gaps have had to be filled by private surveys which, because of their scale, could not provide reliable information on individual industry groups.

DATA DEFICIENCIES

The shortage of data on individual industrial groups, to which we have just referred, was only one of the statistical problems encountered in the present study. Complaints about the inadequacy of available data are of course quite commonplace among economic researchers; but the present exercise does seem to have attracted more than its rightful share of difficulties in this respect. For example, at the time the statistical analysis was being carried out, the DBS had fallen several years behind its normal schedule of publication of manufacturing statistics. This was one reason why the period examined was brought to an end at 1962.[6] But a more serious problem was that official statistics often give no detail for individual provinces. For instance, the Board of Transport Commissioners' *Waybill Analysis* gives data for a "Maritime Zone" which includes Newfoundland, Prince Edward Island, New Brunswick, and part of Quebec as well as Nova Scotia, from which information about individual provinces cannot be disentangled. (Since the data are gathered on a sample basis, provincial information might at any rate be unreliable, even if it were given separately.)

The non-comparability of some official data because of the timing and scope of inquiries upon which they are based, also caused some trouble. In two of the principal sources of information, *General Review of the Manufacturing Industries of Canada* and *Earnings and Hours of Work in Manufacturing*,[7] the former is based upon the annual census

6 There was however another reason. The supporting studies (which will be referred to very shortly) were carried out in 1962 and 1965 and related to the year 1962. Hence, although the DBS subsequently made up most of the delay, the analysis could not be carried past 1962 without the various parts falling out of step.

7 DBS, catalogue numbers 31–201 and 72–204 respectively.

of manufactures which refers to twelve months' operation and has virtually universal coverage, while the latter is based upon a snapshot inquiry taken late each October and covers only the larger establishments.

Then, as in any study extending over a fairly long period, breaks in the continuity of statistical series caused by changes in definitions, coverage, and patterns of analysis led to difficulties. In the series relevant to this study there were plenty. Some were relatively minor and may be expected to have affected both regions to much the same extent; and so, as we are concerned primarily with comparisons between regions, no harm was done. However, two major changes in industrial classification took place, one in 1951 and one in 1960, which made some time-comparisons difficult, and far-reaching changes affecting the reporting unit effectively broke the series in 1961 and 1962. Where possible and necessary, attempts have been made to splice the series together. Occasionally, too, life was made difficult by gaps left when surveys were not undertaken for one or two years (as happened to *Earnings and Hours of Work in Manufacturing* in 1961 and 1962) or when they were dropped completely (as was done with the surveys on capital after 1943).

Finally, information which might have answered some of the important questions is simply unobtainable. For instance, the annual census of manufactures collects no information about the cost of transporting finished products from the factory to the customer. While the situation has improved greatly in recent years, there is still a long way to go before an economic researcher will feel adequately catered for.

The analysis which follows therefore takes the form of a detective hunt in which such clues which can be discovered are drawn together in the hope that, while each may be inconclusive in itself, together they may provide fairly convincing evidence on the various issues. Where official statistics provide no enlightenment on an important point, attempts have been made by three special studies to fill the gaps.[8] These studies also provide information which serves to check the results obtained from the analysis of official data.

Two studies were undertaken in 1962 and 1965 specifically for this purpose. The first,[9] referred to hereafter as the Multiplant Firm Study, was an attempt to discover the relative costs of production in Nova

8 These studies, made by the author, are described in some detail in Appendix A.
9 R. E. George, "Costs of Manufacturing in Alternative Locations: Nova Scotia Compared with Ontario and Quebec," in *Cahiers de l'institut de science économique appliquée*, series L, 16, no. 170 (Feb. 1966), pp. 115–60, as "Coûts de production dans les localisations distinctes : comparaison entre la Nouvelle-Ecosse, l'Ontario et le Québec."

Scotia and Quebec-Ontario using information obtained from multiplant firms with experience of operating in both regions. The second,[10] later referred to as the Site-Choice Study, sought to establish the extent to which firms examine all the various locations open to them before coming to a decision as to where to build new plants; it also collected information on the factors which apparently influence a firm's choice of site. The third,[11] referred to as the Selected Local Areas Study, was undertaken in 1961 for a different purpose but, though it covered only two of the three principal industrial areas of Nova Scotia, its findings seem relevant and are used on occasion.

HYPOTHESIS

This is an exploratory exercise in measurement. Once the results have been obtained, an explanation of the different stages of development of manufacturing industries in Nova Scotia and Quebec-Ontario will be worked out and the policy implications explored. For the benefit of readers who prefer to approach investigations by first formulating hypotheses, we shall take the null hypothesis that the cost of producing manufactured goods and distributing them to customers in the Quebec-Ontario region is the same whether the producing plant is situated in Nova Scotia or in the Quebec-Ontario region.

10 George, "The Attraction of Quebec and Ontario for New Manufacturing Industry," mimeo., Department of Commerce, Dalhousie University, Halifax.
11 George, "A Study of Employment in Manufacturing Industry in Colchester, Pictou and Cape Breton Counties," commissioned by the Joint Federal-Provincial Committee on Seasonal Unemployment, 1961, unpublished.

3   Labour

Though labour usually takes pride of place in discussions about the factors of production, wages do not constitute the major part of firms' costs. On the average labour costs made up only about 21 or 22 per cent of the selling value of factory shipments[1] between 1946 and 1962 (see Table 3/1). The percentage apparently shrank a little in both regions during the period; Nova Scotia was about 1.5 per cent in excess of Quebec-Ontario in 1946 but the gap had been nearly closed by 1951 and remained tiny for the rest of the period. The Multiplant Firm Study obtained information which seems consistent with Table 3/1. In that study, inquiries were made about the proportion that labour costs (including fringe benefits, training costs, and other expenses) represented of all costs in 1962 in the Nova Scotian factories of the firms concerned. The median proportion was apparently 22 per cent which is virtually the same as the 21.8 per cent shown in Table 3/1. But the proportions ranged from as little as 5 per cent in one firm to as much as 50 per cent in another. At one extreme were highly capitalistic firms (certain chemical-type firms, for instance) with large through-puts of material and low value-added to each unit of input; at the other were metal-working firms which used cheap material and added greatly to its value by the application of high-priced labour.

On the average, therefore, labour costs represented just a little more

1 This was called "gross value of production" before 1952. Gross value of production and selling value of factory shipments are the only convenient approximations to total costs that official statistics provide. However, they exclude product transportation costs from the factory to the customer and they include profit. If one wished to arrive at total costs in the conventional sense, one would have to add between 2 and 3 per cent for transportation (see chap. 7) and deduct 5 to 7 per cent for profit (see chap. 10).

TABLE 3 / 1

Wages and salaries paid by manufacturing
establishments as percentage of selling value of
factory shipments, Nova Scotia and
Quebec-Ontario, 1946–62 (selected years)

	Nova Scotia	Quebec-Ontario
1946	24.1	22.6
1951	21.1	20.6
1956	21.8	21.5
1961	22.3	21.7
1962	21.8	21.1

SOURCE: Derived from Tables B/15 and B/28.

than one-fifth of all costs. While they were not the most important element of costs (we shall see later that that distinction belonged to materials costs), they still seem to have been large enough to influence the location of industry, if wage-rates had varied significantly from one region to another. It may appear strange, therefore, that differences in wage-rates so seldom influenced firms covered in the Site-Choice Study when making decisions about where to locate new factories. The level of wage-rates was only mentioned five times out of the 149 times that reasons for their choice were given by firms that considered provinces other than the ones they eventually chose.[2] It seems likely that the reason was that the sites chosen were generally in areas of relatively high wage-rates – not because wage-rates themselves were of no importance, but because in those particular locations other favourable features counterbalanced them.[3]

COSTS OF LABOUR

A first approximation to the comparative costs of labour in the two regions may be obtained by relating wages and salaries to the number of persons employed. Table 3/2 indicates the results of doing this for the years 1946–62. In both Nova Scotia and the Quebec-Ontario region, wages and salaries per employee increased markedly during the period. But the increase was rather greater in Quebec-Ontario (161

2 This was in contrast to the opinions of most of the 239 Michigan manufacturers interviewed in 1961 and reported in E. Mueller, A. Wilken, and M. Wood, *Location Decisions and Industrial Mobility in Michigan, 1961* (Ann Arbor, Mich., 1961). That study (p. 4) put labour costs at the top of the list of the most important locational factors.
3 The inability of studies such as the Site-Choice Study to rule out any factor as irrelevant to the location of industry is discussed in Appendix A.

TABLE 3 / 2

*Wages and salaries per employee in manufacturing industry,
Nova Scotia and Quebec-Ontario, 1946–62 (selected years)*

	Nova Scotia (dollars)	Quebec-Ontario (dollars)	Nova Scotia as percentage of Quebec-Ontario
1946	1,449	1,650	87.8
1951	2,097	2,631	79.7
1956	2,714	3,409	79.6
1961	3,280	4,148	79.1
1962	3,393	4,314	78.7

SOURCE: Derived from Tables B/11 and B/15.

per cent compared with 134 per cent in Nova Scotia). Consequently, while the Nova Scotian level was only 88 per cent of that of Quebec-Ontario in 1946, the gap had widened considerably by 1962 when the percentage had fallen to 79.[4] The comparative deterioration in Nova Scotian rates was mainly in the immediate postwar years, and was no doubt largely due to the dismantling of the wartime wage controls which had allowed rates to rise more readily in the lower-wage areas than in those regions with relatively high wages.

While the percentages in the last column of Table 3/2 may serve as a first approximation to the relative levels of wage-rates in the two regions, we need to ensure that the differences in earnings were not merely because of differences between the two regions in working hours, the mix of industries, the male-female composition of the labour forces, and labour quality. We shall therefore now examine each of these facets of the matter in turn.

4 Most of the gap was due to the relatively very low wages and salaries paid in the smaller Nova Scotian centres of population. Comparing wages and salaries per employee in the municipality of Halifax with those in the municipalities of Montreal and Toronto, one finds much smaller differences, as follows:

	Halifax (dollars)	Montreal-Toronto (dollars)	Halifax as percentage of Montreal-Toronto
1946	1,666	1,688	98.7
1951	2,239	2,582	86.7
1956	2,840	3,327	85.4
1961	3,855	4,017	96.0
1962	3,880	4,335	89.5

Derived from DBS, *Manufacturing Industries of Canada: Geographical Distribution*, 31-209, appropriate years (data for 1946 came from DBS, *Manufacturing Industries of Maritime Provinces*, 31-D-23; *Ontario*, 31-D-26; *Quebec*, 31-D-27).

1 *Hours of work*

Immediately after the war Nova Scotian workers were putting in more hours of work than their counterparts in the Quebec-Ontario region[5] (see Table 3/3). But the gap steadily narrowed until by 1956 virtual equality had been achieved. It seems, therefore, that in 1946 Nova Scotian workers had to work 4.8 per cent more hours in order to earn wages and salaries equivalent to 87.8 per cent of those earned in the Quebec-Ontario region. If they had been working the same number of hours, it is clear that their earnings would have been even poorer relative to those received in Quebec-Ontario. How much poorer depends upon the extent to which the extra hours attracted overtime rates. If none did, then the Nova Scotian rates would have been 83.9 per cent of those in Quebec-Ontario. If all were paid at time-and-a-half, then the percentage would have been 82.1. After 1951, when the hours of work in the two regions became almost the same, very little adjustment is required. Consequently, it seems that the deterioration in Nova Scotia's relative position in respect of earnings (which appears from Table 3/2 to have been from about 88 per cent to 79 per cent of Quebec-Ontario rates) would have been from only about 84 or 82 percent to about 79 per cent, if the same hours had been worked in the two regions throughout the period.

TABLE 3 / 3

Average hours of work[a] in manufacturing establishments employing fifteen or more persons, Nova Scotia and Quebec-Ontario, last pay weeks in October,[b] 1946–62 (selected years)

	Nova Scotia	Quebec-Ontario	Nova Scotia as percentage of Quebec-Ontario
1946	45.4	43.4	104.8
1951	43.1	41.6	103.7
1956	41.2	41.3	99.8
1961[c]	40.6	40.7	99.7
1962[c]	40.8	40.9	99.7

SOURCE: Derived from Tables B/13, B/14, B/19, and B/20.

a Average weekly hours are weighted averages of weekly hours for wage-earners and salaried employees.

b Last pay week in November 1946.

c Figures for 1961 and 1962 have beeni nterpolated (survey was not carried out in those years).

5 It was the salaried workers and female wage-earners who kept the Nova Scotian average up during the early postwar period, male wage-earners having achieved equality with their Quebec-Ontario opposite numbers by 1949 or 1950. Later in the period the levelling process spread to all categories of workers.

2 The mix of industries

Interregional comparisons of earnings might well have been distorted by the mix of industries. If, for instance, earnings per employee in each Nova Scotian industry had been exactly the same as earnings per employee in the corresponding industry in the Quebec-Ontario region, average overall earnings might have been significantly lower in Nova Scotia if that province had had a disproportionately large percentage of low-wage industries. To test this possibility, the average earnings per employee in Nova Scotia were standardized to the Quebec-Ontario distribution of employees within industrial groups. After this standardization, the relationships between Nova Scotia and Quebec-Ontario rates during the period were as shown in Table 3/4. It seems clear that, except in the immediate postwar years, the different mix of industries in the two provinces caused some part of the differences between them in average earnings per employee. In 1962 it accounted for about 8 of the 21 percentage points difference in earnings. In the early part of the period the effect of this factor was less marked; indeed, in 1946 the gap was actually widened by the standardization process. These different results may be attributed largely to the changeover in Nova Scotia immediately after the war from high-wage shipbuilding and other defence manufacturing to low-wage industries such as logging and knitting.

TABLE 3/4

Average wages and salaries in manufacturing industry, Nova Scotia as percentage of Quebec-Ontario, actual and standardized to Quebec-Ontario mix of industrial groups, 1946–62 (selected years)

	Actual	Standardized[a]	Standardized minus actual
1946	87.8	84.0	−3.8
1951	79.7	81.0	+1.3
1956	79.6	88.3	+8.7
1961[b]	79.7	85.9	+6.2
1962[b]	79.3	87.2	+7.9

SOURCE: DBS, *General Review of the Manufacturing Industries of Canada*, 31–201 (data for 1946 appeared in *The Manufacturing Industries of Canada*).

a If $a_1, a_2 \cdots a_{20}$ = average wages and salaries paid in each industrial group in Nova Scotia, $b_1, b_2 \cdots b_{20}$ = numbers of employees in each industrial group in Quebec-Ontario, and W = actual Quebec-Ontario wage and salary bill, then $(a_1b_1 + a_2b_2 \cdots + a_{20}b_{20})/W$ per cent = average wages and salaries in Nova Scotia as percentage of those in Quebec-Ontario, standardized to the Quebec-Ontario industrial mix.

b Data have not been adjusted for changes in industrial classification and in reporting unit.

TABLE 3 / 5

Earnings per hour[a] in manufacturing establishments employing fifteen or more persons, Nova Scotia and Quebec-Ontario, last pay weeks in October,[b] 1946–62 (selected years)

	Men		Women		Women as percentage of men		Nova Scotia as percentage of Quebec-Ontario	
	Nova Scotia (cents)	Quebec-Ontario (cents)	Nova Scotia (cents)	Quebec-Ontario (cents)	Nova Scotia	Quebec-Ontario	Men	Women
1946	76	87	43	54	55.8	61.0	86.8	79.4
1951	116	142	57	88	49.1	62.0	81.6	64.6
1956	148	185	71	109	48.3	59.1	79.9	65.3
1961[c]	181	225	90	131	49.9	58.2	80.3	68.9
1962[c]	185	233	92	136	50.1	58.3	79.4	68.2

SOURCE: Derived from Tables B/13, B/14, B/17, B/18, B/19, and B/20.

a Earnings per hour are weighted averages of earnings per hour of wage-earners and salaried employees.

b Figures for 1946 refer to last pay week in November.

c Values for 1961 and 1962 have been interpolated (survey was not carried out in those years).

3 *Male-female composition of the labour force*
As Table 3/5 demonstrates, women in each region earned substantially less than did men. In Nova Scotia their earnings per hour were throughout the period only about half of those of men. In Quebec-Ontario, the relationship remained very stable at about 60 per cent. These great discrepancies between the earnings of men and women in each region could have contributed to the differences in overall earnings in the two regions. If, for instance, the Nova Scotia labour force had contained a higher proportion of women than did the Quebec-Ontario labour force, then even if the rates for men had been identical in the two regions and the same had been true for women, the overall average would still have been lower in Nova Scotia than in Quebec-Ontario.

In fact, the opposite was the case: the Quebec-Ontario region's labour force had the higher female content (see Table 3/6). In 1946 only 15 per cent of the Nova Scotia labour force was female compared with 27 per cent in Quebec-Ontario. There were signs that the gap was narrowing as the period proceeded, but in 1962 Nova Scotia still drew only 17 per cent of its labour force from the female section of the community, compared with Quebec-Ontario's 25 per cent.

TABLE 3 / 6

Female workers as percentage of manufacturing labour force, Nova Scotia and Quebec-Ontario, 1946–62 (selected years)

	Nova Scotia	Quebec-Ontario
1946	15.3	27.0
1951	14.4	24.5
1956	15.1	24.1
1961	17.9	24.7
1962	17.4	24.8

SOURCE: Derived from Table B/11.

If the wages and salaries for Nova Scotia were standardized to the Quebec-Ontario male-female mix, one arrives at the results shown in Table 3/7. It is evident that if the male-female mix had been similar in each region throughout the period, wages and salaries for employees in Nova Scotia would have borne an even less favourable ratio to those in Quebec-Ontario than they actually did. As the female content of the labour force in the two regions tended to draw together, the effect of standardizing was reduced; but even in 1962 it widened the gap between average earnings by 3.7 per cent.

TABLE 3 / 7

Average earnings per hour in establishments employing fifteen or more persons, Nova Scotia as percentage of Quebec-Ontario, actual and standardized to the Quebec-Ontario male-female mix, last pay weeks in October,[a] 1946–62 (selected years)

	Actual[b]	Standardized[c]	Standardized minus actual
1946	94.6	89.4	−5.2
1951	85.5	81.1	−4.4
1956	80.8	76.8	−4.0
1961[d]	81.6	77.9	−3.7
1962[d]	80.7	77.0	−3.7

SOURCE: Derived from DBS, *Earnings and Hours of Work in Manufacturing*, 72–204.

a In 1946 figures relate to last pay weeks in November.

b Figures in the column headed "actual" differ from those in the last column of Table 3/2 because they are from different source documents with different coverages. If Table 3/2 had been computed from census of manufactures data relating only to firms employing fifteen or more persons, the last column of Table 3/2 would have been: 1946, 92.3; 1951, 83.6; 1956, 82.8; 1961, 82.0; 1962, 80.4 (derived from Tables B/12 and B/16). The remaining discrepancy between the two sets of figures may be attributed to the fact that the annual census of manufactures produces data relating to a full year while the survey of earnings and hours of work gives only a snapshot picture of one week towards the end of the year.

c If a_1 and a_2 = average earnings of men and women respectively in Nova Scotia, b_1 and b_2 = number of men and women employed respectively in Quebec-Ontario, W = actual Quebec-Ontario wage and salary bill, then $(a_1 b_1 + a_2 b_2)/W$ per cent = average earnings in Nova Scotia as percentage of those in Quebec-Ontario, standardized on Quebec-Ontario male-female mix.

d Values for 1961 and 1962 have been interpolated (survey was not carried out in those years).

4 The quality of labour

The quality of labour is clearly important to interregional comparisons. If, for instance, an hour's work in Nova Scotia had been of lower quality than an hour's work in the Quebec-Ontario region, then a proposition that Nova Scotian wage-rates were only (say) 80 per cent of those in Quebec-Ontario would have little significance. We would be comparing the prices of different things. Employers are not concerned with how much it costs to buy a man's attendance for an hour, but rather with how much a certain amount of work costs.

A first approximation to quality may be made by relating the value of work done to the number of persons engaged upon it. Table 3/8 shows that value-added per employee in Nova Scotia fluctuated between about 68 and 74 per cent of that of the Quebec-Ontario region during the same period. The figures seem to be consistent with B. S. Keirstead's assertion that lower wage-rates in the Maritime region compared with rates in central Canada were in almost every industry matched by lower

TABLE 3 / 8

Value-added per employee in manufacturing industry, Nova Scotia and Quebec-Ontario, 1946–62 (selected years)

	Nova Scotia (dollars)	Quebec-Ontario (dollars)	Nova Scotia as percentage of Quebec-Ontario
1946	2,414	3,256	74.1
1951	3,916	5,561	70.4
1956	5,166	7,134	72.4
1961	6,050	8,537	70.9
1962	6,196	9,086	68.2

SOURCE: Derived from Tables B/11 and B/27.

productivity; and that what he termed "earning efficiency" was generally uniform.[6] The figures are apparently also supported by a firm of management consultants which reported to the government of Nova Scotia: "Our respondents consider the productivity of labour in Ontario to be the highest of any province and to counterbalance the lower wage-rates that some provinces offer." (Since the report was primarily concerned with Nova Scotia, that province was presumably included in the "some provinces.") It should be noted, however, that Keirstead was referring to the whole Maritime region, of which Nova Scotia is not typical, and that there is reason to suspect the value of the assessment by the consultants' respondents.[7]

Attempts are sometimes made to attribute this apparently low labour quality to low educational standards in the province. For instance, R. I. Logan and G. P. Miller concluded from an examination of figures from the 1961 census that "Nova Scotia workers were less well-educated on the average in 1961 than the Canadian labour force as a whole. This could be an important explanation of the observed productivity differentials in the secondary manufacturing sector ... "[8] However, an examination of Table 3/9 throws doubt upon the relevance of such an explanation to the comparisons with which we are concerned. The median level of education attained was apparently very slightly higher for Nova Scotia than for Quebec-Ontario. And the Economic Council of Canada calculated that the average years of formal schooling of the Nova Scotian labour force in 1961 was about 9.2 compared with about 8.8 for Quebec and about 9.5 for Ontario[9] (thereby suggesting that

6 *The Theory of Economic Change* (Toronto, 1948), p. 309.
7 See n. 9, p. 113.
8 *Plan for Secondary Manufacturing Sector*, Nova Scotia Voluntary Planning Board (Halifax, 1966), p. 68.
9 *Second Annual Review* (Ottawa, 1965), p. 119. Incidentally, the Economic

TABLE 3 / 9

Schooling of labour force, Nova Scotia and
Quebec-Ontario, 1961

Highest grade attended	Percentage of labour force	
	Nova Scotia	Quebec-Ontario
Elementary		
Less than 5	5.4	6.2
5 and over	31.7	36.3
Secondary		
1–2	29.5	21.6
3	14.3	8.6
4–5	11.2	18.8
University		
Some university	4.3	4.0
Degree	3.7	4.6

SOURCE: Derived from DBS, *Census of Canada, 1961*, vol. III, part 1,
no. 10 (94–510).

Nova Scotia would be about equal with Quebec and Ontario combined).
So there seems to be no evidence to support the conclusion that Nova
Scotia's labour force had a relatively low general level of education. It
is true that a smaller proportion of its population had university training,[10] but then a larger proportion had progressed beyond elementary
school. Whether or not this implies that the Nova Scotian labour force
was educationally inferior is a matter of opinion. While one would
expect a shortage of high-grade executives, scientists, and technicians,
there should not have been the problems which arise when a large section of the labour force has little education.

Before trying to explain a low labour productivity in Nova Scotia, we

Council also shows that the average number of years of formal schooling of
the labour force in Nova Scotia was about one-tenth of one year (about
twenty school days) below the average for the whole of Canada – which does
not support very strongly the conclusion of Logan and Miller.

The quality of a person's education is not, of course, solely a function of the
time he spends at school and university, or even of the grade he reaches. It
also depends on other factors, such as the ability and training of teachers, the
facilities provided, the efficiency and imagination of the educational policy-
makers and administrators, and the environment in which the children live.
Interprovincial comparisons of quality are difficult, however, but something
will be said on this matter in chap. 12.

10 There seems little doubt that the shortage of university graduates in the labour
force of Nova Scotia is not because they are not produced but rather because
they leave the province immediately after graduation. Each year there is a
mass exodus of new graduates to jobs in Quebec and Ontario offered by talent
scouts of the large national companies who start recruiting on university
campuses early in each academic year.

should make certain that it really is low. The differences between the two regions in value-added per employee shown by Table 3/8 might have been due, at least in part, to other reasons. First, the working week might have been shorter. This possibility we can dismiss since we found earlier (Table 3/3) that in 1946 and 1951 Nova Scotians worked respectively 4.8 and 3.7 per cent more hours per week. On the contrary this would indicate that value-added per employee in a standard working week in Nova Scotia was then only about 70 per cent of that of Quebec-Ontario in 1946 and 68 per cent in 1951. Thus, during the first few years of the postwar period, allowing for the length of the working week makes the gap wider. As the period proceeded, the working weeks in the two regions drew together, and after 1956 scarcely any allowance is called for. It seems, therefore, that Nova Scotia's value-added per employee in a standard working week fluctuated during the period between about 68 and 73 per cent of that of Quebec-Ontario.[11]

Second, Nova Scotia factories may have been so small that specialization of labour and other internal economies were not attainable to the same degree as in Quebec-Ontario. Table 3/10 leaves no doubt that, on the average, Nova Scotia factories were indeed relatively small. During the whole period, their labour forces were only one-half the size of those in Quebec-Ontario. Indeed, 72 per cent of Nova Scotia establishments in 1962 employed less than fifteen persons, and it is difficult to see how economies of scale could be achieved in such tiny factories. Quebec-Ontario also had small plants, but the proportion of the establishments in that region employing less than fifteen persons was only 63 per cent.

The Economic Council of Canada has cast doubt upon the relevance

TABLE 3 / 10

Average number of employees per manufacturing establishment, Nova Scotia and Quebec-Ontario, 1946–62 (selected years)

	Nova Scotia	Quebec-Ontario
1946	21.3	38.5
1951	20.7	40.9
1956	22.1	42.9
1961	22.0	40.4
1962	23.2	41.5

SOURCE: Derived from Tables B/8 and B/11.

11 The value-added per employee in manufacturing industry, adjusted for the length of the working week, Nova Scotia as a percentage of Quebec-Ontario, is as follows: 1946, 70.8 per cent; 1951, 68.0; 1956, 72.5; 1961, 71.0; 1962, 68.3 (derived from Tables 3/3 and 3/8).

of plant size as an explanation of different levels of productivity and suggests that the degree of diversification is more important.[12] Its evidence comes from a study of fifty large manufacturing industries with plants in Canada and the United States.

This study, however, may have little relevance for interprovincial comparisons since there is no evidence that the degree of diversification is different in Nova Scotia than it is in plants of similar size in Quebec and Ontario. Indeed, the council's explanation for the different degrees of diversification in Canada and the United States – different commercial policies, foreign trade barriers, government buying policies, restrictive practices, and companies legislation – seem to have little relevance within Canada itself.

In an attempt to determine the effect of size in our present interregional comparisons, the value-added per employee in the manufacturing industry of Nova Scotia was standardized[13] to the Quebec-Ontario size distribution of establishments, measured by the size of their labour forces. The results, giving Nova Scotia as a percentage of Quebec-Ontario, are as follows:

1946	77.5
1951	74.3
1956	74.4
1961	71.9
1962	73.5[14]

Comparing these results with the figures in the last column of Table 3/8 (except for 1961 and 1962, see note 14), we find that the size of establishments does seem to explain some of the differences in value-added per employee between Nova Scotia and Quebec-Ontario. It might account for about 3.4 of the 25.9 percentage points difference in the early part of the period, and for about 4.3 of the 31.8 percentage points at the end.

Third, the industry-mix might have been different in the two regions, which is important since value-added per employee varies greatly from industry to industry. If Nova Scotia had a disproportionately large share of industries in which, by their nature, value-added per employee was

12 *Fourth Annual Review* (Ottawa, 1967), p. 153 ff.
13 Using a method similar to that described in n. (*c*) of Table 3/7.
14 The 1961 and 1962 percentages are based upon data unadjusted for changes in concepts and coverage introduced by DBS in 1961, information not being available to permit the adjustment of value-added or numbers of employees. The actual value-added per employee based on unadjusted figures, Nova Scotia as a percentage of Quebec-Ontario, was 69.4 in 1961 and 69.2 in 1962. These are the percentages with which the 1961 and 1962 standardized figures should be compared rather than those in Table 3/8.

always low, then this might account for part of the overall divergence between value-added in the two regions. The following figures[15] demonstrate the effect of industry-mix:

1946	76.1
1951	70.5
1956	81.3
1961	79.9
1962	78.9

Comparing these results with the last column of Table 3/8 (except in 1961 and 1962), it becomes clear that standardizing to the Quebec-Ontario mix of industries closes the value-added gap in 1946 by 2 per cent. In 1951 the effect of standardizing is almost nil. Thus it seems that high value-added industries assumed a greater share of industry in Quebec-Ontario than was the case in Nova Scotia, and standardizing in 1956, 1961, and 1962 reduced the value-added per employee gap between the two regions by 8.9, 10.5, and 9.7 per cent.

Fourth, there might have been substitution of labour, which at least as far as wage-rates are concerned was relatively cheap in Nova Scotia, for other factors which were not. Since labour rates were lower in Nova Scotia while the proportion labour costs comprised of total costs was much the same in both regions, there is little doubt that the physical quantities of labour relative to the physical quantities of other factors was higher in Nova Scotia; so each Nova Scotia worker had less materials, capital, and other factors with which to work. It is tempting to conclude that this may explain at least part of the lower output per man-hour in that province.

This matter should be judged, however, from the quantities of inputs required to produce any given output. Looking at 1962 we find that for each $100 of Nova Scotian output, $58.60 of materials and fuel, $0.75 of purchased electricity, and about $8.00 capital (depreciation and interest) were used, in addition to labour; while, in Quebec-Ontario, $100 of output was produced with $55.00 of materials and fuel, $0.87 of purchased electricity, and about $8.00 capital, plus labour.[16] Since materials and fuel were about 2 per cent cheaper in Quebec-Ontario (see p. 60), the physical input of materials and fuel per unit output seems much the same in the two regions and there is no sign of materials being displaced by labour in Nova Scotia to any significant degree.

15 Value-added per employee in manufacturing industry standardized to the Quebec-Ontario mix of industrial groups, Nova Scotia as a percentage of Quebec-Ontario. Notes 13 and 14 apply to these figures as well.
16 See Tables 4/1, 4/2, and 5/1; also p. 66.

Electricity, when one takes account of its relatively high price in Nova Scotia, must have been used more sparingly. However, Nova Scotian firms tended to generate more electricity for their own use (see p. 61) and to use more fuel (see p. 59); again there is little sign of labour having displaced electricity. And, finally, there is no indication that labour was being used in lieu of capital in Nova Scotia. Indeed, in 1943 (the last year for which provincial estimates of capital stocks in manufacturing were regularly published by the DBS), Nova Scotia was reported to be using $95 capital to achieve each $100 of output compared with only $74 for Quebec-Ontario[17]; and investment from 1946 to 1962 in Nova Scotia per $100 of output in 1962 was $65 compared with only $55 in Quebec-Ontario.[18] If anything, therefore, capital investment seemed to have been applied in even greater doses in Nova Scotia, but apparently to less effect.

It seems clear that the relatively low output per man in Nova Scotia was not due to the substitution of labour for other factors. For any given output, Nova Scotian factories used at least as much materials, fuel, electricity, and capital. The efficiency of labour is therefore properly measured by the output per worker, after allowance is made for the length of the working week, the size of the plant, and the industry-mix. Table 3/11 traces this measure of efficiency over the period, expressing Nova Scotia's value-added per employee as a percentage of that of Quebec-Ontario. It started at just over 76 per cent, sank a little by 1951,

TABLE 3 / 11

Value-added per employee in manufacturing industry, Nova Scotia as percentage of Quebec-Ontario, after application of standardizing procedures, 1946–62 (selected years)

| | Value-added: Nova Scotia as percentage of Quebec-Ontario, adjusted for length of working week (p. 44, n. 11) | Effect of standardization | | Value-added: Nova Scotia as percentage of Quebec-Ontario, after standardization |
		For size distribution of establishments (p. 45)	For industry-mix (p. 46)	
1946	70.8	+3.4	+2.0	76.2
1951	68.0	+3.9	+0.1	72.0
1956	72.5	+2.0	+8.9	83.4
1961	71.0	+2.5	+10.5	84.0
1962	68.3	+4.3	+9.7	82.3

17 DBS, *The Manufacturing Industries of Canada, 1943.*
18 Derived from Tables B/28 (unadjusted data) and B/29.

rose to over 80 per cent in 1956 where it remained fairly constant for the remainder of the period.[19]

Since labour is an important element in firms' costs, we should consider why there was this 20 to 25 per cent gap between the productive efficiency (measured in terms of value-added per employee adjusted for different conditions) in Nova Scotia and in Quebec-Ontario. Investigations which have previously taken place suggest that there really are no great differences between people. C. B. Hoover and B. U. Ratchford, for instance, found that labour in the southern United States, which tradition would have one believe was physically and mentally relatively slow, was in fact just as efficient as non-southern labour with similar equipment and training.[20] R. A. Lester came to similar conclusions following research in the same area.[21] And the responses from Michigan manufacturers questioned in the study reported by Mueller, Wilken, and Wood suggest that alleged differences between workers were really attributable to different skills in management. One respondent complained that Michigan workers "... don't want to work. Want 3 day week and 2 hour day"; another lamented that "wage rates, work rules, featherbedding add up to a bad situation." But another claimed that Michigan's "biggest advantage is in the labor force. It's vital, alive, adaptable. Can be trained readily. The workers are steady and reliable."[22] The bad workman blames his tools.

Much the same assessments were made by the firms in the Multiplant Firm Study. They were asked to give the "output per hour of average Nova Scotia worker as percentage of output per hour of his counterpart in Ontario or Quebec, assuming similar circumstances (e.g., similar machinery, similar type of operation, similar management competency, etc.)." The answers indicated that some found small differences between Nova Scotian and Quebec-Ontario workers, but the median was 100 per cent with very little deviation. Executives of the firms did not deny the widely held opinion that Nova Scotians tend to be lacka-

19 There is some risk that the allowances for the size distribution of establishments and for the industry-mix might be double-counting the same characteristic. This could be so if the industries in which Nova Scotia was deficient were also those which had relatively large production units in which value-added per worker was high. The maximum extent of the double-counting would be 2.0 per cent (1946), 0.1 per cent (1951), 2.0 per cent (1956), 2.5 per cent (1961), and 4.3 per cent (1962). Unfortunately, data are not available to allow a check on this to be made.

20 *Report of Joint Committee on Impact of Federal Policies on the Economy of the South* (Washington, 1949).

21 "Effectiveness of Factory Labor: South-North Comparisons," *Journal of Political Economy*, 54 (1946), pp. 60–75.

22 *Location Decisions and Industrial Mobility in Michigan, 1961*, pp. 41–2.

daisical, and more impressed with the joys of hunting, shooting, and fishing than with monetary advancement; but they said that, while Nova Scotians did not bustle and make outward signs of frantic industry, just as much work was done in the end. They nearly all considered that were an average Nova Scotian worker to be plucked from his present job and dropped into a similar one in Ontario or Quebec, he would again be an average employee in his new position, as far as productivity was concerned. To illustrate how wrong the labour-productivity folklore can be, one executive recounted how his firm had a few years previously moved its productive facilities from a thickly populated city in Ontario to a small town in the same province. He and his colleagues had been warned from all sides about the differences in attitude and performance that they could expect from the labour force in the new locality. However, none of these prophecies had come true. Once the firm had settled down, no differences in labour productivity had been found; and, as this firm went to the trouble of measuring efficiency by rather elaborate means, its assessment must be taken as being unusually reliable. In the same strain, an executive who had managed labour in many parts of New England and was interviewed in the Selected Local Areas Study spoke with enthusiasm of the willingness of Nova Scotian workmen to stay on outside jobs in weather conditions which would have driven indoors the most determined New Englanders. He expressed the belief that a man who is used to living in poverty with little prospect of escaping from it tends to adopt a slow, unimaginative approach to his work; but if he is offered good wages and the possibility of acquiring those goods and services which he sees advertised and which he knows others enjoy, he will usually come to life and be as good a workman as anyone else.

To check that there were no hidden costs of labour in Nova Scotia which the Multiplant Firm Study was overlooking, executives were asked about their firms' training expenses, absenteeism, and turnover. None of the firms seemed to keep accurate records, so the answers were largely the subjective judgments of executives; but one would have expected senior executives to have been aware of any sharp divergences from one plant to another. The executives thought training costs were much the same in each region; anyway, since training was usually given on the job, such costs were of little consequence. Turnover was also apparently much the same in each region. Several executives of firms with well-established factories in Nova Scotia spoke with relief of the stability of their labour force compared with those in their Quebec-Ontario factories. One remarked about the fact that even those employees of his firm's Nova Scotian factory who had to be laid off at the beginning of the winter were usually the same ones who returned in the spring, which was very different from his experience in other provinces. Of course, new factories always tended to have relatively high turnovers until they settled down, and wherever women comprised a high proportion of a labour force the comings and goings were also generally high; but this was equally true everywhere.

The story on absenteeism was much the same, all firms believing that there was no difference between Nova Scotian and Quebec-Ontario employees in this respect. Again, new factories had given trouble, particularly when they were sited in country districts or small towns of Nova Scotia where the population had been unaccustomed to factory discipline and had been somewhat casual about attendance. After the settling down period was over, however, the firms had always found that the attendance record in Nova Scotia was better than that of their employees in Quebec or Ontario. Two executives did remark, however, on the rather different attitude to work in the two regions. In Nova Scotia, they found, workers who were voluntarily absent were more likely to have been "otherwise engaged" than to have been just malingering. One said it was very usual for his firm's Nova Scotian plant to be almost deserted at the onset of the hunting season. Even the local manager was out in the woods with his gun. However, taking the full twelve months into consideration, the periodic absences due to outside attractions seemed to have been balanced by greater reliability at other times.

We are faced with having to explain why the executives in the Multiplant Firm Study thought Nova Scotian labour the equal of that available in Quebec-Ontario while our foregoing analysis showed that it was appreciably less productive. The answer almost certainly lies in differences in terminology. The factor of production traditionally called "labour" in economics performs two very different functions. One of these is the carrying out of manual and clerical operations under direction; the other is the managing of the operations. They are difficult to distinguish in practice and impossible to separate statistically, since some management responsibilities are diffused downward to employees occupying relatively humble positions in the hierarchy and also performing manual or routine clerical operations; and entrepreneurs often undertake management duties, particularly in small firms. But in principle they are quite distinct. What Hoover and Ratchford, Lester, and other observers were referring to in their comparisons was obviously the purely labour role. Indeed, Lester specifically points out that any differences between the productivity of labour in the locations he was examining was due to inferior management or equipment. As several of the Multiplant Firm Study executives remarked, there are no bad workmen – only bad managers.

The Multiplant Firm Study companies were in a special position because they were interprovincial and could therefore draw their managers for their Nova Scotian plants from the same pool which supplied their Quebec-Ontario plants. And once installed, their managers had to conform to standards set by other factories belonging to the firm and by central Canadian executives. Under these circumstances it is not surprising that their Nova Scotian workers performed as well as their Quebec-Ontario workers.

By contrast, the vast majority of Nova Scotian firms included above in our statistical analysis were locally controlled. The pressures which applied in the case of the companies in the Multiplant Firm Study were therefore absent, and it seems fairly clear that management was inferior and consequently labour was less productive. It is impossible to produce conclusive proof of this, but it is a conclusion which seems to be becoming accepted by observers. Louis J. Walinsky blamed a lack of effective competition which produced "higher prices and profit margins on smaller volume, a smugness on the part of management, and inadequate incentive – or compulsion – to innovation and investment to improve products and to lower costs."[23] (He was here linking management and entrepreneurship obviously, as we observed above, because both functions are often discharged by the same person or group of persons. The inferiority of entrepreneurship in Nova Scotia will be discussed later in chapter 10.) Similarly Lavoie, Rourke, and Fisch talked about a "lack of awareness of modern management techniques in small- and medium-sized businesses" in Nova Scotia and a "shortage of competent management specialists with training in and knowledge of the newer techniques."[24] The relatively small number of university graduates in the labour force in Nova Scotia (see Table 3/9) no doubt contributed to this shortage.

If all these opinions are correct, the weak part of the factor "labour" in Nova Scotia is management. While intrinsically Nova Scotians are able and willing to work as hard and as effectively as are people in Quebec and Ontario, they are less expertly and energetically managed. While the conclusions of the last column of Table 3/11 must stand as

23 "Strategy and Policy for Economic Growth in the Atlantic Region," address to the Annual Conference of the Atlantic Provinces Economic Council, mimeo. (Halifax, 1966), p. 10.
24 J. C. Lavoie, P. W. Rourke, and G. G. Fisch, "Management Concepts and Methods in the Smaller Company," Conference on Productivity through New Technology, mimeo. (Halifax, 1966), p. 12.

a description of the present situation, we should remember that if a firm which commands any given management competence is estimating the comparative cost of producing in Nova Scotia and in Quebec-Ontario, it should consider that labour productivity in the two regions will be much the same.

From the foregoing conclusions of this chapter, we may now proceed to compute the comparative cost of a unit of labour services in Nova Scotia and Quebec-Ontario. The first approximation made at the start of the discussion (Table 3/2) relied upon average annual earnings per employee. The adjustments necessary to allow for differences between the two regions in respect of working hours, industry-mixes, male-female mixes, and labour quality were then made. The final results appear on the last line of Table 3/12.[25] Their consistency and nearness to 100 per cent seem to support the conclusion that Nova Scotian labour was being paid in proportion to its effectiveness throughout the period and that a unit of work of given quality costs much the same in both regions.

TABLE 3 / 12

Computation of cost of labour in manufacturing industry, Nova Scotia as percentage of Quebec-Ontario, 1946–62 (selected years)

		1946	1951	1956	1961	1962
A	Average annual wages and salaries per employee (Table 3/2)	87.8	79.7	79.6	79.1	78.7
B	Working hours (Table 3/3)	104.8	103.7	99.8	99.7	99.7
C	Labour quality (Table 3/11)	76.2	72.0	83.4	84.0	82.3
D	A ÷ B ÷ C	109.9	106.7	95.6	94.5	95.9
E	Differences in annual wages and salaries attributable to mix of industries (Table 3/4)	−3.8	+1.3	+8.7	+6.2	+7.9
F	Differences in annual wages and salaries attributable to the male-female composition of labour force (Table 3/7)	−5.2	−4.4	−4.0	−3.7	−3.7
G	Cost of labour (D + E + F)	100.9	103.6	100.3	97.0	100.1

25 The problem again arises as to whether or not there might be double-counting. For instance, the adjustment on account of the mix of industries might be simply counting again part of the adjustment made because of differences between working hours. Unfortunately, official statistics are inadequate to allow this matter to be investigated. However, since the adjustments for industry-mix work in opposite directions to the adjustments for labour quality and the male-female mix during most of the period, and it is there that the greatest risk of double-counting would appear to lie, the problem does not seem to be a very big one.

Again, however, it is worth repeating the caution that the relatively low effectiveness of Nova Scotian labour, which brings about this equality even though wage-rates are relatively low in that province, is very likely to be the result of management inadequacy. If this could be corrected, then *ceteris paribus* the cost of a unit of work of given quality in Nova Scotia would have only cost 83.1 per cent as much as in Quebec-Ontario in 1962 and similar proportions in earlier years (see Table 9/2). This seems borne out by the responses from the executives interviewed in the Multiplant Firm Study when they were asked to express the average rate per hour in their Nova Scotia plants as a percentage of the average rate per hour for similar work done in their Quebec-Ontario plants. The median was 88 per cent (86 per cent for workers, 100 per cent for executives). This was rather higher than the 83.1 per cent just submitted, no doubt because of the interprovincial nature of the firms concerned, since unions tend always to exert pressure to equalize wage-rates in factories belonging to the same firm, wherever situated.[26]

SUPPLY OF LABOUR

The supply of labour is often considered as a matter quite distinct from the cost of labour. In the Site-Choice Study, for instance, while the cost of labour was only cited as an important factor four times by firms which considered more than one province as possible locations for their new plants, the availability of labour was mentioned twenty times.[27] The supply of executives, who are probably best considered as a specialized type of labour, was mentioned three times.

In principle, the supply of labour and the cost of labour are really different facets of the same thing. In any location a firm were to choose in Canada, however remote or undesirable as a place to live, it could obtain all the labour it was ever likely to need – at a price. However, in the smaller communities, the supply curve of labour to a particular firm may be kinked, at least in the short run. So long as the firm's labour requirements are small relative to the total supply in the district, then it should be able to get what it needs at the prevailing rate. But if its requirements are relatively large, then it might be able to fill only part of them at the prevailing rates. To obtain more labour would in-

26 The fact that our estimates turned out to be below those obtained in the Multiplant Firm Study also helps to still any fears of double-counting.
27 This accords with the findings of the study of Mueller, Wilken, and Wood, *Location Decisions and Industrial Mobility in Michigan, 1961,* in which Michigan manufacturers mentioned the availability of labour skills as one of the two most important factors in choosing the location of their plants.

volve raiding other firms or enticing people from a distance. This would often require offering rates in excess of those previously prevailing locally. Once the local supply is exhausted, therefore, the marginal cost of labour shoots upwards. This might apply to the overall supply of labour in that community. For instance, a firm setting up a factory requiring five hundred employees at Cheticamp (a town of twelve hundred persons situated on the northwest coast of Cape Breton) would simply not be able to hire locally all the hands it needed. But another firm requiring only ten employees for a plant in Halifax might be in the same predicament, if those ten had to be able to do unusually difficult types of welding or operate especially sophisticated machine-tools. Where the shortage is in certain specialized types of labour, the position may sometimes be met by training local people. This avoids forcing up local rates to attract in outsiders but still effectively means paying more for labour. The supply and price of labour thus really boil down to the same thing. However, firms tend to think of price in terms of the rates prevailing in a certain area and, if higher rates have to be offered to attract additional labour, the situation is often described as one of labour shortage rather than of high rates.

There have been a number of instances of firms establishing plants during recent years in Nova Scotia having suffered "shortages" of certain types of labour. One firm included in the Selected Local Areas Study had great difficulty in building up a reasonably well-disciplined labour force in a district where factory work was unfamiliar; another firm requiring high-grade welders found a great dearth of them in Nova Scotia; another firm (one of those in the Multiplant Firm Study) experienced a shortage of labour willing to undertake hard unfamiliar tasks; and another had to go shopping abroad on a big scale for skilled tradesmen.

Some of the Nova Scotian plants of firms included in the Multiplant Firm Study had also had labour supply difficulties due to the reluctance of non-Maritimers to come to Nova Scotia. Natives of Quebec and Ontario often, apparently, need high bribes to abandon what they tend to regard as "civilization" for a life in the Maritime "bush."[28] One firm

28 An analysis of some ten thousand personnel files of P. S. Ross and Partners, Management Consultants, with branches across Canada, indicated that only 0.5 per cent of the executives listed had expressed a preference for working in the Maritimes. While the consultants' personnel files cannot be considered a representative sample of all Canadian executives, and the picture was blurred because 25 per cent of the executives had expressed no preference for any particular area, nevertheless there does seem to be a strong bias against the Maritimes.

The attitude of non-Maritimers to the Atlantic region is also well illustrated by a report in the Halifax *Mail-Star* of March 17, 1966. Apparently, a native had to go as far as to "crack the whip" (as the informant put it) to induce an Ontario man to take up the management of its Nova Scotian plant.

The availability of labour, therefore, may sometimes be one of the most important influences on the location of manufacturing industry. But Nova Scotia has towns and cities with labour forces big enough to man all but the largest plants, and nowadays few manufacturing processes demand special skills not generally available.

OTHER FACTORS AFFECTING LABOUR COSTS

Other considerations relative to labour costs, quite distinct from those already mentioned, might influence the choice of a site if the firm concerned already operated one or more plants. Let us suppose, for example, that the proposed new plant is to be a small branch of the main plant. Then the additional cost of managing the new plant (which is properly considered as part of its labour costs) will depend upon the position of the new plant relative to the old. If the new plant is sited near the older one ("near" in terms of the time and expense of travelling between them rather than the geographical distance separating them), then the firm's existing executives may be able, with some assistance, to control both effectively. If the two plants are far apart, then this no longer will be possible. Either it will be attempted and result in looser control of both plants and lowering of the executives' general efficiency due to fatigue, or a separate set of executives will have to be appointed who, because of the small size of the new plant, will be either inferior to the existing ones or else underemployed.[29] Whatever

of Calgary announced to his friends that Air Canada, his employer, was transferring him to Nova Scotia. Their reaction was to ask him what he had done wrong. Such prejudices probably owe their origin partly to impressions gained during the two world wars by servicemen who spent miserable years away from home in a grossly overcrowded Halifax. While they were suffering the humiliations of the military feudal system and the loneliness of being cut off from their families, they were scorned by many of the local population and preyed upon by local landlords. Their feelings were vented by serious rioting on VE Day.

Maritimers are no less prejudiced. They tend to regard "Upper Canada," a term nowadays applied loosely to all of southern Ontario and most of southern Quebec, as the modern equivalent of Sodom and Gomorrah, and to dismiss the rest of Canada, excepting perhaps British Columbia, as a lonely wilderness.

29 The development of air travel has radically altered the feasibility of management from a distance. An executive can be at a branch plant two hundred miles away from his office in two and a half hours. And because the speed of jet aircraft is so great and a significant part of the total travelling time is taken in getting to and from airports, extra distance is of little consequence. Increas-

happens, the total cost of labour required to achieve a certain output at a distant plant will be greater than at a nearby plant, if all circumstances other than management are the same. However, in the Site-Choice Study, the difficulties of combining the management of two or more factories did not emerge as an important influence upon the choice of location to those firms which considered more than one province. It came only seventh on the list. This is not surprising because only one plant in seven covered by that study was set up by a firm which already had a plant in the Quebec-Ontario region.

The second consideration may arise when the firm is facing the prospect of placing a factory in a part of the country where a different language is spoken. While labour costs in two provinces may be equal, as far as established factories are concerned, a firm searching for the best site for a new plant may believe that language difficulties between executives of the firm and people working at the new plant would lead to confusion and consequently to high labour costs. However, this was only mentioned four times in the Site-Choice Study as an important consideration in determining the choice of site by firms which set up plants in Quebec or Ontario after considering locations in other provinces.

The third consideration concerns the problems of maintaining close contact with customers when the firm operates a long way from its main markets. This was the second most important reason influencing the eventual choice of site by the firms in the Site-Choice Study which considered other provinces.[30] Firms seem to claim that close contact affords several advantages: it builds up a personal relationship with the customers and thus makes salesmanship easier; it makes it possible to detect any changes in the tastes of the customers so that product modification may be undertaken in good time; it gives early warning of any threat from competitors and permits any defensive action which may be necessary; it enables a customer's grievances to be dealt with before they fester; and it reveals when a customer is involved in financial difficulties which might make him a bad credit risk. None of these

ing the distance from two hundred to two thousand miles will do little more than double the time the journey takes. However, and for the same reason, full advantage of air travel can only be enjoyed if the plants the executives are to manage are near main airports. This effectively reduces the list of appropriate locations.

30 The Economist Intelligence Unit, *Atlantic Provinces Transportation Study* (Ottawa, 1967), v, p. 93, was also impressed with the difficulties and costliness of distribution which Maritime producers have to face when they try to supply the central Canadian market. Its views are discussed later (see pp. 72–3) when some doubts are raised regarding the validity of the supporting arguments.

points, however, would compel a firm to put its plant near the market. All the alleged advantages of close personal contact with customers could be achieved by a firm producing a long way from the market if it were prepared to appoint local representatives of sufficient calibre. But high-calibre representatives are expensive. It therefore boils down to a simple matter of cost, and firms advancing this reason presumably meant that they were drawn to their chosen location by the promise of being able to avoid some of the cost of maintaining local representatives. However, this does not seem to have been a big problem for Nova Scotian manufacturers. Only two of the twenty-nine firms included in the Selected Local Areas Study which marketed part of their output in central Canada found it necessary to maintain local representatives there, and none of the rest felt at any disadvantage by not having them; yet only five of those twenty-nine had any association with other organizations in that region.

4 Materials and Fuel

When goods and services bought by manufacturing firms are divided into categories for statistical purposes, fuel is usually lumped together with electricity. This is perhaps to be expected since they are both used to heat and light factories, to drive machinery, and to supply heat for processing; and they can often be substituted one for the other. However, the two are in several respects quite dissimilar. Coal, oil, and most other fuels are shipped in much the same form and manner as are materials used in processes; indeed, in some industries, they are themselves the materials of the production processes. And the expenses of their transportation are usually a clearly identifiable element of their delivered cost. Electricity, by contrast, is obtained merely in the form of energy transmitted along a cable connected to the nearest supply point. If any categorization has to be done, a case might easily be made out for putting materials and fuel in the same category, leaving electricity by itself. We shall adopt this basis since it will be very convenient in the analysis which follows, mainly because it will enable us to draw on the Multiplant Firm Study, which used the same basis, for information which is not otherwise available.

Table 4/1 indicates the importance of the cost of materials and what a consistent relationship it bore to the value of output. In both Nova Scotia and Quebec-Ontario it accounted for a little over one-half of the value of firms' output throughout the whole period. In Nova Scotia the proportion was slightly higher than in Quebec-Ontario. About one-half of this difference seems to have been due to higher prices (which will be discussed shortly) while the rest may be attributable to different types of materials being required by the different assortment of industries in the two regions or to the higher degree of vertical integration in the larger establishments of Quebec-Ontario.

TABLE 4 / 1

Cost of materials purchased by manufacturing
industry as percentage of selling value of
factory shipments, Nova Scotia and
Quebec-Ontario, 1946–62 (selected years)

	Nova Scotia	Quebec-Ontario
1946	56.1	52.8
1951	56.7	54.1
1956	55.9	53.8
1961	55.4	53.3
1962	57.0	53.9

SOURCE: Derived from Tables B/21 and B/28.

Table 4/2 expresses the cost of fuel as a proportion of the value of output. In Nova Scotia the proportion rose slightly from about 3 per cent at the beginning of the period, then declined spectacularly, undoubtedly because of the substitution of electricity for coal as a source of power in factories. In the Quebec-Ontario region fuel costs were relatively much less important.

Taken together, the cost of materials and fuel delivered to Nova Scotian plants made up between 57 and 60 per cent of the value of output during the period, while the percentage for Quebec-Ontario plants varied within the range of 54 to 56. The Nova Scotian proportion was consistent with the replies received in the Multiplant Firm Study, when the median percentage for all firms surveyed in 1962 was 58.

The Multiplant Firm Study is the only source of information available to us upon which we may form a comparison between the cost of materials and fuel in Nova Scotia and Quebec-Ontario. Executives were asked to compare the cost of materials (including fuel) used in

TABLE 4 / 2

Cost of fuel purchased by manufacturing industry
as percentage of selling value of factory shipments,
Nova Scotia and Quebec-Ontario,
1946–62 (selected years)

	Nova Scotia	Quebec-Ontario
1946	2.9	1.6
1951	3.2	1.5
1956	2.7	1.5
1961	1.6	1.1
1962	1.6	1.1

SOURCE: Derived from Tables B/26 and B/28.

their firms' Nova Scotian factories in 1962 with the cost of similar materials in Quebec and Ontario. The answers varied considerably. For one factory processing a bulky, low-value material available in abundance in Nova Scotia but not produced in Quebec and Ontario the answer was 60 per cent; but another firm which had to face the high costs of bringing heavy containers into Nova Scotia from central Canadian suppliers quoted a proportion of 150 per cent. The median of all firms was 102 per cent, the extra cost in Nova Scotia being invariably attributed to transportation charges.

There is little reason to believe that the relative position was significantly different earlier in the period. We shall see later (Table 7/6) that rises in the cost of transporting one ton of manufactured goods within the Atlantic provinces kept step with rises in the cost of transporting one ton within the central Canadian region. If the transportation costs of materials and fuel moved in a similar fashion and most materials and fuel were obtained locally or from abroad by manufacturers in each region (the Nova Scotian plants covered by the Multiplant Firm Study were bringing in only about 8 per cent of their materials and fuel from Quebec-Ontario), the 102 per cent derived for 1962 must have remained almost constant throughout the period.

While the difference in the cost of materials and fuel in the two regions was evidently not great, the importance of materials costs in firms' outlays makes even this small difference of some significance. It caused an inflation of Nova Scotia's total costs by 1.2 per cent throughout the period.

The importance of materials and fuel costs was confirmed by the Site-Choice Study in which they were mentioned fifteen times as being amongst the three most important factors which had led firms which considered other provinces to choose the site upon which they actually built their new factories. They were the fourth most important location-deciding factor. However, this prominence was due solely to materials costs, fuel costs not being mentioned once.

5 Electricity

IMPORTANCE OF ELECTRICITY COSTS

Electricity costs are important to firms using heat treatment for the production of ferro-alloys and special steels, to firms such as aluminum manufacturers which employ electrolytic processes, and to a few others. But to the average firm, which uses electricity only for lighting and heating buildings and for driving and controlling machinery, its cost is of minor consequence.

Table 5/1 illustrates that in Nova Scotia the cost of electricity did not exceed 0.92 per cent of the value of output in any year,[1] and while some fluctuation did occur during the period, no trend is apparent.

TABLE 5/1

Cost of electricity purchased by manufacturing industry as percentage of selling value of factory shipments, Nova Scotia and Quebec-Ontario, 1946–62 (selected years)

	Nova Scotia	Quebec-Ontario
1946	0.84	1.09
1951	0.76	0.82
1956	0.80	0.89
1961	0.92	0.92
1962	0.75	0.87

SOURCE: Derived from Tables B/23 and B/28.

1 A greater proportion of electricity used in Nova Scotia was generated by the factories themselves than was the case in Quebec-Ontario (see Tables B/22 and B/24). Had electricity generated for own use been included at the same price per k.w.h. as was charged for purchased electricity, the proportions for Nova Scotia shown in Table 5/1 would, in all cases, have been a little higher than for Quebec-Ontario.

This proportion is reasonably consistent with the findings of the Multi-plant Firm Study. While one firm examined in that study reported that power represented 4 per cent of total costs, others gave theirs as between 0.5 and 1.5 per cent, so that the median was one per cent.[2]

In Quebec-Ontario there was no sign of a clear trend except between 1946 and 1951 when a sharp drop occurred. Since the prices charged there for electricity were relatively low, it is clear that plants in that region must have used much greater quantities than did Nova Scotian plants. Some of this excess was no doubt due to the substitution of electricity for fuel.

COMPARATIVE COST OF ELECTRICITY

Table 5/2 shows how much more expensive electricity was in Nova Scotia than in Quebec-Ontario. In 1949 (the first year for which data are available), it was more than twice the price. During the next thirteen years Nova Scotian prices fluctuated up and down but ended up where they had been in the beginning. However, during the same period, Quebec-Ontario prices rose by almost 60 per cent and so, in 1962, Nova Scotia rates were only 140 per cent of those in Quebec-Ontario. While this was still a very large differential, it represented a big improvement during the period in Nova Scotia's relative position.

The purpose of Table 5/3 is to confirm that the higher charges for electricity in Nova Scotia were not simply the outcome of manufacturers in that province consuming smaller quantities and therefore not qualifying for the discounts traditionally given larger customers. It leaves no doubt that it was the character of the tariff which led to the

TABLE 5/2

Average cost per kilowatt-hour of electricity purchased by manufacturing industry, Nova Scotia and Quebec-Ontario, 1949–62 (selected years)

	Nova Scotia	Quebec-Ontario	Nova Scotia as percentage of
	(mills per k.w.h.)		Quebec-Ontario
1949	8.02	3.61	222.2
1951	7.97	3.73	213.7
1956	8.39	4.74	177.0
1961	8.99	5.42	166.0
1962	8.00	5.71	140.2

SOURCE: Derived from Tables B/22 and B/23.

2 Water costs were included in these figures, but they are believed to be too small to influence the results significantly.

TABLE 5 / 3
*Index of price of electricity (unrestricted twenty-four-hour power) purchased in
Montreal and Toronto metropolitan areas, 1962
(consumption, k.w.h. per month; Halifax metropolitan area = 100)*

Metro-politan area	Billed load 5 k.w.			Billed load 50 k.w.			Billed load 100 k.w.		
	500	1,000	1,500	5,000	10,000	15,000	10,000	20,000	30,000
Montreal	73	62	53	73	62	53	69	59	50
Toronto	73	59	51	73	59	51	73	59	51

SOURCE: Derived from Table B/25.

higher charges – at least in the main metropolitan areas.[3] In 1962, at every level of consumption, a Halifax user would have been paying between 137 and 200 per cent of what he would have been charged in Montreal or Toronto.

The Multiplant Firm Study also sought evidence on the relative level of electricity charges in the two regions. The results obtained were at variance with Table 5/2; for whereas some firms did remark upon the high charges in Nova Scotia (one firm operating a chemical-type process gave the cost of electricity at its Nova Scotian factory as 180 per cent of what it would have paid for the same service in Quebec or Ontario), most were aware of little difference between the tariffs in the two regions. The median was 100 per cent. The only explanation for the discrepancy would appear to be that electricity costs were so tiny relative to overall costs that firms did not concern themselves with them. So long as a reliable supply was available, that was all they worried about.

In spite of the results of the Multiplant Firm Study there seems little doubt that electricity costs were relatively very high in Nova Scotia. But as they made up less than one per cent of the value of output, they inflated total costs by only one per cent at the beginning of the period and 0.3 per cent at the end. It should come as no surprise, therefore, that in the Site-Choice Study not one firm which had considered locating outside the province it actually chose for its new plant mentioned the cost of electricity as a principal factor influencing its choice.[4]

3 The metropolitan areas are not entirely typical of the provinces as a whole. Rates in both Montreal and Toronto are the lowest in their provinces while Halifax prices are midway between the very high ones in the Sydney area and those of the Truro and New Glasgow areas, which compare well with those in central Canada.

4 Even in the aluminum industry, which has traditionally been quoted as an industry whose location is determined by the cost and availability of electric power, other factors are becoming more important. See, for instance, G. Schramm, "The Effects of Low-Cost Hydro Power on Industrial Location," *Canadian Journal of Economics*, II, no. 2 (May 1969), pp. 210–29.

6 Capital

The cost to any firm of employing the factor "capital" is a function of the quantity of buildings, equipment, and inventories in use, their prices, the rate at which they decrease in value due to use or obsolescence, and the rate of interest on the moneys used to buy them. Measurement is fraught with theoretical difficulties about the valuation of assets at different points in time and the calculation of imputed interest on firms' own funds tied up in capital assets. There are also the practical difficulties of obtaining meaningful data. For most of our period there was no regular flow of information on the matter from official sources and data obtained from firms themselves are produced by arbitrary accounting procedures which are conceived more for practical simplicity than economic significance and vary from one firm to another and from one point in time to another. We shall have to make do, however, with such fragmentary information as we can pick up.

IMPORTANCE OF CAPITAL COSTS

For Canadian manufacturing industry as a whole in the year 1949, the sum of capital consumption allowances and investment income was almost 11 per cent of the value of output at producers' prices.[1] This proportion really represents a mixture of profits in the economic sense, depreciation of equipment, and interest payable on the funds tied up in the firms' fixed and working capital – funds which belong to their proprietors and others. We shall have to try to disentangle some of these parts.

1 DBS, *Supplement to Inter-Industry Flow of Goods and Services, 1949*, 13–513, Table I.

When we come to examine the return to entrepreneurship, we shall find that the taxable corporation income of Nova Scotian manufacturers was almost 6 per cent of the selling value of factory shipments in 1962 (see Table 10/1). This was a mixture of profit and interest on proprietors' own capital. We know therefore that profit plus proprietors' interest equals almost 6 per cent, and that profit plus interest on proprietors' and borrowed funds plus depreciation equals 11 per cent (assuming that the DBS estimate of capital consumption allowances and investment income applied equally to Nova Scotia and had not changed significantly by 1962). Since the interest paid by manufacturing firms to outsiders is believed to be tiny,[2] we can obtain values for profit and then for depreciation if we can estimate imputed interest on proprietors' funds.

We may obtain an estimate of the interest imputed to funds tied up in fixed assets in Nova Scotia in 1962 by adding together the investment carried out in that province between 1946 and 1961 (see Table B/29) after writing off each year's total on a fifteen-year straight-line basis. This yields a figure of $157 million which at 6 per cent (which seems a typical rate for such funds at that time) represents 2.2 per cent of the selling value of 1962 factory shipments of Nova Scotian manufacturers.[3]

For funds tied up in working capital, we shall confine our attention to inventories, since the only other sizable item involving working capi-

TABLE 6 / 1

Capital investment (excluding repairs) in manu-
facturing industry as percentage of selling value of
factory shipments, Nova Scotia and Quebec-Ontario,
1946–62 (selected years)

	Nova Scotia	Quebec-Ontario
1946	4.5	4.9
1951	4.1	4.6
1956	6.6	5.6
1961	10.9	4.3
1962	4.5	4.6
1946–62[a]	5.0	4.7

SOURCE: Derived from Tables B/28 and B/29.
a Investment 1946–62 as percentage of total factory shipments
during period.

2 The Economic Council of Canada put it at "a fraction of 1% of total sales." *Fourth Annual Review* (Ottawa, 1967), p. 160.
3 Selling value of factory shipments unadjusted for changes in definitions and reporting unit (see n. (*a*) Appendix B) to correspond to investment and inventory data which cannot be adjusted owing to lack of information.

tal is accounts receivable, which are largely counterbalanced by accounts payable. Table B/30 gives us a figure of $54 million for inventories held at Nova Scotian plants and plant warehouses in 1962 (which must be the bulk of all inventories held at that time). At the same 6 per cent rate of interest, this would represent 0.75 per cent of the selling value of factory shipments.

The total interest which should be imputed to funds tied up in capital in Nova Scotian manufacturing firms in 1962 would be therefore of the order of 3 per cent.[4] The remaining 3 per cent of the 6 per cent taxable corporation income would be profit, and the 11 per cent capital consumption allowances and investment income must comprise about 3 per cent profit, 3 per cent interest, and 5 per cent depreciation allowances.[5] Capital costs as such may therefore be taken as 8 per cent (depreciation and interest).[6]

Data are not available to permit similar computations to be made for early years in our period; but the relative stability of depreciation practices and the rates of profit and interest on industrial capital funds during the period seem to make it safe to use a figure of 8 per cent for capital costs throughout.

COMPARATIVE COST OF CAPITAL

1 *Buildings and equipment*
For a comparison of the cost of an input of one unit of capital in the two regions we shall have to turn to the Multiplant Firm Study. Firms covered by that study were asked in the first place to compare the cost of erecting a factory building in Nova Scotia with the cost of a similar building in Ontario or Quebec. If they did not own their present factories, they were asked to use the rents payable for similar factory space in the two regions as the basis of comparison. The answers indicated that some firms did find differences but the median was 100 per cent (that the cost in Nova Scotia was the same as in Quebec or On-

4 Calculated on the same bases, the corresponding figure for Quebec-Ontario is 2.7 per cent.
5 Since the 5 per cent depreciation allowances correspond roughly to the rate of new investment during the period (Table 6/1), it looks as if the capital-to-output ratio was just being maintained and gives an assurance that our estimates cannot be very far astray.
6 In the Multiplant Firm Study firms were asked about the proportion capital costs made up of their total costs. The median of the proportions given in their answers was 9 per cent. As this would not include imputed interest, their answers appear to be high relative to the above estimates. However, the proportions given by these firms did include rent, which happened to be a sizable item for several of the firms. This may well account for part of the discrepancy.

tario). Firms which did find Nova Scotian costs higher and volunteered reasons why this was so always pointed to the expense of bringing in building materials which were not produced in the province. No firm considered that Nova Scotian contractors were less efficient.

Secondly, firms were questioned about the cost of equipment. They were asked to express the cost of equipment required for their Nova Scotian factories as a percentage of the cost of equipment for similar factories in Quebec or Ontario. Their answers again indicated that there were differences from one firm to another, but they yielded a median of 100 per cent, again suggesting there was no significant difference between the two regions. As much of the equipment had to be imported from the United States or Europe, this result may well have been expected.

It seems therefore that, by and large, capital goods could be obtained in Nova Scotia at much the same cost as in Quebec-Ontario. It is not surprising that of all the 149 reasons given in the Site-Choice Study by firms which sited their new factories in Quebec or Ontario after considering other provinces, the cost of machinery and equipment was not mentioned once as influencing their choice, and the cost of premises or sites was mentioned only three times.

2 Capital funds

There is reason to believe that during the whole period funds were available to Nova Scotian manufacturers just as readily and at the same rates of interest as they were to firms of similar size and credit-standing in the Quebec-Ontario region. The Selected Local Areas Study seemed to confirm that the availability of long- or medium-term funds did not hold back Nova Scotian industry.[7] The seventy-one manufacturing firms included in that study were asked if they had at any time suffered from a lack of investment funds. Seven reported that they had. Upon further inquiry, however, it became apparent that five of these seven, though complaining of shortage of investment funds,

7 This is in accord with the findings of John F. Graham, *Fiscal Adjustment and Economic Development: A Case Study of Nova Scotia* (Toronto, 1963), p. 113, but there is some evidence that shortage of capital may sometimes have been a relevant factor in the United States. M. L. Greenhut, *Plant Location in Theory and Practise: The Economics of Space* (Chapel Hill, NC, 1956), reported that a chemical firm he studied had found it so; George H. Ellis, "Why New Manufacturing Establishments Located in New England, August 1945–June 1948," *Monthly Review: Federal Reserve Bank of Boston*, 31, no. 4 (April 1949), described it as being of importance; and G. E. McLaughlin and S. Robock *Why Industry Moves South* (Washington, 1949), found that it influenced the Kraft and Pet Milk companies to go south – not that they themselves found capital-raising easier there, but because they expected that their suppliers would.

really meant that they resented being asked to pay interest of 5.5 per cent or 6 per cent when they did not expect the investments to yield much more than that. Of the other two, one had been going downhill for some time and it was hardly surprising that investors were unwilling to back a pretty certain loser; and the last was a tiny firm which, though long-established had been almost stagnant for a long time and had no assets of any consequence.

During the whole period, relatively small firms (and small firms always tend to be more difficult to finance than larger ones) which were not able to obtain long or medium funds from ordinary sources at reasonable rates could have always gone to the Industrial Development Bank. If their plans seemed reasonably assured of success,[8] funds would be made available at rates usually charged by private lenders to large, well-established corporations. And these facilities were, of course, extended to firms seeking to establish or expand in Nova Scotia on just the same basis as firms in Quebec-Ontario.

Also, after 1957, Industrial Estates Limited, a Nova Scotian Crown corporation, was eager to build plants to the specification of firms wishing to start or extend manufacturing activities in the province. The plants were let to the clients at rentals which were intended to do no more than cover costs. In this way, the capital requirements of the firms concerned were significantly reduced. In addition, Industrial Estates Limited was prepared to make long-term loans or to guarantee bonds.

The two bank officials interviewed in the Selected Local Areas Study offered some additional information relevant to this matter. They claimed that Nova Scotian businessmen were more reluctant to get into debt than were businessmen in central Canada. They seemed to harbour a deep-seated longing to own their premises and concentrated their energies on paying back any moneys borrowed for the initial construction and equipping of their factories. Consequently, they tied up much of their firms' own funds in bricks and mortar. Had they viewed things differently, they could have borrowed quite readily for further expansion. A good example of such a businessman was encountered during the Selected Local Areas Study. He was a food manufacturer –

---

8 F. E. Lounsbury, *Financing Industrial Development in the Atlantic Provinces*, Atlantic Provinces Economic Council (Fredericton, 1960), suggests that the requirement that applicants should appear to have a reasonable chance of success discriminates against Atlantic provinces firms. One of the criteria applied by the Industrial Development Bank is that the applicant should have an adequate equity base and not be relying too heavily upon fixed interest debt. Lounsbury considers that funds for equity are unusually difficult to find in the Atlantic provinces, though he does not offer any evidence on this point.

a modest, hard-working man who had slowly and painfully over his lifetime built up a business employing some fifty persons. He was quite certain that his credit had been good enough for many years to have allowed him to borrow much more than he had in fact borrowed; and he was convinced that, had he taken up more of the funds available to him, he would have reached his existing size much sooner and more easily, and might well have become much larger than he actually had become. But he had always had a fear of being in debt and had set himself a rule never to seek additional funds until any debt previously incurred had been cleared.

Statistics of capital investment also suggest that Nova Scotia firms and potential firms were not held back lack of long- or medium-term investment funds at reasonable rates. Table 6/1 demonstrates that, related to its size, Nova Scotian industry carried on as much capital investment as its Quebec-Ontario counterpart. As one would expect in a smaller economy, Nova Scotia's investment was more erratic, but average investment per year relative to the average yearly output (last line of Table 6/1) was rather higher than in Quebec-Ontario.

The story Table 6/1 tells is very different from the one generally recounted when investment in Nova Scotian industry is under discussion. Comparisons are usually made on a per capita basis and Nova Scotia shows up badly relative to provinces outside the Atlantic region.[9] But this is only because Nova Scotia's manufacturing industry has been small relative to its population. Its industry, though small, was evidently not investing any less pro rata to its size than was industry in Quebec-Ontario. If investment in Nova Scotia had been equal per capita to investment in Quebec-Ontario, this would have resulted in an expansion in Nova Scotia much more rapid than took place in Quebec-Ontario. A lower investment per capita, though it has the ring of decline, could well have meant a relative advance in Nova Scotia.

As further confirmation that the shortage of investment funds was not a significant factor in the choice of locations for new plants, we have the evidence of the Site-Choice Study. In that study, of all the 149 times when reasons were given by firms setting up plants in Quebec or Ontario after considering sites elsewhere, not once was either the availability of investment funds or the rate of interest charged for such funds mentioned as having influenced the choice.

The foregoing discussion has been directed towards long- or me-

9 See, for instance, *ibid.*, p. 239: "For the decade [1949–58] total per capita new industrial fixed investment in the region [Atlantic provinces] was $1,135. This was 47.2 per cent of the $2,407 invested in Canada as a whole on a per capita basis."

dium-term investment. Similar conclusions appear, however, to apply to short-term funds.[10] The chartered banks are the main source of such funds and the branch banking system in operation in Canada makes funds readily mobile throughout the whole country. Interest rates charged by banks are generally believed to be uniform in all regions and banks claim that their standards of judging the merit of an application for credit are consistent everywhere.[11] It is true that murmurs are sometimes heard in Nova Scotia that banks are unaccommodating to local firms. But the Selected Local Areas Study turned up only four firms which had ever been squeezed by lack of working capital. For two of them, this had happened when they had been going through hard times and it was not surprising that banks should have doubted the wisdom of getting too far involved. The two others felt that they had suffered merely because of unsympathetic managers who had happened to be in charge of the local branches of their banks for a period.[12] Their problems had apparently disappeared when these managers had moved on.[13]

REGIONAL DIFFERENCES IN CAPITAL
REQUIREMENTS

Before leaving our interregional comparisons of the cost of capital, it is necessary to ensure that a Nova Scotian firm, by virtue of its distance

10 As A. K. Cairncross reported in 1961, "It was also evident that, with some exceptions, bank finance was not regarded as one of the major obstacles to economic growth in the Atlantic Provinces. It repeatedly happened that when I tried to get people to talk about tight money, they hopped quickly to some other topic and brought forward other, and (in their view) more fundamental impediments to industrial development." *Economic Development and the Atlantic Provinces*, Atlantic Provinces Research Board (February, 1961), p. 10.

11 In the Selected Local Area Study, two senior bank managers with experience in many parts of the country were quite definite that this was true; and in an unpublished DBA thesis at Harvard University (1966), "The Availability of Institutional Credit for Small Business in Nova Scotia, with Special Reference to Small Manufacturing Firms," John T. Sears recounts interviews with four bank officials who maintained that Nova Scotian firms actually received more generous credit treatment than did their central Canadian counterparts.

An attempt to obtain less subjective information, however, came to nothing. The head offices of all the chartered banks were asked to indicate the total amounts of loans made to manufacturing industry in Nova Scotia, Quebec, and Ontario during the period 1946 to 1962 and the average rate of interest charged on them. They all replied to the effect that they did not keep figures on an industrial and provincial basis.

12 The findings of Sears, *ibid.*, suggest that this might well have been the case. He found that bank managers in Nova Scotia were generally conservative and ignorant of any satisfactory criteria by which applications for loans might be consistently judged.

13 The experience of Canadian companies seems to have been somewhat at vari-

from the main centres of population and industry, did not require more units of capital for each unit of output than did a firm in the Quebec-Ontario region. Would it not have needed to have kept larger stocks of replacement parts at the ready in case of breakdown to avoid having to wait for spares to be sent from manufacturers in central Canada? Or would it not have needed to have held standby plant to keep production going while maintenance men were on their way from the larger centres?

It is not possible to dismiss these points completely, but not one of the seventy-one Nova Scotian manufacturing firms included in the Selected Local Areas Study suggested that it was at any special disadvantage on this account compared with its opposite number in Quebec-Ontario. Presumably a firm's own maintenance men found most equipment easy enough to service and a small range of spares sufficed to give security against most eventualities. And there was always air transport which could get a spare part or a technical representative from Montreal to Halifax in the same time as it would have taken to reach Sarnia. The cost would obviously have been greater, but the chance of having to incur it was so small that the keeping of unusually large stocks of spares or additional standby equipment seemed unnecessary.

For another thing, would it not have been necessary for a Nova Scotia firm to have kept large inventories of finished goods to enable it to supply distant customers quickly? Local manufacturers can sometimes supply rush orders directly from the production line within a reasonably short time, but would not a Nova Scotian manufacturer a thousand miles from his main markets have been obliged to keep large inventories? Was this not the only way he could ensure that the delivery delay should be no longer than the time the goods were in transit? Further, would not a Nova Scotian firm, which so often relied upon central Canadian suppliers for its supplies of raw and semi-finished materials, have been obliged to keep larger stocks of them, knowing that it would have had a long time to wait for further supplies should they have been wanted in a hurry?

ance with that in the United States. In 1926 John D. Black, *Introduction to Production Economics* (New York, 1926), described big differences between rates of interest existing at that time in the northern and southern states. And A. Losch, *The Economics of Location* (New Haven, Conn., 1954), reported that in 1936 he had found that interest rates had risen as firms had gone farther away from Federal Reserve cities. Though the development of financial institutions may have been expected to have reduced these differences, McLaughlin and Robock in *Why Industry Moves South*, found that they still existed in 1949 and were secondary influences in the determination of industrial location. However, the improvement in communications and the further development of the American Federal Reserve system may well have largely eliminated these differences. In Canada, branch banking probably prevented such differences ever arising to any marked degree.

Table 6/2 shows that Nova Scotian manufacturers did not, as a general rule, keep greater inventories of either finished goods or raw materials than did manufacturers in Quebec-Ontario; indeed, they seem to have held less. As far as raw materials are concerned, these data seem fairly conclusive. However, they refer only to inventories held at plants or plant warehouses and they do not rule out the possibility that Nova Scotian manufacturers might have held high inventories of finished goods near to the Quebec-Ontario market to be able to service customers. The Economist Intelligence Unit seemed to assume that this was the case and was concerned with the difficulties and expense this created. Its concern came as a "... result of extensive field research" which demonstrated that "... firms in the Maritimes which are associated with central Canadian companies have fewer marketing problems than their Maritime based counterparts ... because they are able to use the distributive facilities of their associated company in central Canada." From this evidence it concluded that "... it is the distribution costs of the Maritime company which is its major difficulty," reminding the reader that "... total distribution cost also included warehousing costs, [and] costs of holding additional stock for local requirements, ..."[14]

While this conclusion may be true, it does not seem to follow from the evidence that firms have less difficulty in distributing their products in distant markets if they can use the established marketing organization of an associated company. Marketing is normally a tedious and demanding part of a firm's activity and it comes as no surprise that executives of a Maritime company should find their problems eased if they could fob off these responsibilities on to someone else; indeed, it is known that some Maritime producers market all their goods through

TABLE 6 / 2

Inventories of raw materials and finished goods held at year-ends in manufacturing industry as percentages of selling value of factory shipments, Nova Scotia and Quebec-Ontario, 1954–62 (selected years)

	Raw materials		Finished goods	
	Nova Scotia	Quebec-Ontario	Nova Scotia	Quebec-Ontario
1954[a]	9.16	9.40	5.77	5.78
1956	7.67	8.79	5.46	5.44
1961	8.98	7.49	6.34	6.65
1962	7.22	7.39	5.46	6.32

SOURCE: Derived from Tables B/28 and B/30.

a Previous figures are not available.

14 *Atlantic Provinces Transportation Study* (Ottawa, 1967), v, p. 92.

brokers. No doubt central Canadian manufacturers would be glad to do the same if they could come to satisfactory arrangements with a company which had an already established marketing organization.

No firm evidence seems to be available to indicate that Nova Scotian manufacturers did, in fact, find it necessary to hold inventories of finished goods in central Canada. Of the twenty-nine firms included in the Selected Local Areas Study which sold in central Canada, only one held such inventories, though another indicated that it thought it might have to do so one day.

The conclusion can be drawn, then, that the cost of a unit of capital input, including depreciation, obsolescence, and interest, appears to have been similar in both regions. Capital costs seem to have made up about 8 per cent of the value of Nova Scotian output.

7 Product Transportation

Nova Scotia had few economic links with the rest of Canada until well after Confederation. Tariffs on interprovincial trade did not help, but the real reason for its isolation was the cost and difficulty of transportation. The St Lawrence was frozen over for two or three months every year and access by water to the interior was impossible even in the "open season" until the necessary locks and canals were built. Overland transportation to Montreal and Toronto was difficult, dangerous, slow, and expensive, especially in winter. In 1879 the Intercolonial Railway was completed and joined Nova Scotia to central Canada. However, despite this link and the favoured treatment that traffic on it has received for a good deal of the time since, Nova Scotians have never really felt that they have received their proper due. They particularly resented the nibbling away of the rate advantages they had enjoyed up to 1912 on rail movements between their province and central Canada, advantages to which they claimed to have been entitled under the terms of the British North America Act. By 1923 these advantages had virtually disappeared. The position was more or less restored in 1927 by the Maritime Freight Rates Act, but the development of road competition benefited central Canada more than Nova Scotia, and a series of increases starting in 1948 bore down more heavily on Nova Scotian manufacturers because transportation costs formed a relatively high percentage of their overall costs. An increase in the MFRA subsidy in 1957 probably helped a little, though the precise effect is difficult to assess;[1] and the Freight Rates Reduction Act passed in 1959 to freeze railway class rates probably limited increases to some degree. But the

---

1 See The Economist Intelligence Unit, *Atlantic Provinces Transportation Study* (Ottawa, 1967), v, p. 14 ff., for a discussion of the effects of the MFRA.

periodic interventions of the federal government have not eliminated Nova Scotia's sense of grievance and strong pleas for relief from the burden of high transportation costs have been made continually.[2]

By the time our period opens, Nova Scotian manufacturers were able to send their products to the main Canadian markets by air, water, road, and rail. We shall consider the importance and relative cost of each in turn, though the first two will not detain us very long. Our examination will be hampered, however, by the inadequacy of published data. In place of statistics relating to the transportation of manufactured goods, we shall sometimes have to make do with information relating to all commodities; and, instead of figures on goods transported within, to, and from Nova Scotia, data relating to the Atlantic provinces as a whole will sometimes be our only guide.[3]

AIR AND WATER

Air freight was of such little quantitative significance to manufacturing industry that it may safely be ignored. Even at the end of the period, when air transportation was more highly developed than at any previous time, only about 5,000 tons of freight of all kinds were sent by air from Nova Scotian airports[4] compared with the 10.5 million tons of manufactured and miscellaneous freight that went by rail.[5] According to The Economist Intelligence Unit, Nova Scotian manufacturers seem to use air freight mainly for bringing in urgently needed machine parts, dispatching occasional rush orders, and sometimes shipping relatively high value goods out. Few use it continuously.[6]

By contrast, water transportation was far from insignificant. Coastal

2 See, for instance, the brief submitted in 1960 to the Royal Commission on Transportation (MacPherson Commission) by the Maritimes Transportation Commission, and *The Basic Elements of an Atlantic Provinces Transportation Policy*, a joint report by the premiers of the Atlantic provinces to the federal Minister of Transport (Moncton, 1969).

3 The paucity of statistics about regional transportation movements has been commented upon continuously by researchers. For instance, in *Plan for the Transportation and Communication Sector* (Halifax, 1966), the Nova Scotia Voluntary Planning Board remarked that "... anyone who has delved into the Nova Scotia trucking industry will know that accurate statistical measures are hard to find ... There is a dearth of origin-destination material which is needed to properly measure the flow of goods into, out of, and through the province" (p. 29). The same sort of complaint might be directed against statistics on rail traffic within, into, and out of Nova Scotia.

4 The Economist Intelligence Unit indicated that "... in 1963 about 5,500 tons [of freight] were landed in the province and about 5,000 tons originated at Nova Scotian airports." *Atlantic Provinces Transportation Study*, II, p. 107.

5 DBS, *Railway Freight Traffic, 1962*, 52–205, p. 33.

6 *Atlantic Provinces Transportation Study*, II, p. 113.

traffic originating in Nova Scotian ports in 1962 was a little over 4 million tons. Manufactured goods, however, accounted for only about 1.9 million tons, and of this over 1.6 million tons consisted of petroleum products shipped from the Dartmouth refinery to other ports in the Atlantic provinces.[7] Since we shall be concerned in our analysis solely with the cost of transporting goods to the main Canadian markets, it seems reasonable to leave sea transportation out of the calculations. This is just as well, since figures upon which cost comparisons could be made are not available. It should be remembered, however, that if in fact Nova Scotian industry were to set out to manufacture primarily for the Quebec-Ontario market and petroleum were one of the commodities it produced, water might well offer a cheaper medium of transportation. Consequently, the final conclusion reached through ignoring water transportation will probably show Nova Scotia in a more unfavourable position than it actually is.

ROAD AND RAIL

1 *Division of traffic*
Unfortunately, separate figures for road traffic in manufactured goods are not available and we shall have to rely upon statistics which relate to all goods carried. Table 7/1 indicates the shares of the traffic which road and rail held during that part of our period which is covered by published statistics. It is clear that, while railways had the lion's share in both regions, road transport was particularly undeveloped in Nova Scotia. By 1957 trucks were carrying one-quarter of all Quebec-Ontario's traffic but only 8 per cent of Nova Scotia's. And, during the last five years of our period, trucking made further advances in Quebec-Ontario, reaching 32 per cent, while in Nova Scotia it rose only to 9 per cent.[8]

The major part of road transport service in Quebec-Ontario was carried out by trucking companies, while in Nova Scotia most of it was done by firms' own fleets.[9] As the period proceeded, the difference

7 DBS, *Shipping Report, Part III: Coastwise Shipping, 1962*, 54–204.
8 In 1966 The Economist Intelligence Unit still found only "about 100 truck journeys a week into and out of Nova Scotia to and from central Canada in each direction by for-hire vehicles. ... There are only three or four trucking companies which operate on a regular basis ... " *Atlantic Provinces Transportation Study*, II, p. 87.
9 The Nova Scotia Voluntary Planning Board's *Plan for the Transportation and Communication Sector* (p. 28) tentatively suggests that the growth of private trucking was the result of inadequate for-hire services, of the goods transported being predominantly in an unprocessed form, poor highways, and provincial motor vehicle regulations. It is difficult to see why any of these reasons, with the possible exception of the last, could explain why private trucking should be more attractive than for-hire trucking.

TABLE 7/1

Freight transported by rail and truck, Nova Scotia and Quebec-Ontario, 1957, 1961, and 1962

Province of origin and year	Truck traffic[b] (millions of net ton-miles)			Railway traffic			Truck traffic as percentage of truck plus rail traffic
	For hire	Private	Total	Weight (millions of tons)	Average haul (miles)	Weight times average haul (millions of ton-miles)	
	(%)	(%)	(%)				
Nova Scotia							
1957[a]	113 (44)	142 (56)	255 (100)	11	269[c]	2,887	8.1
1961	75 (26)	208 (74)	283 (100)	10	268[c]	2,628	9.7
1962	74 (28)	191 (72)	265 (100)	10	257[c]	2,689	9.0
Quebec-Ontario							
1957[a]	4,234 (53)	3,701 (47)	7,935 (100)	81	297	24,083	24.8
1961	6,552 (62)	4,022 (38)	10,573 (100)	71	286	20,236	34.3
1962	6,518 (62)	4,051 (38)	10,569 (100)	75	294	20,145	32.3

SOURCE: DBS, Motor Transport Traffic: Atlantic Provinces, 53–208; Quebec, 53–209; Ontario, 53–210; DBS, Railway Freight Traffic, 52–205; Board of Transport Commissioners, Waybill Analysis; appropriate years.

a Data for previous years are not available.

b Figures for truck traffic refer to traffic carried by trucks registered in the provinces indicated. As interprovincial truck traffic is very small (see p. 80) the figures given approximate to net ton-miles actually carried within each province.

c Avarage hauls are from Waybill Analysis and refer to all the Atlantic provinces and eastern Quebec, not just to Nova Scotia. Because of the geographical distribution of industrial production in the region, the average hauls from Nova Scotia may well be greater than those indicated in the table, and the figures relating to the Nova Scotia final column may be overstated. However, since much freight remains within the province of production and Nova Scotia is geographically compact compared with eastern Quebec, New Brunswick, and Newfoundland, any such overstatement would be partially or wholly counterbalanced.

between the two regions became more and more marked; while Nova
Scotian firms increasingly undertook their own road transportation,
Quebec-Ontario firms tended to do less themselves and give more out
to trucking companies.

The MacPherson Commission in 1962 assigned much of the blame
for the slow development of road transportation in the Atlantic provinces to the Maritime Freight Rates Act.[10] It alleged that, by subsidizing the rail transportation of most traffic originating within the Atlantic
provinces, the act made investment in for-hire road transportation unattractive. The Economist Intelligence Unit endorsed this view very
strongly, claiming that the Maritime Freight Rates Act together with
the Freight Rates Reductions Act had kept truck rates too low to support a vigorous industry.[11]

Another reason for the slow development of the trucking industry in
Nova Scotia has been almost certainly the nature of the roads in that
province. It is true (see Table B/34) that the rate of extension of paved

TABLE 7 / 2

Mileage of paved highways and rural roads per
one thousand population, Nova Scotia and
Quebec-Ontario, 1946–62 (selected years)

	Nova Scotia	Quebec-Ontario
1946	1.58	1.64
1951	2.02	1.98
1956	2.93	2.15
1961	4.56	2.88
1962	4.72	2.87

SOURCE: Derived from Tables B/1 and B/34.

10 The MFRA 1927 was a result of the Royal Commission on Maritime Claims
   (Duncan Commission) 1926. It provided for a 20 per cent subsidy on "preferred movements" of freight in the "select territory" (which meant in the
   Maritime provinces and in Quebec east of Lévis and south of the St Lawrence).
   "Preferred movements" were rail movements entirely within "select territory,"
   rail or rail/water movements originating in "select territory" and destined to
   other parts of Canada (the subsidy being payable only on that part of the
   journey which took place by rail within "select territory"), and movements
   originating in "select territory" and destined for overseas which passed
   through an ocean port within "select territory" (the subsidy again being
   payable only on the rail portion of the journey). Movements of freight east-
   bound to "select territory," of freight destined for the United States, and of
   passenger and express freight were specifically excluded (though express
   freight was included in 1969). Newfoundland was added to the "select territory" in 1949 and the subsidy on freight outward bound to other parts of
   Canada was increased to 30 per cent in 1957 as a result of a recommendation
   of the Royal Commission on Canada's Economic Prospects (Gordon Commission).
11 *Atlantic Provinces Transportation Study*; see, for instance, II, p. 80.

highways and rural roads in Nova Scotia was approximately 9 per cent per annum (from 959 miles at the beginning of 1946 to 3,518 miles at the end of 1962), compared with only about 6 per cent per annum in Quebec-Ontario (from 12,692 to 33,581). It is also true that the mileage of paved highways and rural roads per head of the population was much higher in Nova Scotia than in Quebec-Ontario – the two regions were abreast of each other in 1946 with about 1.6 miles per person, but by the end of the period Nova Scotia's mileage per head had tripled while Quebec-Ontario's had risen by only 75 per cent. However, between 1946 and 1962, Quebec-Ontario spent almost exactly one and a half times as much per mile as did Nova Scotia.[12] Assuming that land costs did not differ greatly and that construction costs were similar (and opinions gained from various sources suggest that they were), it seems to follow that roads built since the war in Quebec-Ontario are much bigger affairs than those built in Nova Scotia. Even a cursory personal examination confirms that to be true. While Nova Scotia's roads are generally good enough for automobile traffic between the main centres of population, they are inadequate for high speed trucks. They are comparatively narrow and poorly surfaced, have sharp bends and steep gradients, and have to cross numerous narrow bridges. Nowhere has Nova Scotia anything to compare with the great Highway 401 which links the main industrial centres of Ontario. It is roads such as this that make fast, long-distance haulage an attractive investment.

Other difficulties face Nova Scotian truckers. They pay more for their diesel fuel, partly because the provincial tax is about 20 per cent higher than in central Canada. Then, since Nova Scotia does not yet have a complete network of all-weather roads connecting the main centres, truckers have to observe spring load restrictions which inflate their costs greatly for a period of about one month each year. The Economist Intelligence Unit reported that "most interests stated that it took six months to wipe out the deficit and loss during this period."[13] And perhaps most important of all is the low industrial and population density of the province. In the Quebec-Ontario industrial belt there is a heavy and continuous flow of goods in both directions which permits

12 Derived from Table B/34. The cost per mile in Nova Scotia was $80,092 while for Quebec-Ontario it was $125,610.

13 *Atlantic Provinces Transportation Study*, II, p. 77. The Economist Intelligence Unit also mentioned difficulties of obtaining capital funds at under 9 per cent interest for trucking operations in the Atlantic provinces (*ibid.*, v, p. 145). There is no evidence, however, that this is not the same sort of difficulty experienced in every region by small enterprises belonging to a relatively unstable industry.

regular trucking services to travel with near-capacity loads on outward and return journeys. But in Nova Scotia outward loads are uncertain and return loads at other than giveaway prices unlikely.

So we find a picture of a relatively undeveloped road haulage industry in Nova Scotia. Most petroleum products destined for depots and local outlets were carried by road, as was a good deal of lumber and some perishables. By and large, however, manufacturers were forced to rely mainly on the railways; indeed, outside the Halifax, Truro, and New Glasgow areas, few manufacturers had a regular and reliable for-hire service to call upon. This was true for trade within the province but the position was even more extreme for trade with central Canada. In 1962 only 80,000 tons of all kinds of freight were carried from the Atlantic provinces to destinations in Quebec-Ontario by road,[14] compared to 16.6 million tons by rail.[15] Road traffic in the opposite direction was of the same insignificant proportions.

2 Comparative costs

(a) Intraregional traffic: During the latter part of the period (the only part for which data are available), Nova Scotian shippers were charged appreciably more for the intraregional transportation of their goods by road than were Quebec-Ontario shippers. Table 7/3 (which refers to all goods, separate figures for manufactures not being available) shows that the rates in Nova Scotia were almost 40 per cent higher in 1957 and that by 1962 they had grown to over 50 per cent higher. As interregional road transportation may be dismissed as insignificant, these figures may be taken to indicate the relative cost of goods shipped by road to destinations within the same region.

For information on the average cost of transportation by rail, one must rely upon the Waybill Analysis published in 1949 and annually since 1951 by the Board of Transport Commissioners. Unfortunately, it gives details only by broad geographical regions. The "Eastern Zone" corresponds closely enough to the Quebec-Ontario region, but Nova Scotia is lumped into a "Maritime Zone" together with Newfoundland, Prince Edward Island, New Brunswick, and Quebec east of Lévis and south of the St Lawrence. Though Nova Scotia accounts for only about one-third of the traffic of this zone, there is nothing to be done except to examine the figures relating to the whole zone. However, since we are at present concerned with traffic within the Maritime Zone, which

14 DBS, Motor Transport Traffic, Canada, 1962, 53–207.
15 Derived from Board of Transport Commissioners, Waybill Analysis, 1962. Since goods carried by road were probably relatively high-value, interprovincial road transportation may not have been quite so insignificant in value terms as the volume figures imply.

TABLE 7/3

Average revenue per net ton-mile earned by for-hire trucks,[a]
Nova Scotia and Quebec-Ontario, 1957, 1961, and 1962

	Nova Scotia (cents)	Quebec-Ontario (cents)	Nova Scotia as percentage of Quebec-Ontario
1957	10.1	7.3	138
1961	10.0	6.9	145
1962	10.5	7.0	150

SOURCE: Derived from Table B/33.

a We shall shortly find that the costs per ton-mile for rail movement of manufactured freight are only about a quarter of those shown in the first two
columns of this table. When interpreting this, we should remember the caution
of the submission of the Canadian Trucking Associations Incorporated to
the MacPherson Royal Commission on Transportation: "the ton-mile measure, which is recognised as the best indicator of output of any transport
industry, and which is quite suitable as an index of output changes of the
industry or any particular part of it, has severe limitations if it is used for the
comparison of outputs of two dissimilar transport media, each with its own
particular service patterns. Ton-miles performed are an indicator of the net
output of the industry; this does not necessarily correspond to the value of
the product which different transport industries sell to the customer, or to the
production unit of different industries" (p. 3.2). Truckers tend to concentrate
on the relatively high-value, short-haul traffic; and they usually give a door-
to-door service. There is no indication that they charge more than do the
railways for similar services. The Economist Intelligence Unit, *Atlantic
Provinces Transportation Study*, vol. II, p. 59, found in 1966 that road and rail
rates for traffic in secondary manufactures within Nova Scotia were comparable and little different on manufactures leaving the province. It also
declared that "... there is a premium which shippers are prepared to pay for
the better service which they state is generally received from truck transportation. This premium is of the order of 10 to 15 per cent" (p. 81).

probably means largely intraprovincial movements, there seems no
reason why the average cost figures for Nova Scotia should be very
different from corresponding figures for the whole zone.

The first two columns of Table 7/4 show the charge per ton-mile
levied on traffic carried within the Maritime region and within the
Eastern region from 1949 to 1962. Intra-Maritime traffic evidently
bore charges which increased by 42 per cent while charges within the
Eastern region rose by only 28 per cent. In 1949 a ton-mile of traffic
moving within the Maritimes cost its shippers 91 per cent as much as
shippers of a ton-mile of freight within the Eastern Zone had to pay.
Taking into account the MFRA subsidy, the railway was even then receiving more per ton-mile for Maritime shipments than it was from
Eastern Zone movements. During the 1950s, comparative rates moved
against intra-Maritime traffic until in 1961 railways were charging
shippers almost 20 per cent per ton more for it. This differential, added
to the 20 per cent subsidy, indicated that the railways were receiving a

TABLE 7/4

Average revenue per ton-mile received by railways for transportation of manufactured goods in car-load lots, Maritime and Eastern Zones, 1949–62 (selected years)

	Within Maritime (cents)	Within Eastern (cents)	Maritime-Eastern (cents)	Eastern-Maritime (cents)	Within Maritime as percentage of within Eastern	Maritime-Eastern as percentage of Eastern-Maritime	Maritime-Eastern as percentage of within Eastern	Eastern-Maritime as percentage of within Eastern
1949[a]	1.848	2.036	0.873	1.160	90.8	75.3	42.9	57.0
1951[a]	2.336	2.415	1.118	1.421	96.7	78.7	46.3	58.8
1956	2.736	2.659	1.402	1.741	102.9	80.5	52.7	65.5
1961	2.872	2.421	1.483	2.257	118.6	65.7	61.3	93.2
1962	2.627	2.610	1.464	2.429	100.7	60.3	56.1	93.1
1962 as percentage of 1949	142	128	168	209	—	—	—	—

SOURCE: Derived from *Waybill Analysis*.[b]

a Up to 1953, figures were supplied for a separate "Superior Zone." After that year, this zone was absorbed in the Eastern Zone. In Table 7/4 the figures for the Superior Zone for 1949 and 1951 have therefore been combined with those for the Eastern Zone.

b The *Waybill Analysis* includes a class of commodity called "manufactures and miscellaneous." This is not produced, however, on the same definitions as the DBS uses in its publications. So Table 7/4 and other later tables which relate to manufactured goods and for which the source is listed as *Waybill Analysis* have been compiled by extracting information on goods which would be classified as manufactures by the DBS.

substantial premium per ton-mile for Maritime freight. Only in 1962 did it show signs of decreasing. Presumably, competition from road hauliers had prevented the charges for intra-Eastern traffic rising as much as increases in class rates sanctioned by the Board of Transport Commissioners, but there was no such brake on the increases for intra-Maritime traffic.[16]

It might be thought that the higher rates charged for rail freight within the Maritime Zone during the latter part of the period were because of Maritime producers being small and therefore having to dispatch more of their goods in less-than-carload (LCL) quantities. However, this was not the case. In the Maritimes, LCL traffic was only 2.3 per cent of all traffic at the beginning of the period and fell to an even more insignificant proportion (1.4 per cent) by 1962. The corresponding figures for Quebec-Ontario were 3.6 and 0.7 per cent.[17] Even if this LCL freight had all been in manufactured goods, it would have made up only about 5 per cent of all manufactured goods carried by rail in 1962.

Table 7/5 shows the mechanism by which the relatively cheap rates charged to shippers from one point to another within the Eastern Zone were arranged. In 1949, 91 per cent of traffic within the Maritime Zone was shipped at non-competitive rates compared with only 75 per cent of the Eastern-Eastern traffic. Already, then, railways had been obliged to offer lower rates for traffic within the Eastern Zone to compete with other forms of transportation, but they had felt little necessity to offer competitive rates for traffic within the Maritimes. Between 1949 and 1962 the force of competition was felt in both regions, but again to a greater extent within the Eastern Zone. By 1962 the proportion of all rail traffic within the Maritime Zone going by non-competitive rates had fallen to 59 per cent, but within the Eastern Zone it had dropped to a mere 33 per cent. The almost wholesale granting of agreed rates (special rates governed by contracts made with individual shippers) within the Eastern Zone until they accounted for 34 per cent of the traffic was not matched within the Maritimes where only 15 per cent of traffic went at agreed rates. Such was evidently the effect of competition from road hauliers.

In its brief submitted in 1960 to the (MacPherson) Royal Commission on Transportation, the Maritime Transportation Commission

16 Another possible explanation for part of the increase in the charges on intra-Maritime shipments relative to those levied on intra-Eastern traffic is that road haulage was skimming off some of the higher value cargoes which usually attract the higher rail charges, leaving the railway with low-rate freight.

17 Derived from DBS, *Railway Freight Traffic, 1946 and 1962.*

TABLE 7/5

Ton-miles of railway freight going at various types of rates[a] as percentage of all railway traffic, Maritime and Eastern Zones, 1949-62 (selected years)

	Non-competitive (class and commodity)	Competitive	Agreed	Total
Maritime-Maritime				
1949	90.9	8.9	0.2	100
1951	87.1	12.6	0.3	100
1956	70.9	28.4	0.6	100
1961	61.0	24.9	14.1	100
1962	59.2	25.8	15.0	100
Eastern-Eastern				
1949	74.5	22.2	3.3	100
1951	82.3	13.8	3.9	100
1956	54.4	39.3	6.2	100
1961	33.5	33.8	32.7	100
1962	32.7	33.6	33.7	100
Maritime-Eastern				
1949	94.0	6.0	—	100
1951	90.5	9.5	—	100
1956	81.0	13.2	5.8	100
1961	55.8	13.9	30.3	100
1962	54.2	13.5	32.3	100
Eastern-Maritime				
1949	68.6	31.3	0.1	100
1951	99.4	0.5	0.1	100
1956	87.7	11.5	0.7	100
1961	79.7	11.7	8.6	100
1962	69.2	14.3	16.5	100

SOURCE: *Waybill Analysis.*

a Class rates were the maximum charges that the law permitted to be levied. Commodity rates were special rates offered on certain types of traffic to meet competition from other modes of transport. Competitive rates were rates based upon class rates but were net of discounts granted for large shipments. Agreed charges were those levied under the terms of contracts made between the railways and shippers, the latter agreeing to send by rail a specified minimum quantity of freight or a minimum percentage of their total shipments.

gave another indicator of the relatively weak bargaining position of Maritime Zone firms. Its examination of agreed charges which had become effective up to July 31, 1960,[18] revealed that only 15.8 per cent of the Maritime firms involved had been able to avoid having the "deferred escalator" clause written into their contracts for agreed charges, while 25 per cent of firms elsewhere in Canada had succeeded in avoiding it.[19] This deferred escalator clause allowed the agreed charges to rise in sympathy with general rises authorized by the Board of Transport Commissioners, and it seems clear that railway companies would only have omitted the clause if the shippers had been in a strong bargaining position because of alternative means of transportation.

(b) *Interregional traffic*: Since, as already observed, interprovincial road freight traffic was insignificant, comparisons of the cost of transporting goods between the Nova Scotia and Quebec-Ontario regions may be confined to the relative cost of rail freight. Data relating to such traffic are just as limited as are figures of intraregional traffic. But looking again at Table 7/4, we find the average cost per ton-mile of manufactured goods carried from the Maritime Zone to the Eastern Zone in 1949 was 75 per cent of the corresponding cost of traffic flowing in the opposite direction.

As the period progressed there was some sign of the gap closing but it widened again perhaps partly, but certainly not wholly, because of the increase from 20 to 30 per cent in the MFRA subsidy on Maritime Zone traffic destined for Canadian points outside the zone. In 1961 and 1962, therefore, Maritime Zone manufacturers sending freight by rail to the Eastern Zone were paying, per ton-mile, only two-thirds what Eastern Zone manufacturers were paying for traffic in the reverse direction. This was a big differential in favour of the Maritime manufacturer.

However, we should not forget our assumption that, in order that Nova Scotia should realize its hope of closing the gap between the two regions, its manufacturing firms must be capable of competing in the markets of Quebec and Ontario. For this reason, the most significant comparison is that between the charge for goods shipped by Quebec-Ontario manufacturers to the market (that is, for traffic within the

18 This means from September 17, 1958, when the first deferred escalator clause appeared. It was an amendment to the Transport Act in 1955 which allowed railways greater freedom to make agreed charges.

19 The contracts examined were for freight to be carried not only within the Maritime Zone, but also from it to points beyond. Separate details were not given for exclusively intra-Maritime Zone traffic.

Eastern Zone) and the charge for manufactures shipped to the Eastern Zone from Nova Scotia.

Separate figures for Nova Scotia not being available, we shall have to continue to use data relating to the whole Maritime Zone as our guide. Table 7/4 shows that the average cost per ton-mile of manufactured goods sent by rail[20] from the Maritime Zone to the Eastern Zone was, in 1949, only 43 per cent of the average cost per ton-mile of manufactured goods sent from one part of the Eastern Zone to another. This percentage increased during the period to 56, but a marked differential in favour of the Maritime manufacturer remained, due to the longer Maritime to Eastern hauls and partly perhaps also to the effect of the Maritime Freight Rates Act.

While rates per ton-mile are important, so also are the lengths of the hauls. The two acting together determine the cost of transporting a product from the factory in which it is made to its market. The second and third columns of Table 7/6 therefore show the charges to shippers per ton of freight carried by rail within the Eastern Zone and from the Maritime to the Eastern Zone. This may be taken to reflect the product transportation burden upon a Maritime Zone manufacturer in selling in the Quebec-Ontario market, relative to the burden upon a Quebec-Ontario manufacturer supplying the same market. It seems to have varied from about 150 to about 180 per cent. Up to 1961 there seemed to be a fairly consistent trend to the detriment of Maritime-Eastern traffic, but this was reversed by a relatively big increase in Eastern-Eastern charges in 1962.

This is the appropriate comparison if the plant we are considering is typical of those Nova Scotian plants which were, in the years indicated, actually sending their products to the main Canadian markets. But suppose these plants were not typical of all manufacturing plants. Or suppose that Nova Scotian plants in general tended to have been selected in some way because the value-weight or value-bulk ratio of their products was high and that they were therefore at relatively little

20 Since about one-third of the traffic within the Eastern Zone was going by road at the end of the period (Table 7/1), we should perhaps try and find a way to combine the average cost of road and rail traffic in that zone. However, as already observed (see n. (a), Table 7/3), road hauliers provide a somewhat different service and comparing a wholly rail system with a part-rail and part-road system is likely to lead to misleading results. Nevertheless, figures for rail traffic carried within the Eastern Zone are likely to be depressed because some of the high-value traffic has been diverted to road leaving the railways with only the low-value, and therefore usually the lower rate, traffic. So we should bear in mind that our comparisons may be unnecessarily unfavourable to Nova Scotia.

TABLE 7/6

Average cost to shipper of consigning one ton of manufactured freight by railway, Maritime and Eastern Zones, 1949–62 (selected years)

	Maritime-Maritime (dollars)	Eastern-Eastern (dollars)	Maritime-Eastern (dollars)	Eastern-Maritime (dollars)	Maritime-Eastern as percentage of Eastern-Eastern	Maritime-Maritime as percentage of Eastern-Maritime
1949	3.300	4.582	7.462	9.418	162.9	35.0
1951	4.181	5.582	9.894	11.911	177.2	35.1
1956	5.014	6.206	10.884	14.005	175.4	35.8
1961	5.008	6.012	10.960	18.922	182.3	26.5
1962	5.258	7.188	10.711	18.256	149.0	28.8
1962 as percentage of 1949	159	157	144	194		

source: Derived from *Waybill Analysis*.

disadvantage by being hundreds of miles from the main Canadian markets. Or suppose that Nova Scotian manufacturers in general were typical of all manufacturing industry but that those Nova Scotian plants which actually exported to the main Canadian markets were not typical of all plants in that province.

To test these possibilities, a weighted average of the revenue per ton of freight which went from the Maritime to the Eastern Zone was computed for 1962. The weights used were the selling value of factory shipments in Quebec-Ontario manufacturing groups. (Since Quebec and Ontario produce 80 per cent of all manufactures, the industrial mix of their output may be taken as typical of all Canadian manufacturing.) The result was $13.925 which is significantly higher than the $10.711 of Table 7/6, indicating that Maritime exports to central Canada were from industrial groups which produce goods which were relatively cheap to ship.

The basis of comparison of this figure should be the revenue per ton carried in that year between points in the Eastern Zone weighted to the same industrial mix as before – the selling value of factory shipments of Quebec-Ontario manufacturing. The figure so computed was $9.137, which is again much higher than the corresponding figure of Table 7/6 ($7.188), indicating that Quebec-Ontario manufacturers were buying more rail transportation services for goods which were relatively cheap to transport. Other goods, presumably those with low value-weight or value-bulk ratios, were evidently sold to customers situated nearer to the producing plants – which is what one would expect.

Comparing the two figures we have just derived produces a figure of 152.4 per cent ($13.925 as per cent of $9.137). This indicates the average charge per ton of manufactures moving from the Maritime to the Eastern Zone as a percentage of the revenue per ton of manufactures consigned from one point to another in the Eastern Zone, standardized to the Quebec-Ontario mix of factory shipments. This figure is so close to the original 149 per cent of Table 7/6 that substitution of this standardized comparison could not affect our ultimate calculations by more than 0.2 per cent.

We may be reasonably satisfied, therefore, that the comparative costs of transportation at which we previously arrived are relevant to our model. However, as the average haul from Nova Scotia is probably a little longer than the average haul from the Maritime Zone, the relative burden on Nova Scotian manufacturers might have been a little greater than the next to last column of Table 7/6 suggests.

IMPORTANCE OF PRODUCT TRANSPORTATION COSTS

Official statistics give no indication of the relative importance to manu-facturing firms of product transportation costs. We have, however, two other sources upon which we may draw. First, we have the Multiplant Firm Study. The firms included in that study were asked for the pro-portion which product transportation costs constituted of the overall costs of their Nova Scotia plants in 1962. Their answers varied from a negligible proportion to 16 per cent, the median being 3 per cent. This did refer, however, to a situation in which they were sending only 13 per cent of their output outside the Atlantic provinces (including one per cent to western Canada). Had they been consigning all of it to Quebec-Ontario, which is what our model envisages, then product transportation costs would become relatively more important. Table 7/6 told us that the average cost of shipping one ton of freight from the Maritime Zone to the Eastern Zone in 1962 was $10.71. This was almost exactly twice the $5.26 which was the corresponding figure for freight moving within the Maritime Zone. Consequently, had all output been sent to the Eastern Zone, then product transportation costs would have been of the order of 5.3 per cent.[21]

The second source is the *Atlantic Provinces Transportation Study,* which also collected information about transportation costs and quoted instances in which transportation costs (presumably the costs of bring-ing materials in as well as shipping products out, although this is not always clear from the text) varied between 2 and 15 per cent of overall costs.[22] In a section entitled "The Marketing Problems of Industry in the Atlantic Provinces" (and therefore presumably referring to prod-uct transportation only), it was stated that "... for a large part of sec-ondary industry it appears that transportation costs are commonly

---

21 If 13 per cent sent to Quebec-Ontario at $10.71 per ton (ignoring for simplicity that one per cent carried on to western Canada) and 87 per cent sent to Mari-time customers at $5.26 per ton entails product transportation costs equal to 3 per cent of selling value of factory shipments, then 100 per cent sent to Quebec-Ontario at $10.71 per ton would raise these costs to:

$$3\% \times (100 \times \$10.71)/[(13 \times \$10.71) + (87 \times \$5.26)] = 5.4\%$$

Since total costs would also rise by 2.4 per cent, transportation costs as a pro-portion of total costs would become $5.4\% \times 100/102.4 = 5.3\%$. (The as-sumption of one market and consequent rise in the relative importance of product transportation costs to Nova Scotian plants really call for revision of our estimates made elsewhere of the importance of other factor inputs in cost structures. But the effect of such a revision would have been tiny.)

22 II, p. 34 ff.

around 5 per'cent of total costs and may even be lower than this."[23]
Since the transportation costs of the two most important manufacturing
firms which might not be considered "secondary" in this context seem
to be relatively low (for instance, costs at the Sydney steel plant were
put at "4–5 per cent of turnover"[24] and "... almost every fishing interest interviewed in Nova Scotia had transportation costs accounting
for 7 per cent of total sales, covering all operations"[25]), and since the
firms covered in the study could usually be identified by a reader with
some local knowledge as larger firms which sent most of their products
to markets outside the province, the result of this study and the 5.3 per
cent suggested above seem fairly consistent.

It might seem reasonable to expect that transportation costs, in
keeping with the historical trend, would have become less important as
the period progressed, and that therefore in 1946 the percentage would
have been greater than in 1962. However, this does not seem to have
been the case. For 1949, Table 7/6 tells us that the cost of consigning
one ton of freight from the Maritime Zone was $7.46. This was 70 per
cent of the $10.71 which it cost to do the same thing in 1962.[26] How-
ever, the price of fully or chiefly manufactured goods in 1949 was 80
per cent of their price in 1962.[27] So, during the period, the cost of sending one dollar of manufactured goods from the Maritimes to Quebec-
Ontario actually rose, and in 1949 was only about 4.6 per cent of the
selling value of factory shipments.[28] Similar calculations for 1951,
1956, and 1961 yield proportions of 5.0, 5.8, and 5.6 per cent
respectively.

CONCLUSION

Since (a) air and water freight transportation between Nova Scotia
and Quebec-Ontario was insignificant, (b) road transportation between those regions was generally not competitive with rail transportation, (c) road and rail competed energetically in Quebec-Ontario and

23 *Ibid.*, v, p. 91.
24 *Ibid.*, II, p. 46.
25 *Ibid.*, II, p. 44.
26 If, as seems to be the general impression, manufactured goods of any type are
   tending to become lighter due to the use of lighter materials and improvements
   in design, then relationships over time between the cost of transporting a given
   weight of goods would not be relevant. However, no information is available
   on this matter, and general impressions are often unreliable.
27 Computed from DBS, *Prices and Price Indexes, Dec. 1960* and *Feb. 1963,*
   62-002. The dangers of applying national indexes to regions have been mentioned before (see p. 17, n. 8); but they afford the only guide to price changes
   which is available.
28 $5.3 × 70%/80%.

therefore must have charged similar prices for similar services, and (*d*) Maritime region freight rates could not have differed much from the rates levied on Nova Scotian traffic, it follows that the final column of Table 7/6 may be taken to indicate the cost of sending products manufactured in Nova Scotia to the Quebec-Ontario market relative to the cost of doing the same thing from plants in Quebec-Ontario.[29]

The Multiplant Firm Study provided some check upon the proportion of 149 per cent given for 1962 in Table 7/6. In that study, firms were asked the hypothetical question: "Supposing your Nova Scotia factory were called upon to supply both its present market and also the customers who are now supplied from your Quebec or Ontario factory (assuming it were capable of producing sufficient output), how would costs of transportation compare with those which would arise if it supplied this same enlarged market but was located in Ontario or Quebec? (Please answer by expressing the costs of transportation from Nova Scotia as a percentage of costs of transportation if located in Ontario or Quebec.)" The answers showed a very large variance. Some of the Nova Scotian factories already exported a good proportion of their outputs and some produced a light article which was sent by the mail at much the same cost whatever the distance within Canada. The answers for such factories were therefore "100 per cent" or near to that proportion. By contrast, one firm marketing a low value-high bulk commodity answered "400 per cent." The median of all firms was 125 per cent. Four-fifths of the gap between this proportion and the 149 per cent of Table 7/6 is attributable to the differences in the bases on which they were computed. The Multiplant Firm Study percentage assumed that the Nova Scotian plant would still be supplying the Atlantic provinces market as well as Quebec and Ontario, while Table 7/6 assumed that all Nova Scotian output would be sent to the Quebec-Ontario region. Similarly, the Multiplant Firm Study assumed that Quebec-Ontario plants would, in the same way, be taking care of the Atlantic provinces as well as Quebec-Ontario while Table 7/6 assumed that only the local market would be covered. So the Multiplant Firm Study produced a proportion based upon a deflated Nova Scotian figure

29 If our comparisons had been between a Nova Scotian plant distributing its products over the central Canadian and Atlantic provinces markets in proportion to the personal income of those two regions (that is, 91 per cent in central Canada and 9 per cent in the Atlantic provinces) and a plant in Quebec-Ontario doing the same, then the 149 per cent would have dropped to 138.2 per cent. In 1962, the cost per ton of freight shipped between two places within the Maritime Zone was only 29 per cent of the cost per ton of freight transferred from the Eastern to the Maritime Zones (see Table 7/6). Similar computations yield figures of 148.6, 164.4, 162.8, and 168.3 per cent for 1949, 1951, 1956, and 1961 respectively.

and an inflated Quebec-Ontario figure (that is, deflated or inflated relative to those which would have resulted from applying the basis used in Table 7/6).

The 149 per cent for 1962 therefore seems fairly reliable. For the figures relating to previous years in Table 7/6, no confirmation is available. As they were derived on the same assumptions and by the same methods, there seems no reason for suspecting their approximate accuracy.

While product transportation costs facing a Nova Scotian plant supplying the Quebec-Ontario market were in 1962 about 150 per cent of the corresponding costs of a Quebec-Ontario plant performing the same operations, we would expect that *ceteris paribus* its overall costs would be 2.6 per cent higher (50 per cent of 5.3 per cent). On the same reasoning, costs would have been 2.9 per cent higher in 1949, 3.9 per cent higher in 1951, 4.4 per cent higher in 1956, and 4.6 per cent higher in 1961. These are very significant percentages and it was therefore not surprising to find that in the Site-Choice Study this factor was mentioned most often when firms which considered locations in more than one province explained their eventual choice of site. Of all the 146 reasons given by these firms, the cost of product transportation was mentioned twenty-four times.

This conclusion might at first seem to conflict with that reached by The Economist Intelligence Unit's *Atlantic Provinces Transportation Study*: "It is traditional to assume that the major handicap to Maritime industry competing in central Canada is the high transport cost involved in shipping the product to the market ... but the indications resulting from the extensive programme of interviews which has been part of this study are that the importance of transport costs are generally overestimated."[30] "The burden of transport costs is not considered to be a major factor in retarding the development of the region ..."[31]

There is no real conflict, however. Though of the several cost disadvantages faced by an average Nova Scotian manufacturer competing in the central Canadian markets which we have so far examined (and we shall find later that our subsequent analysis will not change this) product transportation costs are the biggest, even for the average manufacturer this disadvantage is still not big enough to be called crippling, and in many industries whose products have a high value relative to their weight and bulk, it is insignificant.

We should also remember that most of the assumptions upon which our comparisons were made put the Nova Scotian situation in the

30 v, pp. 90–1.   31 *Ibid.*, p. viii.

worst possible light. We assumed that all production of both Nova Scotia and Quebec-Ontario manufacturers would be sent to central Canada. In fact, some Nova Scotia–produced goods would inevitably be marketed locally, thereby reducing transportation costs; while Quebec-Ontario manufacturers would have to face the relatively high costs of sending some of their production to the Maritimes. In addition, our comparisons of transportation costs were based upon the actual amounts being paid during the period by Nova Scotian and Quebec-Ontario manufacturers for the transportation of their goods by rail; but Quebec-Ontario rates were probably depressed since a relatively large proportion of the high value and short distance traffic of that region was being diverted to road, thereby leaving rail transport with the traffic which attracted lowest rates. And we ignored the possibility that if some goods produced in Nova Scotia were sent to Quebec-Ontario, then water transportation might well provide a cheaper service than the railways. Assumptions less unfavourable to Nova Scotia than these would almost certainly have resulted in the Nova Scotia cost disadvantage due to product transportation being lower than the 2.6 per cent shown.

Apart from the cost of transport, the quality of the services offered is clearly also of importance to a manufacturer. Even if rates were low, a Nova Scotian manufacturer would bear a disadvantage relative to his Quebec-Ontario counterpart if the service was irregular and unreliable. This aspect of the matter, however, was investigated by The Economist Intelligence Unit which discovered relatively few shippers who were preoccupied with the quality of service rather than with rates.[32]

32 *Ibid.*, II, p. 60.

8   Local Taxation

In discussions about the relative attractiveness of different locations for manufacturing industry, attention is often focused upon local taxation. This is perhaps because it constitutes one of the few items which lie, at least partially, within the control of local authorities. In their scramble for industry, local authorities have sometimes offered tax concessions to firms willing to set up new plants in their areas.[1]

No indication of the relative importance of local taxation or the variations in its level from province to province is available from official sources, and we shall have to rely on the evidence provided by the Multiplant Firm Study. In that study firms were asked to express the local taxes they paid as a percentage of their total costs. The median percentage turned out to be 2 per cent. This referred to the year 1962 and no data are available for previous years. Because of the progressive increase in the functions that local authorities have had to discharge and the rapid growth in the cost of education, much of which falls on local authorities, it seems likely that the percentage was somewhat smaller earlier in the period.[2] It is such a tiny item that speculation about precisely how much it was does not seem worthwhile.

1 This practice is perhaps not as widespread as is generally believed. The power of local authorities to grant concessions stems from provincal governments, all of which have permitted such concessions within certain limits. Nova Scotia has done so liberally, Quebec rather less, while Ontario scarcely at all in postwar years. See Stewart Fyfe, *Municipal Assistance to Location of Industry: A Canadian Study of Tax Concessions and Other Inducements* (Halifax, 1961).

2 J. S. Floyd, Jr., *Effects of Taxation on Industrial Location* (Chapel Hill, NC, 1952), provided figures for certain US hosiery, furniture, and tobacco firms which suggested that, in 1946, the median local and state taxes constituted about one per cent of sales.

Firms in the Multiplant Firm Study were also asked to compare the level of local taxes in Nova Scotia with the level in Ontario and Quebec. This was, of course, a particularly difficult comparison to make as similar properties on similar pieces of land within a mile of each other are often assessed at very different amounts for local tax purposes. So firms were asked for what could not be much more than a general impression of how the local taxes they paid on their Nova Scotian plants compared with what the taxes would have been if the plants had been located instead on similar sites in Ontario or Quebec.

The answers followed a fairly well-defined geographical pattern. Nearly all firms whose Nova Scotian factories were in the Halifax-Dartmouth area had the distinct impression that the taxes levied on these activities were relatively high. One such firm gave the Nova Scotia level as 140 per cent of what it would have been in Ontario or Quebec. Firms with plants outside the Halifax-Dartmouth district all considered that they paid the same or less than they would have done in Ontario or Quebec. The median for all firms was 100 per cent – that is, local taxes were at much the same level in the two regions.

The Multiplant Firm Study referred only to 1962 and no evidence is available which might establish the relationship in previous years. However, there seems no reason why it should have altered significantly over the period. Even if it had changed somewhat, the relative unimportance of local taxation in firms' costs ensures that it would still not have been an important factor influencing location. This was confirmed in the Site-Choice Study, when local taxation levels were not mentioned once as a factor which had influenced the choice by those firms which settled in Quebec or Ontario after considering locating in a province other than the one they eventually chose.[3]

3 This is in keeping with the conclusions reached in various studies of the United States economy. In *The Tax System and Industrial Development* (Urbana, Ill., 1938), G. Steiner found no evidence that local taxation either attracted or repelled; in "Taxation of Manufacturing Industry: Help or Hindrance to Regional Development," *University of Alabama Business News*, xx, nos. 3 and 4 (Nov. and Dec. 1949), P. E. Alyea thought it might be a balancing factor but had little general effect. His findings coincided with those of G. E. McLaughlin and S. Robock, in *Why Industry Moves South* (Washington, 1949). J. W. Martin and G. D. Morrow, in *Taxation of Manufacturing in the South* (University, Ala., 1948), declared their belief that firms preferred stable and equitable taxes and good services over tax concessions and poor service. And S. E. Harris, *The Economics of New England* (Cambridge, Mass., 1952), p. 307, declared that "I am not convinced that taxes are as important as is generally assumed. They are only in part costs; and the *differences* among states are not a substantial item." However, some of the Michigan manufacturers interviewed by E. Mueller, A. Wilken, and M. Wood, *Location Decisions and Industrial Mobility in Michigan, 1961* (Ann Arbor, Mich., 1961), said they might be influenced by local taxation levels to

move away from the state; but since the study was carried out in a period of "public controversy about Michigan's tax problems" (p. 6), business leaders were probably so emotionally involved that they were incapable of making a balanced and reliable judgment. Floyd, Jr., *Effects of Taxation on Industrial Location*, did find tax differences between firms in different locations to be as much as 1.9 per cent of sales; but these were individual extremes and the differences between the first and third quartiles never exceeded 0.45 per cent, and, had states or other larger areas instead of districts been the basis of analysis, the differences would have been even less.

9 All Inputs other than Entrepreneurship

The findings of the preceding chapters relating to the importance of the various inputs and their cost in Nova Scotia relative to their cost in the Quebec-Ontario region are drawn together in Table 9/1. Immediately after the war the Quebec-Ontario region evidently had an edge of about 5 per cent. This percentage seems to have risen during the first five postwar years and then fallen back during the following eleven years to a little below its original level.

Labour made a contribution to the result only in 1951, and then only to the extent of about 0.75 per cent. Capital costs and local taxes made no contribution at all. It was the remaining inputs which built up the Nova Scotia disadvantage. Materials and fuel accounted for a little over one per cent, not because there was much difference between their costs in the two regions, but because they constituted such a large proportion of total costs. Electricity costs were tiny, but since electricity prices were so much higher in Nova Scotia than in Quebec-Ontario they had a significant effect, at least at the beginning of the period. Product transportation was the biggest factor in the final analysis. Even in 1962, when the differential was at its lowest point, it contributed over 2.5 of the 4.3 percentage points of the excess of Nova Scotia over Quebec-Ontario.

RELIABILITY OF RESULTS

As the jigsaw was being put together in the preceding chapters, we drew upon as many sources as were available. Usually there was a high degree of agreement between them, which justified confidence in the reliability of the results. But there were one or two points at which

TABLE 9/1

Cost of supplying Quebec-Ontario market with manufactured goods, plants producing in Nova Scotia compared with plants producing in Quebec-Ontario, 1946-62 (selected years)

	Labour		Materials and fuel		Electricity		Capital		Product transportation		Local taxes		All inputs
	$\frac{NS^a}{Q/O}$	w^b	$\frac{NS}{Q/O}$	w	$\frac{NS}{Q/O}$	w	$\frac{NS}{Q/O}$	w	$\frac{NS}{Q/O}$	w	$\frac{NS}{Q/O}$	w	$\frac{NS}{Q/O}$
1946	100.9	24.1	102.0	59.0	222.2	0.8	100.0	8.0	162.9^c	4.6	100.0	2.0	105.3
1951	103.6	21.1	102.0	59.9	213.7	0.8	100.0	8.0	177.2	5.0	100.0	2.0	106.9
1956	100.3	21.8	102.0	58.6	177.0	0.8	100.0	8.0	175.4	5.8	100.0	2.0	106.4
1961	97.0	22.3	102.0	57.0	165.0	0.9	100.0	8.0	182.3	5.6	100.0	2.0	105.9
1962	100.1	21.8	102.0	58.6	140.0	0.8	100.0	8.0	149.0	5.3	100.0	2.0	104.3

SOURCE: Tables 3/1, 3/12, 4/1, 4/2, 5/1, 5/2, and 7/6, and pp. 60, 66, 89-90, and 94-5.

a Nova Scotia as a percentage of Quebec-Ontario.

b Weights (per cent of total costs). Where figures in these columns are derived from official statistics, they are in reality the proportion that the cost of each input represented of the selling value of factory shipments in Nova Scotia. The selling value of factory shipments exceeds total costs (as usually conceived) by profits but falls short of them by the cost of product transportation. As profits were about 6 per cent while transportation costs were about 3 per cent, selling value of factory shipments exceeds total costs by about 3 per cent.

c 1949, since data for 1946 are not available.

information was available from only one source and could consequently not be checked, or there was some disagreement between the
sources. We should therefore re-examine these points and see the
extent to which error may have crept in.

1 *Weights*

As far as the weights are concerned (that is, the percentage that the
cost of each factor input constituted of the total costs of an average
factory in Nova Scotia[1]) there seems to be little cause for concern. The
weights for labour, materials, fuel, and electricity came from DBS statistics, which produced results consistent with those obtained in the
Multiplant Firm Study. Capital costs weights were produced mainly
from official sources; but they depended on some assumptions and
were rather at variance with the results obtained from the Multiplant
Firm Study. However, since there was no difference between the comparative costs of capital in the two regions, even a large error in the
weight given this item would have little effect upon the final result.

Product transportation weights were based upon figures from the
Multiplant Firm Study adjusted to the assumption that the only market
for output from either a Nova Scotian or a Quebec-Ontario factory
would be in central Canada. Evidence was available from semi-official
sources to suggest that they were of the right order, but it is just con-
ceivable that product transportation costs for a Nova Scotian factory in
1962, if all its output had gone to central Canada, could have been as
high as 7 per cent. This would have raised the final result for 1962 to
105 per cent, which would seem to be the maximum possible extent of
the error one might reasonably expect.

Local taxes weights relied solely upon the Multiplant Firm Study
but, so long as there was little difference between taxes in the two regions, an error here would have no significant effect on the final figures.

The closeness of the sum of the weights to 97 per cent in each year
also encourages one to believe that any error must have been small.
(The sum of the costs excluding profit would be expected to be about
97 per cent of the selling value of factory shipments – see note (*b*),
Table 9/1.)

2 *Comparative Costs*

The comparative costs for labour, electricity, and product transportation were all derived from official statistics, and except for electricity

1 The choice of weights in geographical comparisons of our present sort raises
the usual index number problem. The substitution of Quebec-Ontario costs
structures as weights throughout the calculations would, due to the lower
importance of transportation costs in Quebec-Ontario, reduce the differential
between the regions by between one and two percentage points.

there was confirmation of their reliability from the information obtained in the Multiplant Firm Study. In respect of electricity, official
statistics and the Multiplant Firm Study were at variance, but electricity costs are such a small proportion of total costs that the possible
error could not do more than change the final result by two decimal
points.

Comparative costs of materials and fuel came entirely from the
Multiplant Firm Study and there seems to be no way of checking them.
But it seems improbable that the executives who supplied data for the
Multiplant Firm Study could have been as far as 50 per cent out in
their estimates of the comparative disadvantage of Nova Scotia in this
respect; and even this big error would only have affected the final result
by about 0.5 per cent. An error larger than this seems scarcely worth
considering.

For our capital cost comparisons we also had to rely exclusively on
the Multiplant Firm Study. But general knowledge of the problem encourages one to preclude the possibility of any very large difference
here. And since there would have to have been a 12 per cent difference
before the final result would be affected to the extent of one per cent, it
seems unlikely that significant error could have come from this source.

We also had to rely exclusively upon the Multiplant Firm Study for
comparisons between local taxes in the two regions. This was admittedly a difficult matter upon which to make estimates but, since local
taxes formed such a small part of total costs, only a large error could
have affected the final result significantly.

It seems therefore that the only possible source of significant error
was in the cost comparisons relating to materials and fuel and the
weight for product transportation. Even these possible errors could
only have arisen if executives of firms in the Multiplant Firm Study had
committed errors many times greater than they did when they made
estimates in areas which could be checked through official statistics.

AGGLOMERATION EFFECTS

During our discussion of the relative costs of inputs, we took note of a
number of somewhat intangible considerations arising because of the
position of a plant in respect to other plants and to concentrations of
population, which might have affected costs in some way. A firm siting
its plant in an already highly developed industrialized area can usually
count on a pool of skilled labour, can maintain close relationships with
customers, and can often get cheaper insurance and better services;
and it may be close to those city facilities that many entrepreneurs
believe make their personal lives more pleasant. Though it is not pos-

sible to measure the effect of these factors upon the costs of firms,[2] it is necessary to satisfy ourselves that, by not bringing them into our analysis, we are not overlooking the really important determinants of location.

If agglomerating forces had predominated during the period, we should have expected that those districts which had housed the greatest industrial centres or the biggest population at the start of the period would have continued to grow industrially at a faster rate than did other districts in the same general region. To see if this did in fact happen, two correlation exercises were carried out. The index of value-added by manufacture in 1960 (1946 = 100)[3] for each county[4] in Ontario and Quebec was correlated with (a) the value-added in 1946 and (b) the population at the 1951 census. The co-efficient of correlation for (a) proved to be −0.035 and for (b) −0.0014. It seems therefore that there was no significant correlation between the increase in value-added over the period and either value-added at the beginning of the period or the size of the population early in the period.[5] Agglomerating forces were evidently ineffective.[6]

It seems worth considering the possibility that, while the most highly industrialized or most populous counties might not have grown more rapidly than others, there might have been a tendency for industrial or urban centres below a certain size to be left behind in the growth race because they lacked the attractions of larger centres. If, for instance, Nova Scotia centres had been below this "growth point," might not their demise have been expected for this reason alone?

The growth of value-added in counties of Quebec-Ontario with value-added in 1946 equal to, or more than, the value-added in Nova

2 H. S. Perloff et al., Regions, Resources, and Economic Growth (Baltimore, 1960), suggested that the market was exercising a greater and greater pull on industry because of the growing complexity of manufacturing processes.

3 The source was DBS, General Review of the Manufacturing Industries of Canada, 1946 and 1960, 31–201. The year 1960 was the last before changes in the statistical procedures for the collection of the annual census of manufactures effectively broke the series.

4 Counties are the smallest unit for which data covering the whole region are published. There were 129 in all.

5 Neither co-efficient of correlation was significant at the .10 level.

6 These findings are consistent with those of D. B. Creamer in Carter Goodrich et al., Migration and Economic Opportunity (Philadelphia, 1936), who showed that in every census, 1874–1935, a decreasing proportion of manufacturing industry in the United States was within central cities; and with those of E. M. Hoover, Location Theory and the Shoe and Leather Industry (Cambridge, Mass., 1937), who claimed that there was a trend in the United States towards the equalization of the degree of industrialization between cities of different sizes; and with those of D. B. Creamer, Changing Location of Manufacturing Employment (New York, 1963), who showed that in those areas where industrial employment was high it tended to fall and vice versa.

Scotia's main industrial area, Halifax County, was therefore computed. It proved to be 280 per cent, which compares with 379 per cent for other Quebec-Ontario counties. So Nova Scotia had at least one industrial area of a size which might have been expected to have grown more rapidly than the larger industrial areas in Quebec-Ontario. Similarly, the growth of value-added in those counties of Quebec-Ontario with populations in 1951 no larger than that of Halifax County was calculated. It turned out to be 325 per cent compared with 288 per cent for the more populous counties. Nova Scotia, therefore, did have a population centre which should have been large enough to support growth at a rate at least as rapid as took place in the larger centres of population.

These measurements of growth during the period relative to different areas' degrees of industrialization or population at the beginning, seem to confirm that there is no reason to believe that agglomerating forces held sway and invalidated the cost comparisons drawn in Table 9/1.

SIGNIFICANCE OF RESULTS

Faced with cost differences of between 4 per cent and 7 per cent, we are bound to conclude that, though the nature of the data does not allow statistical tests of significance to be carried out, there is at least a prima facie case for refusing to accept the hypothesis that the cost of producing manufactured goods and selling them to consumers in the Quebec-Ontario region is the same whether they are produced in Nova Scotia or in Quebec or Ontario. The relative retardation of Nova Scotia's manufacturing industry looks as if it could well be justified purely on the grounds that it is in a high-cost location. If the standard deviation found to hold in the Multiplant Firm Study (3.4 per cent) may be taken as an indication of the dispersion of firms' individual percentages around the results we have obtained, then only 2 to 10 per cent of all firms would be as well off producing in Nova Scotia. And since about 3.5 per cent of manufacturing firms setting up new plants in the two regions chose Nova Scotia, everything seems to tie up nicely and the least-cost theory is vindicated.

We should remember, however, that these results have been obtained on the basis of rather restrictive assumptions. The effect of relaxing these assumptions will now be considered.

RELAXATION OF ASSUMPTIONS

Of the assumptions previously adopted, two seem of major importance:

1 Assumption of one market

We started from the assumption that the plant would be sending all its output to the Quebec-Ontario market whether it was producing in that region or in Nova Scotia. However, there is an Atlantic provinces market containing about 9 per cent of the total personal income of central and eastern Canada. The plant we are considering would therefore normally send about that proportion of its output to that market. By so doing, a plant located in Nova Scotia would find its unfavourable transportation differential with a plant in Quebec-Ontario significantly reduced (see p. 91, note 29).[7]

2 Assumption of inferior Nova Scotia management

Our calculations showed that the lower efficiency of Nova Scotia labour counterbalanced its lower rate of pay and so left a Nova Scotian factory at no advantage in respect of labour inputs. It became fairly clear, however, that this need not be so if the firm setting up the plant ensured that the management was up to the normal standard of Quebec-Ontario. This would appear to be eminently possible; the companies in the Multiplant Firm Study appeared to have done just that and certified to the fact that an average worker's efficiency in Nova Scotia was as good as that of the average worker in Quebec-Ontario.

By substituting the comparative cost of product transportation, assuming that about 9 per cent of output would go to the Atlantic provinces market, and assuming that labour efficiencies in the two regions are made the same by ensuring equally efficient management, we arrive at Table 9/2. This throws a rather different complexion upon our comparisons. While we cannot rely upon the precise figures produced (for instance, if efficient managers were installed in Nova Scotia, the salaries payable to them might be somewhat higher than are now paid in that province, or there might be a greater pressure for higher wages if the tempo of work in Nova Scotian plants was stepped up), it seems clear that our results provide no grounds for rejecting the hypothesis that the cost of producing manufactured goods and distributing them to customers in the Quebec-Ontario region is the same whether the producing plant is situated in Nova Scotia or in the Quebec-Ontario region.

Our final conclusion after relaxing our assumptions leaves the question: if a typical plant intended to supply the whole of central and

7 The differential would be reduced even more if the export market were taken into account and the policies discussed in Part Three led to the personal incomes in Nova Scotia rising relative to those of Quebec-Ontario.

TABLE 9/2

Costs of manufacturing plants in Nova Scotia compared with costs of plants in Quebec-Ontario, assuming equally efficient management in each region and output being marketed in Quebec-Ontario and Atlantic provinces in the proportion 91 per cent : 9 per cent, 1946-62 (selected years)

	Labour		Materials and fuel		Electricity		Capital		Product transportation		Local taxes		All inputs
	$\frac{NS^a}{Q/o}$	w^b	$\frac{NS}{Q/o}$	w	$\frac{NS}{Q/o}$	w	$\frac{NS}{Q/o}$	w	$\frac{NS}{Q/o}$	w^c	$\frac{NS}{Q/o}$	w	$\frac{NS}{Q/o}$
1946	74.8	24.1	102.0	59.0	222.2	0.8	100.0	8.0	148.6^d	4.6	100.0	2.0	98.3
1951	73.8	21.1	102.0	59.9	213.7	0.8	100.0	8.0	164.4	5.0	100.0	2.0	99.8
1956	84.5	21.8	102.0	58.6	177.0	0.8	100.0	8.0	162.8	5.8	100.0	2.0	102.1
1961	81.8	22.3	102.0	57.0	165.0	0.9	100.0	8.0	168.3	5.6	100.0	2.0	101.6
1962	83.1	21.8	102.0	58.6	140.2	0.8	100.0	8.0	138.2	5.3	100.0	2.0	99.8

SOURCE: Tables 3/1, 3/12, 4/1, 4/2, 5/1 and 5/2, and pp. 60, 66, 89-90, 91 (n. 29), and 94-5,

a See n. (a), Table 9/1.
b See n. (b), Table 9/1.
c The changed figures of relative product transportation cost really call for adjustment of the weights for product transportation (and for that matter, all other weights). But the effect of doing so would have been tiny.
d 1949, because data for 1946 are not available.

eastern Canada is as well off in Nova Scotia as in Quebec-Ontario, why does Nova Scotia not receive its fair share of new manufacturing industry (that is, a share proportionate to its population)? In fact only about fifty new plants were opened in Nova Scotia each year during the period (see Table B/9). This represented only about 3.5 per cent of all plants setting up in the Nova Scotia and Quebec-Ontario regions combined. Nova Scotia merely got the share of new manufacturing establishments proportionate to the number of establishments it had to start with. This did no more than allow it to maintain its original lowly position; it led to no closing of the gap.

The answer to this question is the key to the explanation of Nova Scotia's lag in manufacturing development. It seems established that cost differences of the factor inputs cannot explain the shortage of new plants. Only one possible explanation appears to remain. The reason must be connected with the only factor input not previously dealt with – entrepreneurship. To this we will now turn.

10　Entrepreneurship

An examination of entrepreneurship inevitably runs into conceptual difficulties. To avoid some of these we shall (*a*) consider all returns to entrepreneurs as profit, and (*b*) take the rate of profit to be the earnings of the firms, after payments to other factors, expressed as a proportion of the value of its output.

RETURNS TO ENTREPRENEURSHIP

Table 10/1 shows for Nova Scotia and Quebec-Ontario the proportion that taxable corporation income comprised of the selling value of factory shipments.[1] The period for which data are available is too short to justify firm conclusions. Also, the method of compilation of the official statistics upon which Table 10/1 is based may have caused the gap between the two regions to be understated, since the income of interprovincial firms is merely allocated to the various provinces in proportion to the numbers of persons employed at plants in those provinces; but since the Multiplant Firm Study disclosed that interprovincial firms accounted for only about 20 per cent of Nova Scotia's output in 1962, the error introduced in this way cannot be great.

Notwithstanding data limitations, it does seem that Quebec-Ontario profits were a little higher than those made by manufacturing firms in Nova Scotia.[2] The question is whether or not this may be taken as an indication of a comparative lack of business opportunity or an in-

1 Taxable corporation income is the nearest approximation to profit, as we have defined it, for which official data are available. However, as we observed in chap. 6, about one-half of it must be considered as interest on entrepreneurs' capital funds tied up in the firm.
2 If H. Liebenstein is right in *Economic Theory and Organisational Analysis*

TABLE 10 / 1

Taxable corporation incomes of manufacturing firms
as percentage of selling value of factory shipments,[a]
Nova Scotia and Quebec-Ontario,
1957–62 (selected years)

	Nova Scotia	Quebec-Ontario
1957[b]	6.2	6.9
1961	6.6	6.3
1962	6.2	6.5
1957–62[c]	5.9	6.6

SOURCE: Derived from Tables B/28 and B/31.
a Taxable corporation incomes relate to tax years while
selling value of factory shipments relates to calendar years.
b Data for previous years are not available.
c All taxable corporation incomes 1957–62 divided by selling
value of factory shipments during same period.

feriority of entrepreneurial talent. This is a matter upon which we are
obviously not going to be able to bring reliable proof, but scraps of
evidence of the relative profitability of enterprise in Nova Scotia occasionally come to light. For instance, until the late 1950s no multi-storey
apartment buildings existed in Halifax. Yet, of the eight cities in
Quebec and Ontario for which the DBS published appropriate data,[3]
only in Ottawa, Toronto, London, and perhaps Hamilton were residential rents higher than in Halifax in September 1959 (the first time the
survey was carried out); and as wage-rates in the construction industry
were relatively low in Halifax, it seems likely that opportunities for
profitable apartment building existed there. One entrepreneur eventually appeared on the scene and proved it to be so; development has
been rapid since then. Similarly, supermarkets were slow to come to
Nova Scotia but are generally acknowledged to have been more profitable there than in Quebec-Ontario. And in its 1962 and 1963 annual
reports, Webb and Knapp (Canada) Limited, the large development
corporation with projects in most of the largest Canadian cities and in
the United States, spoke of the building of a shopping centre in Halifax
as "an excellent investment" and noted that "Sales levels of the retailers
since opening had exceeded expectations, and this Shopping Centre is
already secure as a commercial success." This success was apparently
secure within four months of the centre being opened and contrasted
markedly with the financial troubles into which other projects were
leading the corporation at that time.

(New York, 1960), this difference might have been due merely to the difference in the average size of the firms in the two regions.
3 DBS, *Residential Rents in Major Canadian Cities, September 1959*, 62-519.

THE QUALITY OF ENTREPRENEURSHIP

It seems to be the almost unanimous opinion of persons with experience in both regions that such profit that Nova Scotian firms make is the result of comparatively little enterprise. Everyone seems to have a fund of personal stories to illustrate the happy-go-lucky outlook of Nova Scotian firms and their apparent lack of energy in pursuing business. The different pace in the two regions is very obvious. Salesmen remark that if they are interviewing buyers in Toronto or Montreal when lunch-time arrives, sandwiches are usually brought in and the discussions continue; but in Halifax activities are suspended while everyone goes out for a leisurely lunch.

These are, of course, merely subjective judgments, but then the quality of entrepreneurship is difficult to measure objectively. In the Selected Local Areas Study, however, some attempt was made to judge the degree to which firms in Nova Scotia sought after improvement and more profitable ventures (though even here some subjectivity had to be introduced). Firms were asked about the innovations or production improvements they had introduced during the preceding six years. It turned out that a little less than half of the firms had introduced anything which might be remotely considered a new product, the remainder merely accepting without serious consideration that there was no scope for new products. Similarly, only eighteen of the seventy-one firms had done anything by way of extending their factories or modernizing their equipment. And only twenty of the seventy-one firms had sought the advice of consultants – and only then on technical problems, never on how to sell more or manage better.

The reasons for this are largely a matter of speculation. Observers seem to be fairly satisfied now that the fault lies deep in the social fabric of Nova Scotian society. A. L. Levine noted, for instance, that "In parts of the region [the Maritime provinces] it would appear that the social mores and institutions still reflect, to a very considerable extent, those of a colonial outpost of the mid-nineteenth century."[4] He decided that "... it does not seem to be an unreasonable hypothesis that it is this same social milieu which is the one of the more important sources of defective entrepreneurship."[5]

One reason for the poor quality of entrepreneurship in Nova Scotia

4 *Retardation and Entrepreneurship*, Atlantic Provinces Economic Council (Fredericton, 1965), p. 9.
5 *Ibid.*, p. 10. Levine also cast doubt upon the usual excuse offered by Maritime entrepreneurs for their inability to advance more rapidly – that Maritime plants cannot attain a size which allows economies of large-scale production to be achieved.

(though it might perhaps be an effect) is suggested by Table 10/2, which shows that a much greater proportion of Nova Scotian industry was in the hands of individuals or partnerships in 1962. The proportion did fall during the period from 65 to 52 per cent, but the corresponding proportion for Quebec-Ontario fell from 63 to 43 per cent; so Nova Scotia lagged further behind in the movement towards incorporated companies. While family businesses are not necessarily unenterprising, it seems to be a generally accepted belief that by and large they do tend to settle down over the years into a complacent rut.

TABLE 10 / 2

Type of ownership of manufacturing establishments, Nova Scotia and Quebec-Ontario, 1946–62 (selected years)

	Individual and partnerships		Incorporated companies	
	Nova Scotia	Quebec-Ontario	Nova Scotia	Quebec-Ontario
		(Percentage of all establishments)[a]		
1946	65.4	62.6	20.0	33.7
1951	65.8	56.0	28.8	37.3
1956	62.1	50.0	31.5	42.9
1961	53.7	43.8	44.0	53.8
1962	51.7	42.9	45.7	54.8

SOURCE: Derived from Tables B/8 and B/10.

a Percentages do not add to 100 per cent because co-operatives have been omitted.

Louis J. Walinsky pointed to the adverse effect of lack of competition on the quality of management (see p. 51). Certainly competition is much less intense in Nova Scotia. For instance, during the period 1961–7 there were only two attempts by gasoline stations in Halifax or Dartmouth to cut prices below the maximum permitted by the Public Utilities Board, and they were relatively short-lived. By contrast, one has little difficulty finding cut-price gasoline in either Montreal or Toronto. Similarly, salesmanship generally is low-key and householders are not badgered by door-to-door salesmen to anything like the extent they are in the larger centres.

SUPPLY OF ENTREPRENEURSHIP

It seems, therefore, that there is some reason to believe that the profits made in Nova Scotia during the period came with relatively little effort, and that comparatively low-grade, passive entrepreneurs continued to exist in that region. Since the rate of profit in Nova Scotia was little less than in Quebec-Ontario, it seems to follow that opportunities for profit-making by an average entrepreneur in manufacturing industry in Nova Scotia were at least as good as those in Quebec-Ontario.

Yet the supply of entrepreneurship to Nova Scotia seems to have been inadequate and there was a distinct dearth of entrepreneurs willing to set up new plants to take advantage of the opportunities. Table 10/3 indicates that during the last part of the period the number of new manufacturing establishments expressed as a percentage of existing establishments was consistently lower than in Quebec-Ontario. Similarly, as illustrated in Table 10/4, the number of bankruptcies in Nova Scotia was tiny compared with those in Quebec-Ontario.

TABLE 10 / 3

New manufacturing establishments created as
percentage of all manufacturing establishments,
Nova Scotia and Quebec-Ontario,
1957–62 (selected years)

	Nova Scotia	Quebec-Ontario
1957	4.4	7.8
1961	7.2	6.2
1962	4.6	6.2
1957–62[a]	4.5	6.4

SOURCE: Derived from Tables B/8 and B/9.

a Average number of new establishments created per annum 1957–62 as percentage of average of annual number of establishments operating during period.

TABLE 10 / 4

Business failures[a] per one thousand manufacturing
establishments, Nova Scotia and Quebec-Ontario,
1955–62 (selected years)

	Nova Scotia	Quebec-Ontario
1956	0.71	12.44
1961	1.00	11.37
1962	—	12.66
1955–62[b]	1.08	12.34

SOURCE: Derived from Tables B/8 and B/32.

a Reported under the Bankruptcy and Winding Up Acts.
b Average number of business failures as percentage of average of annual number of establishments 1955–62.

The rate of creation and failure of enterprises provides some indication of the urge of entrepreneurs and potential entrepreneurs to chance their hands. Though abortive business ventures waste a nation's resources, it is the readiness of people to try something new that produces progress. One must conclude from the evidence that the supply of entrepreneurship in Nova Scotia was appreciably weaker than in Quebec-Ontario, and that there was a relative shortage of people willing to grasp opportunities.

One would expect the supply of entrepreneurship to Nova Scotia's manufacturing industry to originate both within and outside the province. The weakness of the internal supply is sometimes blamed on the stolid Anglo-Saxon stock from which the province's population principally derives. And it is true that while, in 1961, 71 per cent of Nova Scotia's population was of British Isles origin, the figure for the Quebec-Ontario region was only 37 per cent.[6] It does seem probable, however, that the weakness was due less to the ethnic origin of Nova Scotia's inhabitants than to the province having been for many years an isolated society denied the revitalization of immigration. Table 1/5 shows that during the postwar period to 1962, Quebec-Ontario received over three times as many immigrants from abroad, relative to its population size, as did Nova Scotia. Indeed, not since the first half of the nineteenth century has Nova Scotia received its fair share.

At the same time as Nova Scotian society was aging and missing the revitalization by immigration, it was also losing by emigration many of its most vigorous and enterprising young people (see Table 1/6). In addition, as Levine also suggested, the social climate of the province was suffering from the failure of governments to devote adequate resources to social capital, especially education.[7]

The simple explanation for the weak external supply of entrepreneurship seems to be that the vast majority of entrepreneurs outside Nova Scotia gave no thought to the possibility of setting up a new plant in that province. This is made very clear by Table 10/5 drawn from the Site-Choice Study. Seventy-nine per cent of the firms that set up new manufacturing plants in either Quebec or Ontario between 1959 and 1962 thought that the choice was obvious and did not consider any province but the chosen one. Of the remaining seventy-three firms, only sixteen looked outside the Quebec-Ontario region. Only three thought of Nova Scotia and none of these firms went to the lengths of carefully examining its relative merits. Most entrepreneurs, it seems, have a sort of sheep-instinct. They are apparently compelled to follow the rest of the flock. If the leading sheep demonstrates that one field contains grass, the rest will content itself with that same field even though a richer pasture is waiting for any prepared to explore what lies beyond the gap in the fence. This may be rational action if the avoidance of

6 DBS, *Census of Canada, 1961*, vol. I, part 3, no. 9 (92-560).
7 *Retardation and Entrepreneurship*, p. 10.

TABLE 10 / 5

Extent to which firms which set up new manufacturing establishments in Quebec-Ontario, 1959–62, considered provinces other than the ones in which they sited their new establishments

		Number of firms	
No consideration of other provinces		277	(79%)
General consideration of other provinces:			
Other province of Quebec-Ontario region	50		
Nova Scotia	3		
Other provinces	5	55	(16%)[a]
Detailed examination of other provinces:			
Other province of Quebec-Ontario region	15		
Nova Scotia	0		
Other provinces	8	18	(5%)[b]
		350	(100%)[c]

SOURCE: Site-Choice Study.

a Three firms considered the other province of the Quebec-Ontario region and also Nova Scotia or another outside province. Hence the total is less than the sum of the parts.

b Seven firms examined both the other province of the Quebec-Ontario region and other provinces. The total is therefore less than the sum of the parts. It includes two other firms which carried out detailed examinations of a province or provinces other than the one they chose but which omitted to specify which.

c Ten firms included in the study omitted to specify the extent to which they considered other provinces.

uncertainty is the prime object,[8] but one would expect that some of the sheep would be prepared at least to peek through the gap. Perhaps the smaller and weaker lambs would not have the strength to make the journey to it, but surely the explanation for the flock's behaviour lies in its shortsightedness. It has a small horizon prescribed by its previous experience and it is unaware of, and uninterested in, what lies beyond.

In defence of the entrepreneurs concerned, it might be suggested that they ignored other provinces because previous experience had convinced them of the futility of considering them. But it turned out that only 33 per cent of the firms had had any previous manufacturing experience in Canada at all and two-thirds of these had had no experience outside the province they had chosen. Only 6 per cent of all firms had manufactured outside the Quebec-Ontario region and one solitary firm had first-hand experience in Nova Scotia. Or again it might be suggested that provinces outside Quebec-Ontario were ignored on the advice of

8 The influence of uncertainty in business decisions was rightly stressed by G. Tintner, "The Theory of Choice under Subjective Risk and Uncertainty," *Econometrica*, 9 (1941), pp. 298–304; by K. W. Rothschild, "Price Theory and Oligopoly," *Economic Journal*, LVII (1947), pp. 299–320; and by subsequent writers.

consultants who knew these regions. But only 8 per cent of the firms engaged consultants.[9] And, finally,[10] it might be suggested that, though the firms themselves had not previously manufactured outside the province in which they had set up their new plants, their senior executives had had personal knowledge gained outside their existing firms. To test this possibility, firms were asked to say if any executive who had contributed to the decision about the location of their new plants had visited Nova Scotia during the previous ten years. Fifty-nine per cent replied in the negative. As the visits of some of the remaining 41 per cent were probably limited to vacationing or passing through on the way to Europe, first-hand knowledge of the manufacturing potential of the province must have been slight in most cases.

The Site-Choice Study, therefore, if it did nothing else, stressed the small horizons of firms' policy-makers in the examination of possible locations. Of the large number of firms which set up new manufacturing plants in the Quebec-Ontario region between 1959 and 1962 (there were about fifteen hundred each year – 60 per cent of all new Canadian plants), all but a tiny minority went straight to Quebec or Ontario without considering in even a casual manner the relative merits of other provinces. Scarcely any bothered with Nova Scotia. They did not base their decisions regarding location on previous knowledge or on expert advice – they were just drawn there, almost instinctively. When asked

9 Even consultants seemed to suffer from the affliction of the limited horizon. On only three of the twenty-six occasions when consultants were retained to advise on the location of new plants were sites outside the Quebec-Ontario region considered. While this was a better average than the sixteen out of 350 which were the corresponding figures for all firms studied, it still indicated a rather chronic myopia. They suffered from the same readiness to accept prejudice rather than evidence. For instance, consultants retained by the province of Nova Scotia to advise on development opportunities there were apparently impressed by the opinion that labour productivity in the Maritime provinces was low, on the following evidence: "One company that made a study of labour costs in the Maritime Provinces and Ontario concluded that there would be little or no cost saving in the Maritimes. This conclusion was based on the company's recent experience in constructing and operating a warehouse in the Maritimes. Other respondents who compared the productivity of labour in different provinces also cited specific examples or gave their overall impressions." The construction and operation of a warehouse is scant evidence upon which to make a judgment about the productivity of labour in manufacturing operations (which were the consultants' only concern). And as this "one company" was singled out for special mention, there is an implication that either it was the only one with any first-hand experience, or that the evidence provided by the others was even less convincing.

10 There are a few other possible explanations. Entrepreneurs may benefit from setting up their new activities where they are known and know others. In this location they know the best suppliers, they are on friendly terms with possible customers, and they may be better able to tap sources of capital funds.

why he chose a particular location, one entrepreneur replied simply: "This is my home."[11] Entrepreneurship seems to be one of the least mobile factors of production and each region must, unless it can offer the irresistible attraction of a scarce natural resource, produce its own entrepreneurs.

This lack of an adequate supply of entrepreneurship was a serious matter for Nova Scotia, since the role of the entrepreneur is so crucial to any organization. If new business opportunities are not ferreted out and exploited energetically, the progress of the region is bound to be retarded. And as the entrepreneur often also assumes a role in senior management, especially in the small firms found in Nova Scotia, this same lack of energy and imagination pervades the operation of the firms, reducing the effectiveness of all other factors of production. (We concluded in chapter 3, for instance, that the relatively low labour efficiency in Nova Scotia could very likely be attributed to inadequate management.)

NON-MONETARY RETURNS TO ENTREPRENEURSHIP

We have observed that the rate of monetary returns to entrepreneurship was much the same in Nova Scotia as in Quebec-Ontario; but might not non-monetary returns also be important to entrepreneurs?[12] The pros-

11 This was the same sort of reply as was given by K. C. Irving, New Brunswick's biggest industrialist. When asked why he built a refinery in Saint John, which he claimed was a high-cost location, he replied, "Because I live in Saint John." *Financial Post*, April 20, 1968.
  These observations strongly support those of L. Needleman and B. Scott, in "Regional Problems and Location of Industry Policy in Britain," *Urban Studies*, I, no. 2 (Nov. 1964), pp. 153–73. Their assertion that firms merely look for a "satisfactory" location because they are not particularly interested in maximizing profit does, however, seem suspect. It is known that there is a high rate of mortality among new firms and only a small minority of them survive the first year. While most entrepreneurs seem to be inherently and unjustifiably optimistic, they must realize that they are going to have to strain themselves to the utmost if they are to establish themselves successfully. It therefore seems improbable that, by and large, they would ignore chances of reducing costs or increasing revenue, especially during the critical first year. Firms which are already established might act in a somewhat cavalier fashion (though in the Site-Choice Study there appeared to be no great difference in the degree of energy with which established firms and new ones sought the best sites), but new entrepreneurs surely must wish to find the best sites they can – so long as the search does not involve heavy expenditure and delay.
12 These were recognized by A. Weber, though he did not consider them important; see C. J. Friedrich's *Alfred Weber's Theory of Location of Industries* (Chicago, 1929). M. L. Greenhut, in *Plant Location in Theory and Practise: The Economics of Space* (Chapel Hill, NC, 1956), referred to a steel-fabricating entrepreneur who said that he would want a premium to leave his home district; and in "The Quantitative Study of Factors Determining Business

pect of profits at the North Pole would need to be exceptionally good before an entrepreneur could be persuaded to transplant himself and his family there from metropolitan Toronto. They would miss their friends, their sporting activities, their ballet, their theatre, their cinemas, their television, their schools, and their colleges. If the option is between two regions otherwise similar in facilities, climate, language, and culture, then there would still be a strong incentive for the entrepreneur to set up a new factory where he and his family would not be required to break their social contacts. Consequently, each region offers psychic returns which can only be valued subjectively. Natives of Nova Scotia will nearly always put a high value on the psychic returns which arise from operating in their own province and a low value upon those available in Quebec or Ontario. Natives of Quebec or Ontario will usually feel precisely the opposite. Psychic income in our present comparisons may therefore be of importance to the mobility of entrepreneurs and may partially explain why rates of profit for similar entrepreneurs are not equalized, though they do not explain differences in the supply of home-produced entrepreneurs.

Decisions," *Quarterly Journal of Economics*, XVI, no. 1 (Feb. 1952), G. Katona and J. N. Morgan found that the location of one firm had been due to psychic income.

Part Three
Policy Implications

11 Justification,
Objectives, and Methods
of Policy

The retardation of Nova Scotia's manufacturing industry relative to that of Quebec-Ontario is not a new phenomenon, the gap between the two regions having remained very stable during the 1946–62 period. Nor has the situation altered appreciably since 1962, the selling value of Nova Scotia factory shipments in 1968 per capita being somewhat under 35 per cent of the corresponding figure for Quebec-Ontario,[1] a percentage which was slightly above that for 1962 but rather lower than for 1946.[2] A stable equilibrium seems to have been established soon after the last war, notwithstanding the efforts made by the federal and provincial governments through the Area Development Agency, the Atlantic Development Board, the Cape Breton Development Corporation, the Department of Trade and Commerce, the Nova Scotia Department of Trade and Industry, the Nova Scotia Voluntary Planning Board, and Industrial Estates Limited.

Does this mean that governmental efforts to secure a more even distribution of manufacturing industry over the country had no effect? Or did they merely prevent further deterioration in Nova Scotia's relative position? There is no way of knowing the answer to these questions.

1 Derived from DBS, *Inventories, Shipments and Orders in Manufacturing Industries, Jan. 1969*, 31-001; and DBS, *Estimated Population by Sex and Age Groups, Canada and Provinces, 1968*, 91–202.
2 About 1966 and 1967 there was a feeling in the air that Nova Scotia, together with the other Atlantic provinces, had at last turned the corner. In 1966, for instance, Louis J. Walinsky, "Strategy and Policy for Economic Growth in the Atlantic Region," address to the Annual Conference of the Atlantic Provinces Economic Council, mimeo. (Halifax, 1966), p. 15, spoke of "New Winds of Change." But while there were signs of improvement in some sectors of some provinces, there was no real indication that the situation of Nova Scotia's manufacturing industry had altered.

What is certain, however, is that the government measures did not accomplish their objective. In this and the next three chapters we shall discuss the various possible ways in which the gap between the two regions might be closed, how the previous measures were faulty, and which method holds most promise for the future.

THE DESIRABILITY OF ATTEMPTS TO CLOSE THE GAP

Before proceeding we should consider whether or not we should really be trying to close the gap. If we adhered to classical economic doctrine we should decide against any such attempt, since it is easy enough to demonstrate that, with any given distribution of income, the optimum use of the nation's economic resources can only be achieved if economic forces are left to do their work without interference. We should conclude that the only outcome of steering manufacturing activity into areas where it would not otherwise have gone would be the creation of a high-cost Canadian manufacturing industry and a general lowering of income levels.

Such a doctrine is irrefutable so long as the assumptions upon which it rests are realistic. The first assumption is that the existing distribution of income is ideal; the second is that economic forces really do act freely; the third is that there is one unique low-cost geographical distribution of manufacturing industry; and the fourth is that firms' costs correspond to the social costs of their activities. But, in fact, one cannot be assured that any of these conditions is satisfied in Canada today. It is not possible to demonstrate that the present distribution of income is ideal without resort to subjective judgments which enjoy no universal acceptance. No one pretends that the competitive conditions (including perfect knowledge) necessary before economic forces can fulfil their traditional role exist in every sector of the economy. There is a good deal of evidence (the success of the great majority of firms induced to go into the British development areas, for instance) that many firms are footloose in the sense that they can produce at similar cost in many locations. And, perhaps most important to our present purpose, private costs seldom coincide with public costs. If, for instance, a depressed area holds idle persons, the social cost of using that labour *in situ* will probably be much lower than its cost to a private employer moving into the area. By contrast, the same employer setting up in a prosperous city to which the unemployed are coaxed or driven may well escape the cost of moving or providing services for them.[3] And we know that in

3 If the United Nations' *Economic Survey of Europe in 1954* (Geneva, 1955), p. 156, is right and the average cost per capita of public services starts to rise

Nova Scotia there is a good deal of unemployment and underemployment. Its unemployment rate is always above the Canadian average and the proportion of the population officially considered in the labour force is relatively low because many people, particularly women, simply lack job opportunities. In such circumstances, the public cost of taking jobs to the unemployed will be less than the private cost to the employer who hires them. Indeed, once a society accepts the responsibility of maintaining unemployed people, the cost to the government of recompensing a firm for going to a high-cost area may be less than the unemployment and welfare benefits saved.[4] Nor should one overlook the fact that unemployed persons tend to depreciate rapidly both physically and mentally; so the cost of pushing industry into a high-cost location may be a low price to pay to prevent the depreciation of part of the nation's human resources.

There seems to be no logical ground, therefore, for believing that a locational pattern produced as the result of governmental direction is necessarily inferior to a pattern which would arise in the absence of such direction. In any event, the matter is no longer an open issue. In 1961, for instance, the Special Committee of the Senate on Manpower and Employment concluded that "The massive migration of the population is neither socially nor economically desirable, and we reject this possibility. Therefore, the other course, namely of providing better opportunities for these people in the areas concerned, must be undertaken with determined effort."[5] In the 1968 federal election each party vied with the others to convince the electorate that its proposed programme for economic development of depressed areas would be more effective than the one offered by its opponents. And, for reasons discussed in chapter 1, economic development to most politicians, and for that matter to most economists,[6] means the building up of manufacturing industry.

once a city expands its population beyond 300,000, then the cost to the city of absorbing the inflow of unemployed may well be heavy; yet the employer will pay only a small part of it.

4 T. Wilson, in *Financial Assistance with Regional Development*, Atlantic Provinces Research Board (Fredericton, 1964), p. 61, quoted figures indicating that the net cost of non-repayable government assistance for each worker employed in the factories assisted to locate in British development areas in the early 1960s was only about $750. Even if building and equipment were substantially more expensive in Nova Scotia during that period, the corresponding cost per worker in Nova Scotia could scarcely have exceeded six months' unemployment benefit for a typical family.

5 *Final Report*, no. 25, p. 6.

6 For instance, the Atlantic Provinces Economic Council, *Incentives for Manufacturing Industries* (Fredericton, 1962), p. 12, declared that "secondary industries would seem to offer the most obvious opportunities for expansion of

OBJECTIVE OF POLICY

The proper objectives of a programme of regional development are elusive, and several commentators have drawn attention to the lack of a clear idea on the part of the various federal and provincial departments and agencies of what it is they are really trying to do.[7] Graham remarked that "The situation can still be fairly described as one of programs without policy."[8] In particular, the government policymakers do not yet seem to have decided whether they are trying to maximize personal income per capita in the depressed areas or to minimize the unemployment there. Fortunately, we are saved from becoming embroiled in controversy over this topic since our area of concern has been a narrow one and our object simple. We are concerned merely with closing the gap between the stages of development of manufacturing industry in Nova Scotia and Quebec-Ontario.

THE NATURE OF A POLICY

At the end of our comparison of the costs of the operation of factories in Nova Scotia and Quebec-Ontario, we were left with the conclusion that there was no evidence that cost consideration could justify the gap between the relative stages of development of the manufacturing industries in those regions. Only a weak supply of entrepreneurs seemed to be holding Nova Scotia back. There really is cause, therefore, for governments to intervene on the side of Nova Scotia in the distribution of manufacturing industry only to the extent necessary to correct the shortage of entrepreneurs in the province. A direct government policy would concentrate on clearing away ignorance of the opportunities in Nova Scotia and developing a more enterprising state of mind among its own population. Education and indoctrination are slow processes,

employment opportunities in the Atlantic Region"; John F. Graham, *Fiscal Adjustment and Economic Development: A Case Study of Nova Scotia* (Toronto, 1963), p. 139, submitted that "a considerable expansion of secondary manufacturing industries" was the alternative to increasing out-migration as a way of combating unemployment; and A. K. Cairncross, *Economic Development and the Atlantic Provinces*, Atlantic Provinces Research Board (Fredericton, 1961), seemed to lean towards manufacturing as offering the main hope for Nova Scotia.

7 For a discussion of this topic, see F. T. Walton, "The Formulation of Regional Economic Objectives," a paper presented to the meetings of the Canadian Economics Association, Calgary, June 1968.

8 John F. Graham, "Areas of Economic Stress in the Canadian Federal Context," in W. D. Wood and R. S. Thoman, eds., *Areas of Economic Stress in Canada* (Kingston, 1965), p. 10.

however, requiring perhaps a generation to bring about significant change and a more indirect approach seems to be called for if quick results are required. Measures must be taken so that, given the present state of ignorance and lack of enterprise, entrepreneurs and potential entrepreneurs located within or without the province are persuaded that Nova Scotia is a no less attractive site for manufacturing industry than is the Quebec-Ontario region. This implies monetary incentives of one sort or another which are big enough to attract the attention and whet the appetites of those who make the decisions about where to set up new manufacturing plants. There is unlikely to be unanimity about how big the incentive would have to be to do this, but it seems reasonable to suppose that a carrot amounting to 5 per cent of total costs would be big enough to impress most entrepreneurs or potential entrepreneurs. Such an incentive would be very generous compared with those provided under the British programme which have been estimated to be about 2 per cent of the costs of a firm going into the development areas.[9] It would also be, incidentally, just about the level of subsidy which our previous calculations (see chapter 9) indicated would be necessary to eliminate the cost disadvantage of an average Nova Scotian plant, relative to a plant in Quebec-Ontario, which was producing entirely for the central Canadian market and which continued to operate with Nova Scotia's relatively low quality management.

It also implies that assistance may have to be given on a long-term basis. If entrepreneurs are convinced, even through ignorance, that Nova Scotia is a high-cost location, a short-term subsidy will not seem particularly attractive, unless of course it is on a very big scale. But the idea of long-term subsidies seems repugnant to many people. Wilson, for instance, says "If the measures for regional development are to be as consistent as possible with the long-term requirements of natural growth, then the assistance should not be indefinite in duration";[10] and Graham admits of "a strong argument on economic grounds for the use of federal subsidies" but specifies "for a limited duration."[11] It would without doubt be preferable if Nova Scotia were eventually able to take off into sustained flight after a few years of a subsidy programme; but if we accept that self-sufficiency must await psychological and sociological changes, a short, sharp programme even of great magnitude is unlikely to achieve its effect. The rapid build-up of external economies, upon which short-term programmes seem to rely, may be illusory. In any event, if one accepts the arguments about social costs of manufac-

9 See Wilson, *Financial Assistance with Regional Development*, p. 58.
10 *Ibid.*, p. 30.
11 *Fiscal Adjustment and Economic Development*, p. 140.

turing in areas of unemployment being less than the private costs of the firms concerned, the case against all long-term subsidies seems to be destroyed.

The next decision to be made relates to the type of manufacturing industry which the policy should aim to attract. It is obviously better if the industries steered into Nova Scotia held out the prospect of future growth in that province. Industries which are obviously ill-suited for Nova Scotia should be avoided. The problem lies in trying to discover which are the most desirable industries from this standpoint.[12] It is not difficult to single out a few which are eminently unsuitable if there is to be any hope of competing in Canadian markets. (Monument-making is an obvious example; the costs of transporting the heavy stone from Quebec and the finished product back to central Canada would be prohibitive.) But to find suitable ones is more difficult. Ideally, we should like to find manufacturing activities which do not require large quantities of the expensive Nova Scotian electricity, can find ready markets within and outside the province, and have products with a high value to weight and bulk ratio. But this is not easily done. For instance, the desirability of producing souvenirs for sale to tourists is often mentioned; but souvenirs form a most heterogeneous class of commodities produced in industries ranging from sheet-metal stampers and glass moulders to leather workers and domestic-type garment makers. Which particular branch of the "souvenir" industry is appropriate for Nova Scotia cannot be determined from official statistics. Something can be done in this direction, however, by using official statistics as a means of obtaining hints where individual feasibility studies might be directed. Localization coefficients[13] may suggest industries the productive units of which do not seem to need to concentrate at a small number of points but spread themselves geographically and might therefore be at home tucked away in Nova Scotia; location quotients[14] might point to existing Nova Scotian industries which seem to be able to hold their own in

12 This is perhaps the reason why the Atlantic Development Board largely played safe by confining its activity to improving the Atlantic provinces' infrastructure. It is politically easy to justify the building of a road, and few will question its usefulness once it is finished; but public scorn is shown toward a government body which builds a factory which eventually stands idle. A. O. Hirschman, *The Strategy of Economic Development* (New Haven, Conn., 1958), p. 85, pointed out that "Development planning is a risky business and there is naturally an attraction in undertaking ventures that cannot be proven wrong before they are started and that are unlikely ever to become obvious failures."

13 See P. S. Florence and W. Baldamus, *Investment, Location and Size of Plant* (London, 1948).

14 See E. M. Hoover, "The Measurement of Industrial Localization," *Review of Economic Statistics*, XVIII, no. 4 (Nov. 1936), pp. 162–71. The location quotient seems often to be used on a sort of "heads you win, tails you can't lose"

export markets and are therefore prima facie particularly suitable for Nova Scotia, and to possibilities for new industries which might be brought into Nova Scotia to serve local markets at present supplied by imports. And a study of the patterns of industry in communities similar to those found in Nova Scotia may well suggest particular industries which would find conditions in that province appropriate. One should remember, however, that within industrial groupings for which statistical tests of this sort give no favourable indication, may well be hidden small manufacturing activities eminently suitable for Nova Scotia.

One point that certainly needs stressing is that the search should not be preoccupied with finding industries which are new to the province. Since existing industries have demonstrated that it is possible to survive in Nova Scotia, they have created the presumption that the activity in which they are engaged is suitable for the province. And since entrepreneurs are apparently the least mobile of factors of production, it seems sensible to encourage local industries to expand. As a corollary to this point, it is important to avoid the temptation to protect existing firms by refusing to assist new firms in the same industry. The political pressures to do so are bound to be strong (they were explicitly yielded to when the terms of reference given to Industrial Estates Limited, Nova Scotia's crown corporation charged with attracting industry to the province, specified that assistance might not be extended to industries which would be competitive with existing firms). But if an existing firm refuses offered assistance to expand while an outsider is satisfied that with the same assistance he can operate new capacity profitably, refusal to help the outsider merely protects the unenterprising.

Another highly desirable characteristic to look for in an industry is its ability to produce indirect beneficial effects. For instance, a labour intensive firm will, through the multiplier effect, probably stimulate activity elsewhere in the economy, and a firm which buys semi-finished goods which are produced, or may be produced, locally may set in motion a chain development which may lead eventually to an industrial complex.[15] By contrast, some of the industries which Nova Scotia has

---

basis. If for any area the quotient is high in respect of one industry, then that industry is assumed to be suitable for the area since it has "export potential"; if it is low, then that industry is assumed to be appropriate for "import substitution."

15 This point is not rendered inapplicable because the firm is a low-wage firm. Trade unions in Cape Breton have tended to look down their noses at such firms and have suggested that the region would be better off without them. But if a firm is able to hire labour at low rates, this is a symptom of lack of employment opportunities locally – an unfortunate circumstance which is only cured by out-migration or by increasing the demand for labour. If more such firms could be attracted in, the increased demand for labour would ensure that they would all have to pay rates which unions would regard as more satisfactory.

been so pleased to procure in recent years (heavy water plants and oil refineries in particular) buy nearly all their materials outside the province, employ little labour once construction is completed, and consequently contribute little in the way of stimulation to the districts in which they are located.

To determine the relative desirability of industries calls for cost-benefit analyses of each. This is clearly impossible, but cost-benefit analyses might well be done each time a decision has to be taken regarding assistance to a specific firm. In the calculation, care should be taken to ensure that all the public costs are included as well as all the public benefits. For instance, if the proposal relates to a new potato chip factory whose waste would turn an attractive river into a stinking sewer, the distress caused to the people who lived near the river should be taken into account.

Finally, firms which show inclination to come to Nova Scotia and accept the assistance offered merely as a way of staving off impending collapse are not likely to be particularly beneficial to the province. If they have previously demonstrated their managerial incompetence or in other ways shown inability to compete, their shortcomings are not likely to be rectified by moving to another province. Indeed, even well-established and profitable firms avoid moving production facilities whenever possible.

These, then, seem to be the considerations which should be weighed when deciding which industries and which firms to try to persuade to set up new plants, or to extend existing plants, in Nova Scotia. Having said all this, however, one has to recognize that Nova Scotia, like other have-not areas, is unlikely to be able to pick and choose. There will be no queue of firms seeking to come to Nova Scotia. It will almost certainly be a case of grasping quickly and gratefully at any reasonably promising prospect. But the foregoing discussion is relevant because industrial development organizations such as Industrial Estates Limited need some kind of guide as to the sort of industries and firms for which they should make a pitch. Manufacturing industry, as a whole, with its thousands of firms engaged upon thousands of different activities, constitutes too wide a field in which to plough about aimlessly. Some guidance as to the firms most likely to be suitable for, and most beneficial to, Nova Scotia is obviously called for.

Having considered the type of industries and firms which should best be sought, we next come to the question of where within the province they should be encouraged to settle. The word "encouraged" is the appropriate one since no real obstacle should be put in the way of a firm wishing to establish anywhere in the province, so long as the point about social costs previously mentioned is not overlooked. But may there not be virtue in encouraging firms to cluster their plants so as to secure external economies? There has been a general disposition to believe that this would be a desirable policy. The Economic Council of Canada noted that certain metropolitan areas "clearly constitute the most important focal points for the development of their respective regional areas and for improved regional balance across the country;"[16] and in 1963 the British government, after many years of energetically pursuing area development programmes, gave recognition to the virtue of developing focal points of industry, even when other parts of the region showed greater economic distress.[17]

Our discussions in chapter 9 suggested that external economies were overemphasized, but nevertheless they may well be of consequence in some circumstances. Also, agglomeration may bring a greater stability to the region since the inevitable rise and fall of firms is less catastrophic in a large industrial area than it would be in small towns which come to rely upon a single industry. Certainly, if there is an inclination for firms to be attracted towards certain parts of the province, no attempt should be made to coax them into a remote area merely because its inhabitants appear to be in greatest need. But this is precisely what the Canadian government did until 1969 by denying area development tax holidays or grants to firms setting up or expanding manufacturing plants in the Halifax-Dartmouth area.[18] And it can also be argued that the Maritime Freight Rates Act, by removing part of the penalty of high transportation costs normally imposed upon firms choosing to locate in the remoter areas, has also encouraged economic scatter.

Finally, it is important to keep in mind that Nova Scotia's future

16 *Second Annual Review* (Ottawa, 1965), p. 127.
17 See Scottish Development Department, *Central Scotland: A Programme for Development and Growth* (Edinburgh, 1963).
18 As the Economic Council observed in its *Fifth Annual Review* (Ottawa, 1968), p. 168, "The designation of areas has been based on past recorded economic stagnation rather than future viability or economic potential." In 1969, however, with the coming of the new Department of Regional Economic Expansion, the criteria were made more flexible and any area which was a part of a region which had exceptional inadequacy of opportunities for productive employment could qualify; and since, as Jean Marchand, Minister of Regional Economic Expansion, is reported to have said to newsmen (see the Halifax *Mail-Star* of Feb. 18, 1969), "Halifax, for instance, is a natural growth centre," Halifax-Dartmouth became a designated area. Mr Marchand reflected the new outlook when he went on to observe that "It is useless to spend money on centres that do not have some reasonable possibility of development without it." (It should, however, be noted that the adoption of this new flexible policy was not an unmixed blessing for Nova Scotia because it resulted in a very large band stretching across most of southern Canada becoming "designated.")

industrial development will rely on a satisfactory industrial climate elsewhere in Canada. Table 11/1 shows how Nova Scotia shared in the good and bad times of the rest of Canada during the late 1940s and 1950s. Indeed, Nova Scotia's swings were much more pronounced. In times of high employment, when profits seem relatively easy to come by and factors of production become scarce in the main centres of industry and population, firms are more ready to look farther afield for favourable locations. In economic depressions, when profits seem more difficult to make and factors are readily available, firms tend to be less venturesome and prefer to remain in well-tried locations. Also, depressions take their heaviest toll from the newer and smaller firms; so firms enticed into Nova Scotia will be particularly vulnerable. Consequently, Nova Scotia's chances of catching up with central Canada will be better if generally prosperous conditions can be maintained.

TABLE 11 / 1

Selling value of factory shipments of manufacturing industry, cyclical relatives,[a] Nova Scotia and Canada, 1948–58

	Nova Scotia	Canada
1948	108.6	105.5
1949	98.5	96.5
1950	92.7	96.6
1951	104.4	105.8
1952	108.5	102.9
1953	101.2	100.8
1954	90.2	93.9
1955	93.9	98.9
1956	103.6	105.0
1957	109.4	101.9
1958	101.5	98.4

SOURCE: Derived from DBS, *General Review of the Manufacturing Industries of Canada*, 31–201.
a Selling value of factory shipments as percentage of five-year moving average.

METHODS AVAILABLE

A government in Canada wishing to try to close the gap between the level of manufacturing development in Nova Scotia and the Quebec-Ontario region is denied two important weapons available and extensively used in Britain, France, and many other countries. First, since little manufacturing industry in Canada is government-owned, governments cannot decide location of production units merely by making management decisions. And, second, because of the division of power between the federal and provincial governments, intergovernmental agreement would be necessary before firms could be prevented from setting up new plants or expanding in areas judged to have less need of new industry; and since no provincial government is likely to wish to bar potential new industry from its territory, the chances of such agreement are exceedingly remote.

Consequently, it is a matter of coaxing private enterprise firms to locate in Nova Scotia new plants which they might be otherwise disposed to set up in Quebec or Ontario. Governments may try to do this by increasing the supply of factors of production so that, at any price, the supply might be larger than it now is (or, what is much the same thing, the amount of factors at present being employed could be obtained by Nova Scotian entrepreneurs at prices lower than those now being paid). Or they may seek to increase the demand for products manufactured in Nova Scotia so that manufacturing firms in that province may receive higher revenue from any particular output than is now possible. Or, finally, they may seek to remove any obstacles, such as ignorance or restrictive practices, which hinder the influx of firms to Nova Scotia.

CHOICE OF METHODS

The first criterion by which any particular method of attracting manufacturing industry into Nova Scotia must be judged is whether or not it would be capable of achieving its object. If the approach is by way of reducing the price of inputs by subsidies, then the method adopted must be capable of reducing the overall cost of inputs for an average plant by the appropriate proportion (which has already been suggested might be set at 5 per cent). Of, if another approach is adopted, it should be sufficiently powerful to have a similar effect. It may seem superfluous to make this point, but one must acknowledge that none of the measures previously tried by governments (and the measures have been various and apparently on a large scale) have achieved the results for which they were designed.

The second criterion is that the required effect should be achieved at minimum cost. When we come to consider each method in detail, we shall find that the cost will very largely be determined by the extent to which the action can be accurately focused upon the particular firms for which assistance is intended. Some methods will prove relatively cheap while others may cost four times as much.

The third criterion is that side-benefits which spill over into other sectors of the economy and bring benefits in addition to those directly created by the original action should be maximized. A labour-intensive industry which buys its materials locally is likely to produce large effects via the income multiplier. Similarly, expenditure on education designed to improve the quality of managers and entrepreneurs will very likely benefit many people who will never have any connection with manufacturing industry. Caution is necessary, however, to ensure that one is not misled by side-benefits. All too often a scheme is introduced which is an unnecessarily expensive way of achieving the primary objective, but is justified vaguely by its side-benefits. The extra cost of such a scheme, over and above the cost of the cheapest way of achieving the primary objective, is the cost of the side-benefits; and only if these side-benefits are worth this cost should the scheme go forward. Also, it is important to offset against the benefits any ill-effects which may arise on the side when a new industry attracted to the province harms existing firms or private members of the community.

The administrative and political feasibility of the method proposed is the fourth criterion upon which it should be judged. Though a method might promise to produce the desired effect at low direct cost, it would have to be rejected if it was politically unacceptable or the administrative problems of implementing it too cumbersome or expensive. Under this heading should also be included the question of the ease with which any measures might be reversed if circumstances subsequently seemed to justify such action. Some types of financial assistance are notoriously difficult to withdraw even when the reason which originally gave rise to them has disappeared.

The final criterion is that the method chosen should distort the "natural" distribution of industry to the minimum extent. A subsidy on a factor input will tend to be especially attractive to firms which are heavy users of that factor; and it is therefore important to consider whether the mix of industries achieved is the one which best suits the circumstances in Nova Scotia.

These five criteria appear to be the only ones upon which the choice of methods should rest. It does not seem to matter much to a firm which believes it would be worse off by $100,000 per annum by siting its plant in Nova Scotia whether it receives a counterbalancing $100,000 annual grant in the form of a subsidy upon the cost of the materials it buys or upon the cost of shipping its products to the market. In the past there has been a tendency for Nova Scotians to call for, and policy-makers to grant, help in areas in which the province is at the greatest disadvantage. But there appears to be no justification for this; indeed, it very likely offends the fourth criterion by being of maximum benefit to those firms least suited to the province.

DIRECTING THE POLICY

In the past many government departments and agencies have been concerned with development in Nova Scotia. Co-ordinating federal government activities with those of the Nova Scotia government's Department of Trade and Industry, Voluntary Planning Board, and Industrial Estates Limited is inevitably difficult in the Canadian political context, but even at the federal level the Area Development Agency, the Department of Trade and Commerce, the Atlantic Development Board, and the Cape Breton Development Corporation have all tended to go their own ways. A consistent policy towards development of Nova Scotia's manufacturing industry did not therefore emerge.

It was intended that the Area Development Agency, when it was founded in 1963 within the Department of Industry, would become the co-ordinating body. It did not do so, turning itself instead almost entirely into a simple executive agency for dispensing Area Development Incentives Act grants. Consequently, in 1968 the Economic Council of Canada found it necessary to point out that "... as far as we are aware, nowhere in the federal government structure is there a central focus, not merely to avoid duplication, inconsistency and contradiction of programming, but also to assure the allocation of scarce federal funds to secure maximum benefits for the region and the country as a whole. There is a clear need for a complete reappraisal of administrative and procedural means for putting federal support for Atlantic regional development on a more rational and well-integrated basis."[19]

The phasing out of the Department of Industry (including the ADA) and the Atlantic Development Board, and the setting up of the Department of Regional Economic Expansion in 1969 give some hope that, at least at the federal level, there will be a higher degree of co-ordination.

19 *Fifth Annual Review*, p. 176.

12   Cheapening Inputs

Assistance to lagging areas has generally been by way of subsidies on factor inputs. Before discussing each type of subsidy, something generally may be said about the cost of such programmes if they are to be large enough to be effective. If we continue to assume that a subsidy to the average firm at a rate which equals 5 per cent of the value of its output would be of the order required to impress entrepreneurs enough to overcome the psychological and sociological barriers which seem to have limited the expansion of manufacturing in Nova Scotia, then the cost of various general categories of programmes would be as listed in Table 12/1

The first line (type A subsidy) indicates the cheapest type of programme – one in which the subsidy could be directed exactly where it was needed. A subsidy which was offered only to firms which set up

1 All computations which follow deal with the cost of the various programmes if they had been introduced in 1962 and are therefore based upon the selling value of factory shipments in Nova Scotia in 1962. To estimate the cost of a type A or type B subsidy programme started in a later year, assuming the cost comparisons of Part Two remain valid, it is necessary merely to multiply the 1962 costs by the ratio of the selling value of factory shipments in the later year to the selling value of factory shipments in 1962. For instance, the cost in the first year of a subsidy on the whole of Nova Scotian manufacturing started in 1968 would be the cost in 1962 multiplied by (selling value of factory shipments 1968 divided by selling value of factory shipments 1962), that is, $21 million × 650/427 = $32 million.

Similarly, if a smaller rate of subsidy were contemplated, its cost could be calculated merely by taking the figures of table 12/1 and multiplying by the ratio of the desired rate of subsidy to the 5 per cent postulated in our discussion. Conversion of a type C subsidy to a programme started in a later year merely involves multiplying the appropriate figures of Table 12/1 by the ratio of the gross provincial product in that year to the gross provincial product in 1962.

TABLE 12 / 1

Cost of subsidizing factor inputs to Nova Scotia manufacturing industry to extent of 5 per cent of the selling value of factory shipments, 1962

		Cost of first year of programme	Annual cost when policy achieved its goal
		(millions of dollars)	
A	Subsidy on new manufacturing activity in Nova Scotia only	negligible	47
B	Subsidy on Nova Scotia manufacturing sector only	21	68
C	Subsidy on all sectors of the Nova Scotia economy	140	187

new manufacturing activity would cost very little in the first year since obviously the number of new firms involved would take time to build up. (To be precise, the subsidy should go only to firms setting up new plants which would otherwise not have come to Nova Scotia without the subsidy, but they would be difficult to identify.[2]) If the programme succeeded until Nova Scotia's manufacturing output per head of the population reached the level of Quebec-Ontario (see Tables B/1 and B/28), the cost would rise to $47 million (2.2 times 5 per cent of the 1962 Nova Scotia selling value of factory shipments).[3]

The second line (type B subsidy) would apply where the input subsidy, due to administrative or political reasons, could not be directed only to new manufacturing activity but would have to be extended to all Nova Scotia's manufacturing firms. The cost would be much higher. It would start out in the first year at $21 million (5 per cent of the selling value of Nova Scotia factory shipments, which amounted to $427 million in 1962). If the programme achieved its object, its cost would rise by another $47 million to $68 million (3.2 times $21 million).

2 Under the new (1969) Regional Development Incentives Act grants are to be made only at the discretion of the Minister of Regional Economic Expansion, and the present minister, Jean Marchand, has publicly indicated that he proposes to confine them to firms which would not otherwise establish or expand plants in the development areas. How successful he will be in distinguishing such firms from the others which apply for grants has yet to be seen.

3 There is the distinct probability that, as Nova Scotia's manufacturing industry expanded more rapidly than manufacturing in Quebec-Ontario, manufacturing wage-rates in Nova Scotia would rise nearer to the level of wage-rates in Quebec-Ontario, though they would not be likely to reach that level unless circumstances in other sectors of the Nova Scotian economy improved in the same way. If they did rise relative to those of Quebec-Ontario, then *ceteris paribus* the relative cost position of Nova Scotia's manufacturing industry would deteriorate and the subsidy would have to be raised.

If assistance could not be limited to manufacturing activity but had to be granted as a blanket subsidy on all economic activity (as, for instance, if it was in the form of a general rebate of personal and corporation income tax earned by activity in Nova Scotia), the cost would be according to the last line of the table (type c subsidy). In the first year it would be $140 million. (The gross provincial product of Nova Scotia in 1962 was $1,146 million[4] – 6.6 times the value-added by the manufacturing sector.) It would then rise by the extra $50 million when manufacturing output had achieved its required level (assuming other sectors did not also grow). It is difficult, however, to see why a broad approach such as this would be necessary, but a programme which offered a transportation subsidy which was available upon all Nova Scotian goods would quite likely reach half these figures.

We shall now look at each type of subsidy upon factor inputs which might be used, discussing the extent to which it can be effective, any side-benefits and ill-effects which might be involved, the administrative and political considerations which need to be taken into account, any distortions which might be caused, and the cost entailed. We shall refer to costs as "low," "moderate," or "high" to correspond to the amounts indicated in Table 12/1 for the types a, b, and c subsidy respectively.

LABOUR

We saw previously that labour costs were the second most important element of costs, accounting for about 21 or 22 per cent of the selling value of factory shipments (see Table 3/1); and that the level of wage-rates and the availability of labour were together mentioned most frequently in the Site-Choice Study as being influential in location decisions. To achieve the desired 5 per cent level of cost reduction for the average manufacturing firm, governments would have to relieve it of about 25 per cent of its wage bill. This might be attempted by any of the following:

1 *A payroll subsidy*
The federal and provincial governments have in the past used payroll subsidies to reduce winter unemployment and in some circumstances to encourage training on the job; so payroll subsidies are evidently politically possible, at least sometimes. And they should be fairly easy

4 Estimate by D. B. Das Gupta, *An Approach to a Social Accounting System for the Atlantic Provinces*, Atlantic Provinces Economic Council (Fredericton, 1966), p. 40.

to administer and police because of the rather elaborate wage recording systems which nowadays have to be kept for social security and income tax purposes. It might be possible to limit the subsidy to new manufacturing activity, at least for some years.[5] After that, pre-existing firms that did not qualify might become resentful; but for a considerable time the cost of the programme would be low.

By the action of the multiplier, benefits from such a subsidy would be felt strongly outside the firms which actually received it;[6] so its overall effects would be much greater than those actually directly purchased by governments. And the general improvement in conditions which would result would stimulate local markets and might well make the province more attractive to other firms. Such a subsidy would be most attractive to labour-intensive firms. It is difficult to see anything sinister in this, since these are the type of firms which one would expect "natural" economic forces to push towards a low wage-rate area like Nova Scotia. Also, because of the relatively high levels of unemployment in Nova Scotia, one would expect the social cost of procuring output from a labour-intensive plant in that province to be lower than procuring the same output from a plant set up in an area of full employment.

2 An enlarged education and training programme

Nova Scotia has in the past been proud of the facilities it provided for general education up to the baccalaureate level and for professional training. How far this is justified is difficult to judge objectively, though it is certainly true that its professional schools are well-regarded throughout the world. But there is little doubt that of recent years, when universities have had to look to governments for more and more

---

5 T. Wilson, *Financial Assistance with Regional Development* (Fredericton, 1964), p. 71, suggested a subsidy equivalent to one-quarter of new plants' payrolls for three years. Based upon 1962 labour costs, the total subsidy payment would be of the order of $170 million (wages and salaries 1962 × proportionate increase in output required to raise Nova Scotian manufacturing to the level of Quebec-Ontario × rate of subsidy × number of years, that is, $103 million × 2.2 × ¼ × 3). In 1967, the British Government introduced a sort of payroll subsidy of 7.5 per cent of labour costs, payable to manufacturing activities in development areas for a period of seven years.

6 From this point of view, firms such as clothing manufacturers (whose labour costs comprise about 70 per cent of their overall costs), machine shops (where the percentage is about 40), and similar labour-intensive firms, are particularly valuable. At the other end of the scale, an oil refinery, whose labour costs are only about 5 per cent of its total costs, is least desirable (in addition to which it would import nearly all its materials from outside the province).

of their funds, Nova Scotian universities have had to struggle hard to maintain their relative positions. Expenditure of provincial government funds on higher education in 1961–2 was only $3 per head of the population in Nova Scotia compared with $8.4 per head in Quebec-Ontario.[7] Similarly, government financial inputs into elementary and high schools have been poor relative to those in other provinces and there has been a continuous emigration of teachers to provinces that pay much better salaries, those that remain being relatively ill-trained.[8] In the field of vocational training, Nova Scotia has been as backward as the rest of Canada and only since the federal government entered the field with its cost-sharing programme under the Technical and Vocational Training Assistance Act of 1960 has progress been made.

The extent to which the education system of Nova Scotia would have to be improved to bring about the development required in manufacturing industry cannot be estimated without relying on some dubious assumptions.[9] The Economic Council of Canada suggested that investment in education might well give a rate of return of 10 to 15 per cent. But even if those percentages are applicable to manufacturing in Nova Scotia (of which there is no assurance), it seems improbable that such a return would hold up at that rate as the flow of investment in education rose, or that wage-rates and wages would remain unaffected by increases in skill and productivity per worker; so the chances of achieving the required 5 per cent reduction in costs in this way would seem remote. And education and training cannot very easily be directed so that it is of benefit just in manufacturing industry. General education cannot be denied to a person just because he does

7 Derived from DBS, *Preliminary Statistics of Education, 1962-3*, 81–201, p. 41, and Table B/1. The Atlantic Development Board also gave a little help to Nova Scotian universities by making grants for post-graduate education and applied research. According to a press release from the Department of Forestry and Rural Development, reported in the Halifax *Chronicle-Herald* on Dec. 26, 1968, the ADB had by Oct. 31, 1968, committed itself to grants of $4.4 million for these purposes.

8 See Economic Council of Canada, *Second Annual Review* (Ottawa, 1965), pp. 133-4.

9 The oft-quoted statistics from the Canadian censuses of population showing that, generally speaking, the more highly educated a person is, the higher are his earnings, do not provide convincing evidence of the return to a society for investment in education. Apart from the fallacy of composition which is involved in concluding that a general raising of the level of education would result in a general increase in real earnings (which is the thesis of the Economic Council of Canada's *Second Annual Review*, pp. 90–1), there is no guarantee that the higher educational levels achieved and the higher earnings at present enjoyed by part of the population are not both results of unequal income distribution in the previous generation.

not intend to enter manufacturing. It is true that, by the careful selection of trades in which training is given, vocational training programmes may direct their efforts towards manufacturing industry; and
federal and provincial governments have, through their grants for
training within industry, encouraged training in techniques and practices which might have little application outside the firm in which the
trainees were then employed. But few trades are specific to manufacturing industry. As a consequence, using education and training to
reduce the cost of factor inputs would be a very expensive way of
trying to achieve the objective. However, there seems little doubt that
the side-benefits would be great. All productive activities would presumably gain benefit and the population would (or so it is generally
assumed) reap a rich reward in greater personal fulfilment. Education
and training also have the great advantage that they can scarcely cause
distortion in the pattern of industrial distribution. The economic forces
which are reputed to determine the optimum distribution are less effective the more imperfect knowledge is; so any measures which improve
knowledge must inevitably strengthen economic forces and minimize
any maldistribution of industry. Finally, the public's general acceptance of the virtue of education, and the educational administrative
machinery already established within the province, ensure that en-
largement of the present programme would not encounter undue
political or administrative barriers.

There is little doubt that improvement in education and training in
Nova Scotia, though not a remedy for the retardation of industry,
should be an adjunct of any other measures taken. The Economic
Council of Canada, relying on studies in both Canada and the United
States, concluded that education was one of the most important factors
required for long-term growth.[10] It follows, therefore, that any region
which lags educationally will *ceteris paribus* lag economically. We
noted previously that one of the greatest deficiencies in Nova Scotia
was in the field of managerial skills. The growing size of enterprises
and the increasing sophistication of management tools demand more
and more highly educated persons. Nova Scotia is in a dilemma. Already the province does not derive full benefit from the people it does
educate because lack of suitable local opportunities forces them to go
elsewhere. In turn, this reflects the low quality of existing managers
who do not recognize the potentialities of modern management techniques and the benefit that fresh, trained minds can bring to any
business. Time will obviously be needed to allow the trained persons

10 *Ibid.*, pp. 91–2.

leaving the educational system gradually to infiltrate the business community and to start a cumulative improvement.

3 *An improved infrastructure*

An indirect way of lowering labour costs in Nova Scotia would be by creating circumstances in which persons would be more anxious to live in the province. While people are often blind to the shortcomings of their home towns, outsiders are seldom so. Improvement of the living amenities is therefore one way to ensure that more labour is available at any given level of wage-rates.

Some efforts have been made, of course, to improve the infrastructure in Nova Scotia. Some of the worst slums have been cleared, the network of roads has been greatly upgraded in recent years, and some of the facilities which are a commonplace in large centres have been developed. But much more might be done. One still hears the motto, "flowers make poor soup," repeated in government circles (particularly on municipal councils) and few ratepayers give much heed to town planners' pleas for investment for the future when another line of action promises to bring some extra dollars in rates in the short term; so small industrial communities remain neglected, larger centres miss their chances of becoming attractive places, and the very great potential provided by the province's really beautiful countryside goes largely undeveloped.

Also relevant under the heading of infrastructure improvements which might help to lower the cost of labour is the expansion of facilities for air travel within Nova Scotia and between that province and the main Canadian industrial centres. The stress laid by multiplant firms in the Site-Choice Study upon being able to manage two or more geographically separated establishments was significant. The maintenance of frequent and convenient air line services are of great importance, and the suggestion by the Nova Scotia Voluntary Planning Board that small airstrips be developed for private aircraft[11] seems to be worth following up, now that it has become a commonplace for firms to maintain or hire private planes.

Improvement of infrastructure is a politically acceptable activity; it presents no very great administrative problems, and it also benefits other sectors of the economy. But it could not be much more than a supplement to other programmes. It is a general approach which would bring most benefits outside manufacturing and would therefore be very expensive; and it could scarcely be carried on a scale large enough to

11 *Plan for the Transportation and Communication Sector* (Halifax, 1966), pp. 67–8.

bring the desired effect.[12] However, like education and training, it is probably an essential addition to other measures.

MATERIALS AND FUEL

Materials comprise by far the largest single element of cost, being about 57 per cent of the selling value of factory shipments in Nova Scotia (see Table 4/1). Even a small change in their relative prices from one province to another would have an appreciable effect on relative overall costs. It was not surprising, therefore, to find the cost of obtaining materials was the fourth most frequently mentioned reason influencing the location of the firms included in the Site-Choice Study. A mere 9 per cent reduction in the delivered price at Nova Scotian plants would produce the 5 per cent cost reduction which we are seeking. Fuel costs, on the other hand, are unimportant in firms' cost structures (see Table 4/2), and the Site-Choice Study provided no evidence that they influenced plant location. So there is no prospect of affecting Nova Scotia's position significantly by the subsidization of fuel inputs.

There are two main ways of reducing the cost of materials and fuel to manufacturing industry. One may subsidize the transportation costs of bringing them to the Nova Scotian plant, or one may make a direct subsidy upon the cost of materials used. We shall look at each of these in turn.

1 Subsidy on transportation

Since the relatively high cost of materials and fuel to Nova Scotian manufacturers was apparently attributable to transportation costs (see p. 60), it is perhaps natural to think first of a transportation subsidy. This has been the federal government's approach under the Maritime Freight Rates Act, though the act has only been of benefit where the materials and fuel originated within the Atlantic provinces or eastern Quebec and were carried by rail. Its effect was discussed at some length in chapter 7 and we shall have more to say on this matter later in this chapter when we consider subsidies on product transportation. It will suffice here merely to recall that there is considerable doubt whether the payments under the act really went towards rate reduction or merely constituted a hidden subsidy to railways.

12 T. E. Brewis, *Regional Economic Policies in Canada* (Toronto, 1969), pp. 63–4, puts the points very clearly when he said: "... the pay-off period in the case of many social capital investments is often very long-term and any quantification of the benefits is apt to be highly conjectural. What can be said with certainty is that while expenditures on infra-structure may be a precondition of growth, they are rarely a sufficient condition, and at times are undertaken with more concern for political than economic expediency."

Freight subsidization has become such a part of Canadian life that there would be no great political obstacle to using it further. And while paid directly to the two railway companies, it is a very simple form of subsidy to administer. However, there seem to be signs of a disposition to reduce rather than to extend it. In 1962 the MacPherson Royal Commission recommended the abolition of the 20 per cent MFRA subsidy on goods moving within, but not destined outside, select territory (except Newfoundland); in 1969 the joint report of the Atlantic provinces premiers visualized this subsidy would be continued only in selected cases;[13] and, also in 1969, the federal government, partially following a recommendation of the House of Commons Committee on Transport and Communications, made provision so that it could be withdrawn merely by order-in-council. If this subsidy is withdrawn, there seems little doubt that Nova Scotian manufacturers' materials and fuel costs will rise relative to the corresponding costs of manufacturers in Quebec-Ontario. It is true that materials brought into the province from elsewhere (and these make up the bulk of materials used because of the large imports of oil and metal products) would not be directly affected (though there might be an indirect effect if the Nova Scotian trucking industry developed as a result of its becoming eligible from July 1969 for the 30 per cent MFRA subsidy on traffic leaving the select territory); but the delivered cost of materials originating in the province would probably rise somewhat if all or some of the traffic which both originated and terminated in the Maritime Zone should no longer receive the MFRA subsidy. The commission seemed to accept that this would be the initial effect since it said that the proposed change would "... bring rail rates to a level which is favourable to the encouragement of road traffic." But it apparently expected the effect to be temporary because "... the stimulus given to competition will, over time, confer the same or greater benefits than those now given under the Act to shipments within select territory."[14] However, this seems improbable if the benefits envisaged are measured in terms of the level of charges for transportion, since only if trucking were to be highly competitive and subject to unusually great economies of scale would a subsequent fall in rates to their original level be possible. It is unlikely that both conditions would be satisfied; indeed they are probably mutually incompatible.[15] And, the lack of any sign that the extension

13 *The Basic Elements of an Atlantic Provinces Transportation Policy* (Moncton, 1969).
14 *Report of the Royal Commission on Transportation* (Ottawa, 1961), II, pp. 212–13.
15 There are the customary signs that in one way or another the Nova Scotian trucking industry will become less, rather than more, competitive as time

to truckers of the 30 per cent MFRA subsidy in July 1969 had been passed on to shippers reinforces this point.

However, even if there was an official disposition to use further transportation subsidies to bring down the cost of materials and fuel to Nova Scotian manufacturers by, for instance, making certain materials entering the select territory eligible for subsidy (as the joint report of the Atlantic provinces premiers to the federal Minister of Transport suggested), such subsidies could not be big enough to achieve the effect desired. We found earlier (p. 89) that transportation charges on finished products being sent from Nova Scotian factories to customers made up only 3 per cent of the factories' total costs. If freight costs of materials and fuel used by those factories were about the same percentage, then, even if transportation was supplied free, the overall cost saving would be less than the 5 per cent which we are seeking. In any event, free transportation would be politically impossible. Even going part of the way would be expensive since it would be politically difficult to limit the enlarged subsidy to manufacturing firms. And while other sectors of the Nova Scotian economy would benefit from any general increase in subsidy, some firms would be badly hit if manufactures from central Canada were carried into the province at lower cost and broke into local markets at present protected by high transport costs.

Transportation subsidies on materials and fuel would also seem to have the disadvantage that they would create the greatest distortion of the "natural" pattern of industrial distribution in the country. They would bring greatest benefit to firms using heavy materials and fuel not available in Nova Scotia and therefore would attract to the province those firms which were least suited to be there.

2 Direct subsidy

One way of meeting some of these problems would be by paying subsidies directly to firms upon the cost of the materials and fuel they use. Admittedly, having to deal directly with many small firms and checking

passes. For instance, the Nova Scotia Voluntary Planning Board, in *Plan for the Transportation and Communication Sector*, endorsed recommendations to put obstacles in the way of small truckers who were sometimes apparently guilty of rate-cutting (pp. 35–6), of out-of-province truckers (p. 38), and of private fleet operators (pp. 43–4). According to The Economist Intelligence Unit, *Atlantic Provinces Transportation Study* (Ottawa, 1967), v, pp. 148–9, it is apparently already difficult to obtain licences to enter the trucking business in Nova Scotia. But while warning against the dangers of restriction of competition, The Economist Intelligence Unit surprisingly gave support, be it only lukewarm, to a policy of control of entry into the industry in the interests of stability (v, p. 161). Surely every restrictive practice ever devised can be justified on the same ground.

their claims would be much more administratively laborious; but since the subsidy need not be tied in any way to transportation costs, it could be pitched at a level high enough to achieve the objective. One amounting to 9 per cent of the cost of materials and fuel would bring down the overall costs of the average firm by the required 5 per cent. It might also be possible, at least for several years, to limit it to new manufacturing firms, and so the cost would be low. And, finally, there would be no danger of the subsidy helping competitive manufactures to enter the province from central Canada.

This method therefore seems to have its attractions. Only two objections seem to arise: the administrative difficulties would be relatively great, and there would remain the danger of distorting the country's pattern of production by attracting plants which were least suitable to the province.

ELECTRICITY

Electric power produced in Nova Scotia has in the past attracted generous financial support, as coal used in generating stations has been heavily subsidized by the federal government. However, as the subsidies were designed to encourage the use of coal where it would otherwise be displaced by oil, their incidence was probably mainly upon coal-mining rather on the generation or use of electricity. But government moneys are being applied in other ways to try to reduce the cost of electricity to Nova Scotian manufacturers (as well as to other users). Large projects financed by the federal government are being planned for the Bay of Fundy; and the federal government is also contributing towards the construction of thermal electricity generating stations.[16] These projects could turn out to be sound commercial ventures and not merely subsidization measures, but, as electricity concerns show no eagerness to commit their own funds to such projects, their commercial soundness is rather suspect.

Further subsidization of electricity does not promise to go very far in achieving the required 5 per cent reduction in manufacturers' costs. While it might well be politically possible to limit the subsidy to new manufacturing activity and thereby keep the cost of the subsidy low, and there seems no great administrative difficulties in such an arrangement, yet even if electricity were supplied free of charge to manufacturers (which is unthinkable) their costs would on average diminish by

16 A Department of Forestry and Rural Development press release stated that the ADB had committed $12.1 million to electric power projects to Oct. 31, 1968.

a mere three-quarters of one per cent (the proportion that outlay on electricity by Nova Scotian manufacturing firms constituted of their total costs in 1962).

Electricity is therefore one area which may be ignored in the search for an appropriate method of reducing the cost of Nova Scotia manufacturers' factor inputs. Not once was it mentioned in the Site-Choice Study as an important factor influencing plant location.

PRODUCT TRANSPORTATION

We have now come to the item which, while relatively unimportant in Nova Scotia firms' outlays (product transportation costs constitute only about 3 per cent of firms' total costs, a percentage which would still rise only to about 5.3 per cent even if all output was shipped to central Canada), nevertheless exercises an important influence on plants' location. It was mentioned most often in the Site-Choice Study as a determinant of location and was the factor input in respect of which Nova Scotian firms were at the greatest disadvantage vis-à-vis their Quebec-Ontario opposite numbers.

There are plenty of possible ways of approaching the problem of eliminating or reducing this disadvantage. The principal ones seem to be the following:

1 Subsidize carriers

This has been the favourite way, probably because it was administratively easy (so long, anyway, as only the two railway companies were involved – as was the case until 1969), and it was something that the federal government could do without being accused of encroaching on the jurisdiction of the provincial governments. Since 1927 the federal government has paid the CNR and CPR subsidies under the Maritime Freight Rates Act of up to 30 per cent of the freight charges for most traffic originating in the "Select Territory" (see p. 78, note 10); and since 1969 the subsidies have been paid on goods carried by truckers. There seems great doubt whether all this subsidy accrued to the shipper in lower charges; rather, it probably served merely to increase the railways' profits or reduce their deficits. (This matter was discussed in chapter 7.) However, in 1969 the premiers of the Atlantic provinces seemed ready to accept a discriminatory system.[17] They advocated that a federal-provincial committee should be set up to administer transportation subsidies, and that this committee should have the power to grant or withhold subsidies for traffic confined to the Atlantic provinces,

17 The Elements of an Atlantic Provinces Transportation Policy.

according to its judgment of the importance of the industry concerned to the region and of the importance of transportation costs to that industry. Later the same year the federal government made certain provisions so that the beginnings of such a scheme might be brought about.

Even if freight subsidies succeeded in lowering the transportation costs of Nova Scotian manufacturers, they would still have the undesirable features that would tend to distort the national pattern of production by attracting firms producing goods with low value to weight or bulk ratios – firms which are usually least suited to Nova Scotia.

An important question still remains. Even if subsidies to carriers could be devised which had no distorting effects and which were all passed on as reduced charges to shippers, could such subsidies be big enough to achieve the 5 per cent overall cost reduction for which we are looking? The answer seems almost certain to be in the negative, since it would be necessary to carry products virtually free of charge. This would be unthinkable.

Also, such a subsidy could not very well be confined to products shipped by new manufacturing firms or even simply to manufactured products in general. The sense of grievance about transportation costs is so general in Nova Scotia that giving concessions just to new comers would be politically most difficult; and the problem of setting up and policing a generally acceptable scheme applicable only to the transportation of manufactured goods would cause great difficulty. So the cost of such a scheme would be high relative to the benefits it brought to Nova Scotian manufacturers. Of course, this high cost would be partly offset by the benefits which would accrue to non-manufacturing concerns which were covered.

Another form of government assistance which would seem logically to call for inclusion under the heading of subsidies to carriers is the improvement of roads. Improvement of Nova Scotian roads would reduce the costs of truckers by cutting down their costs of labour, fuel, tires, and vehicle maintenance. Indeed, a lot has already been done towards this end, as we saw in chapter 7, some of it due to the federal government's input of financial resources through the Trans-Canada Highway and Roads to Resources schemes, and by way of the Atlantic Development Board.[18] But the Nova Scotian highway system is still

18 According to the Department of Forestry and Rural Development press release the ADB had committed itself up to Oct. 31, 1968 to grants of $19.5 million to trunk highway development. If the Atlantic provinces premiers have their way as submitted in their joint report, the federal government will continue to provide financial aid for highway development on a long-term basis. In this, they were supported by the House of Commons Standing Committee on Transport and Communications which also recommended that the federal government provide short-term help while policies for the long term are being worked out.

much less conducive to truck operation than is the one found in the industrial part of Quebec-Ontario. In particular, the loss incurred by truckers each year on account of spring load restrictions due to inadequate highways is apparently serious for them.[19] While large-scale road-building in Nova Scotia would undoubtedly benefit the local road transport business and might indirectly reduce the freight charges on manufactured goods, it would be a very expensive way of trying to achieve the objective we set for ourselves. Roads, when built, could not for political reasons be confined to trucks carrying just manufactured goods, or even to the trucking business as a whole. The cost would therefore be high, though other sectors of the community would benefit from the better roads. But the effects upon manufacturing industry in the province would be so indirect that it obviously could not achieve the desired object. The best roads in the world would not lead to the setting up of a trucking industry which would be prepared to carry manufactured goods free of charge. In addition, improved roads might produce a backlash which would be harmful to some manufacturers and other sectors of the Nova Scotian economy, for they would encourage the importation into the Nova Scotian market of goods produced in Quebec-Ontario. The local monopolies enjoyed because of transportation costs would be threatened.[20] But road-building has been a politically easy activity,[21] and it produces relatively few administrative headaches; so it might be used as a supplement to other forms of subsidy, though it would be expensive relative to the slight impact it would have upon the costs of manufacturing concerns.

Still another line of action which would be equivalent in nature to a subsidy payable to a carrier (or rather the reduction of a negative subsidy) would be the removal of certain special financial penalties at present levied upon trucking in Nova Scotia. Fuel taxes in Nova Scotia are unusually high, licence fees for truckers tend to be somewhat above those existing elsewhere, and the obligation upon a trucker carrying

19 The Economist Intelligence Unit, *Atlantic Provinces Transportation Study*, II, p. 77, found a trucker who operated at a loss of 6.5 per cent during this period each year compared with a profit of about 15 per cent the remainder of the time.

20 An obvious example of this would be the construction of a road from New Brunswick by direct route to Montreal via Maine, a project often advocated by Nova Scotians. However, a feasibility study carried out by The Economist Intelligence Unit found that its cost could not be justified by the likely benefits. See *Atlantic Provinces Transportation Study*, X.

21 Nevertheless the "shared-cost" nature of the programmes under which the federal government's participation was engineered may be less acceptable in the future because of the new temper of provincial governments and because the federal government has become alarmed by the unlimited liability it assumes under such programmes.

interprovincial traffic to take out licences in provinces outside the Atlantic region because of the absence of reciprocal agreements, all send up road transport costs. These are very marginal matters, however, and complete elimination of all such taxes and impediments would have little effect upon the transportation costs of Nova Scotian manufacturers.

2 Subsidize shippers

In principle, there is no reason why any subsidy which is intended to reduce manufacturers' product transportation costs should not be given directly to the manufacturers who ship the goods.[22] In this way, at least, one may be sure that the subsidy rests where it is directed rather than being diverted, as some of the MFRA subsidies almost certainly are, into the pockets of the carriers.

However, the administrative difficulties of dealing with large numbers of small firms would be formidable. And policing the scheme so that firms eligible for subsidies did not set themselves up as transshipment agents for firms that were not, would be difficult, and the administrative cost would likely be high. Also, like subsidies payable to carriers, subsidies to shippers could not be large enough to achieve the results required, and they would probably give rise to the same political problems and distorting effects.

3 Improve the quality of transportation

An improvement in the quality of transportation is the equivalent of lowering its price. While there seems little evidence that adequacy of service is of primary concern to Nova Scotian manufacturers,[23] it is clear that more frequent and speedy transportation services would improve their relative position. We have already mentioned the improvement of roads in Nova Scotia as a means of subsidizing the trucker. It would also presumably improve the transportation services available to manufacturers in the province. Trucks would complete their journeys more quickly and road transport services which are not available in the Annapolis Valley, Cape Breton, and other parts of the province might develop.

22 This method was favoured by The Economist Intelligence Unit, *Atlantic Provinces Transportation Study*, v, p. 88 ff., and recommended in 1969 by the Atlantic provinces premiers in their joint report, *The Elements of an Atlantic Provinces Transportation Policy* – a recommendation supported by the House of Commons Standing Committee on Transport and Communications. Even the Canadian National Railways supported the idea in its submission to that committee.

23 *Ibid.*, II, p. 60.

Similarly, both rail and water facilities might be improved; and developments in the two media of transportation might go hand in hand. Halifax, the main port of the province, has been consistently declining in importance and needs rebuilding if it is to attract back the traffic it has lost; and the long haul by conventional rail services has caused importers and exporters of goods into and out of central Canada to risk the St Lawrence ice during the winter or to use American ports. Halifax harbour, however, apparently does possess the depth of water which makes it one of the two suitable east coast ports in North America for handling the 400,000-ton ships now being planned. The traffic could be containerized and carried to and from Halifax in fast "integral trains."[24] While this scheme is primarily designed to revive the port of Halifax, it nevertheless would incidentally provide a uniquely fast and efficient type of transportation to central Canada and beyond for the products of Nova Scotian manufacturers.

And again, air services could be improved. While air freight is at present of interest only to a few firms, its importance is growing rapidly.

Improving transportation services is therefore one avenue by which costs of inputs for Nova Scotian manufacturers might be reduced. However, clearly it is no more than a make-weight – something which would have to be justified primarily on grounds other than as a subsidy to manufacturers. The benefits they would feel would be tiny relative to the cost of such projects.

CAPITAL

We found previously that capital costs represented about 8 per cent of total costs in 1962. The location of the factory did not appear to affect the price of a unit of capital input significantly, and capital costs were scarcely mentioned in the Site-Choice Study as one of the factors influencing location. Of all the 149 reasons given for choosing a particular site after considering alternatives in other provinces, the cost of suitable sites and premises was listed only three times, while no mention whatsoever was made of the cost of obtaining machinery and other equipment, of the supply of investment funds, or of the rate of interest at which investment funds were available. However, because of the

24 This is the sort of scheme recommended by Theodore J. Kaufeld, a New York consultant retained by the government of Nova Scotia, the city of Halifax, and the Port of Halifax Authority in 1966. The matter has since been studied by other consultants and the parties are planning a start on the project in a small way. Already a regular container service between Halifax and Europe has been inaugurated.

importance of capital in firms' cost structures, it provides plenty of scope as an avenue for subsidization. There are several forms it might take:

1 *Grants*

The obvious and most direct way is to make outright grants towards the investment necessary to set up a new manufacturing plant in Nova Scotia. This is exactly what the federal government has been doing since 1965 under the Area Development Incentives Act. Up to 1969 grants were automatically given to any firm setting up new manufacturing activity in any part of Nova Scotia other than the Halifax-Dartmouth area. They were for amounts up to 33⅓ per cent of capital costs for new factories for which total investment did not exceed $250,000. Lesser proportions were granted for larger investments, but the proportion could not fall below 20 per cent unless the investment exceeded $25 million. For expansions of existing plants a slightly lower rate applied. In 1969 the Regional Development Incentives Act raised the limits for both new manufacturing activity and expansion of existing activity to provide, at the discretion of the Minister of Regional Economic Expansion (no firm will have the right to aid), for 25 per cent of capital costs plus $5,000 for each job created, subject to three maxima: $12 million, $30,000 per job created, and 50 per cent of capital costs. From that date, grants could also be made for modernization of existing plant up to 20 per cent of capital costs or $6 million, whichever was less.[25]

These grants appear to be very attractive.[26] They are quite large and, coming in the form of lump sums near the beginning of a new plant's life, they are made when most needed. In addition, small or rapidly growing firms seem to find the availability of capital funds their biggest problem and it must be very nice to have government departments assume responsibility for 20 to 30 per cent of the amounts required. However, the scheme does not appear to have achieved the results its sponsors hoped for. While the Area Development Agency claimed that about eight thousand jobs were created by the plants set up with the

25 The federal government has also made provision for grants to assist the setting up of warehousing facilities and the purchase of specialized transportation equipment. These grants would be made through a federal-provincial government agency and would not be confined to manufacturing industry or to firms setting up new plants or expanding or modernizing existing processes.
26 The attractiveness of the grants is enhanced by the provision that depreciation is still claimable for tax purposes based upon the total investment – not just upon the proportion borne by the firm. Before 1965 there was no such provision and grants offered then were therefore worth much less.

aid of ADIA grants by about the end of 1968, there are two reasons to doubt if they really steered industry to the poorer regions. First, some of the grants must have gone to firms which would have set up their new plants or extensions in the development areas anyway.[27] And, second, most of the new plants were built in the poorer parts of prosperous provinces rather than in the depressed regions of the country. About 60 per cent of these new jobs were in Quebec and Ontario – which corresponds closely with the proportion of new firms which went to those provinces even before the ADIA grants. The grants have obviously not been powerful enough to induce firms to go far from the main centres of industry and population.[28]

The lack of success of the ADIA grants in steering industry to Nova Scotia (as to the other Atlantic provinces) may be attributed to several reasons. They were once-for-all grants; but if a firm was really convinced that any plant built in Nova Scotia would be at a permanent cost disadvantage, it was bound to be concerned about its future position. The effect of the grants would be felt to a maximum extent during the life of the original assets, and after about ten years when they would have to be replaced, the firm would have to stand entirely on its own feet.

Firms also seem to have been deterred by the delays and administrative tedium with which they allegedly had to contend when they applied for grants. And even when everything was cleared, the grants did not become available at once but were payable over a period which could be as much as two and a half years after commercial production had actually commenced.[29] Care in the use of public moneys was obviously essential, but the delays entailed decreased the attractiveness of the grants.

Then, the part of Nova Scotia which has proved to be the most attractive to new industry, the Halifax-Dartmouth area, was not until 1969 made into a designated area. Its exclusion almost certainly reduced the effectiveness of the ADIA grants in attracting manufacturing

27 In its *Fifth Annual Review* (Ottawa, 1968), p. 169, the Economic Council of Canada declared that "... there is good reason to believe that the decision to invest would have been taken (perhaps at a date further in the future) and the particular location chosen, even in the absence of the subsidy."

28 The tendency of firms receiving development grants to move the minimum distance from the places where they would normally have established new plants was also observed in Britain by B. J. Loasby, "Making Location Policy Work," *Lloyds Bank Review*, no. 83 (Jan. 1967), pp. 34–7.

29 In Nova Scotia, Industrial Estates Limited made loans to bridge part of the gap between the time the ADIA grants were approved and the time they became payable.

plants to Nova Scotia. And it broke one of the rules for any incentive scheme: that industry should be encouraged to cluster so as to build up external economies.

A last reason for failure of the ADIA grants in respect of Nova Scotia was simply that industrialists were often scarcely aware that they existed. This was one manifestation of the ignorance which is another barrier to regional development – a matter we shall be taking up shortly.

In addition to the grants provided under the Area Development Incentives Act, grants have also been made available by the Atlantic Development Board and Industrial Estates Limited. The best known example was the case of the Clairtone Corporation which received substantial grants and other assistance from both those bodies, in addition to the usual ADIA assistance.

Notwithstanding the somewhat disappointing results achieved by schemes which offer grants on a scale which must be considered as generous relative to anything previously available in Canada and even to those offered in other countries with long-established policies for regional development, this method of steering industry to relatively poor areas has much to recommend it. It is politically acceptable and administratively simple. There seems no reason why it could not be made large enough to have the effect of reducing costs by 5 per cent, though it would have to be prepared to shoulder rather more than half the cost of the capital investment of the new activity and perhaps find some way to extend its effect past the lives of the original assets. Its cost is low since it is very easy to direct the grants precisely where they are wanted. To satisfy our particular aim, they could be given only for new manufacturing activity which would not otherwise locate in Nova Scotia – as is the declared aim of the present Minister of Regional Economic Expansion, using discretion given him under the Regional Development Incentives Act 1969, though he is likely to find difficulty in deciding which activity falls in this category. And the value of a grant to a small growing firm with difficulty in raising funds is often much greater than the cost to the government, which can borrow at the lowest rates in operation. Indeed, for this reason, a capital grants scheme, instead of tending to distort the distribution of industry as do some other methods, may actually improve distribution by compensating for the imperfections of the capital market which tends to channel money readily into clumsy industrial giants while refusing finance to growing and efficient firms.

Though the Minister of Regional Economic Expansion has stated that, in exercising his discretion under the Regional Development Incentives Act (he may make or withhold grants to firms locating in development areas as he sees fit), he will consider multiplier effects, nevertheless such grants are, like other subsidies on capital inputs, most attractive to capital-intensive firms which often bring little in the way of indirect benefits to the areas in which they locate. The multiplier effect is less than that produced by labour-intensive firms, and it often seems to follow in practice that the most capital-intensive firms rely mainly upon imported materials, again limiting the effect upon the local community.

2 *Loans*

The classification of loan-granting as a method of subsidizing capital inputs would not be appropriate if the granting body charged the market rate for such loans. But official agencies seldom do charge the market rate. Indeed, they only exist because money is not available at the usual interest rates from private sources to the firms requiring the assistance. It is true that in good times official lenders may with luck break even; but in a business turn-down they stand to lose more than would private lenders because of the kind of risks they have assumed.

Governments and their agencies have been in the money-lending business for some years. Manufacturing firms in Nova Scotia requiring capital funds have, like firms elsewhere and in other industries, been able to turn to government agencies if capital funds were not available to them at normal rates. The Industrial Development Bank, Industrial Estates Limited (which is the main channel through which the government of Nova Scotia supplies loans for new industry), and the Nova Scotia Department of Trade and Industry (which administers the Industrial Expansion Act and the Industrial Loan Act) are the main examples. They have all, no doubt, had some success in encouraging the development of manufacturing industry in Nova Scotia over the years. But they have their limitations. The Industrial Development Bank is limited in the size of loan it can make and, anyway, does not bestow benefits on firms coming to Nova Scotia any greater than on those going anywhere; Industrial Estates Limited at present relies on funds from the provincial government and probably could not continue to provide loans so freely if firms did start flowing into the province in larger numbers; and the Industrial Loan and Industrial Expansion acts are very small fry. Most important, the provision of loans cannot very well have sufficient impact to achieve the 5 per cent decrease in costs for which we are looking. The Economic Council of Canada estimated that interest actually paid by Canadian manufacturing firms was only a fraction of one per cent of total costs.[30] Provision of interest-free loans,

30 *Fourth Annual Review* (Ottawa, 1967), p. 160.

even if they were politically possible, would not therefore affect the situation greatly. Even if interest imputed to proprietors' own investment were taken into account (perhaps the smaller or growing firm cannot rely for its funds on undistributed profits to the extent that firms generally can), interest-free loans would still only reduce overall costs by about 3 per cent.

It is nevertheless an attractive method of subsidization even if it can do no more than contribute toward the required result. Though it may be somewhat costly to administer because of the work required in processing applications and collecting repayments and interest, it is a low-cost method of subsidization because it may be directed accurately at new manufacturing industry. There also seem to be no great political difficulties raised by operating these money-lending schemes and there are no indirect ill-effects. Like capital grants, they are of most interest to capital-intensive firms which tend to bring less benefits via the multiplier to the districts in which they operate; but, again like capital grants, they may well improve the distribution of industry rather than distorting it.

In the category of loans, one should include special provisions for accelerated depreciation such as were available between 1961 and 1967. These had much the same advantages and disadvantages of straightforward loans but they were easier to administer because they were applied through the income tax system. However, they were really not loans at all to firms whose Nova Scotian plants did not make profits during the first few years' operation – which is what usually seems to happen.[31]

3 *Industrial estates*

This method is an old one, popular with governments and certain private concerns like railway companies as a means of enticing industry to the places where it is wanted. In Nova Scotia, Industrial Estates Limited, the Atlantic Development Board, and municipal governments have all done work in this field, though it cannot be described yet as being widespread.[32] It is therefore obviously politically possible, and,

31 The study of certain British branch factories reported by W. F. Luttrell in *Factory Location and Industrial Movement* (London, 1962), appeared to confirm that plants have high costs during the first years and yield no profit until they have been established some considerable period. This point was given explicit recognition in the RDIA 1969 which authorized the Minister of Regional Economic Expansion to make grants to firms to assist them in their settling-in period.

32 Up to Oct. 31, 1968, the ADB had committed itself to grants for industrial parks amounting to $10.2 million. Department of Forestry and Rural Development press release.

apart from processing applications and collecting interest and repayments, the administration would not seem particularly difficult.

It might again be objected that it is inappropriate to classify industrial estates as a form of subsidization; but the answer must be much the same as that given above when loans were discussed. If industrial estates were conducted purely on a commercial basis (as they are when private developers are responsible for them), the objection would be justified; but governments tend to provide land and premises on terms that private firms would consider unattractive, and it appears unlikely that costs are all recoverable.[33]

There are indications that industrial estates are sometimes a very effective and inexpensive way of attracting industry to particular areas. They remove much of the risk from the firm, they reduce the firm's requirements for capital funds, and, if they are built on a speculative basis, they cut down the time a firm has to wait and the worry it has to suffer in obtaining land and building its own factory. In the Site-Choice Study, the availability of suitable sites or premises exactly when needed was described as a strong determinant of location, being the sixth most frequently mentioned reason for firms choosing particular locations. And in other countries the same situation has been observed.[34]

Since capital costs seem to be only about 8 per cent of total costs of the typical firm (see p. 66), and buildings account for perhaps half of this (Multiplant Firm Study), industrial estates would have to be let rent free if the object of reducing firms' costs by 5 per cent were to be approached. This might not be too easy politically, but it might not be impossible.[35]

In other respects, industrial estates programmes have the same ad-

---

33 Though the detailed workings of Industrial Estates Limited are not made public, it is known that 10 per cent of its clients have failed and some persons close to the scene suspect that several others are not meeting their interest and repayment commitments.

34 See, for instance, Arthur D. Little Inc., *Report on Ten-Year Industrial Plan for Puerto Rico* (Washington, 1951), in which it is observed that "The lack of good factory space on an immediately available basis is frequently a major reason for prospective manufacturers to decide against locating in a particular community. Many of Puerto Rico's own prospects have lost enthusiasm on learning of the present shortage of first-class buildings" (p. 29).

35 J. E. Moes, "The Subsidization of Industry by Local Communities in the South," *Southern Economic Journal*, 28 (1961–2), pp. 187–93, is enthusiastic about the example of the town of Natchez, Miss., which rented a factory to Armstrong Tire and Rubber Company for almost nothing, yet apparently gained a return of 100 per cent per year on its investment. He quotes other US examples to support his view that the subsidization of industry by municipalities, including the industrial estates type of subsidy, bears enormous dividends.

vantages and disadvantages as capital grants. They are not especially good when it comes to creating indirect advantages, but neither do they tend to distort the pattern of industry to any great extent or produce any other ill-effects. Perhaps most important, since land, premises, and plant need only be granted to selected firms, the programme may be directed at new manufacturing industry and could therefore be low-cost.

4 *Other methods*

It might be possible to introduce monetary and fiscal measures which are discriminatory in favour of Nova Scotian manufacturing industry. The Economic Council of Canada gave tentative support to the idea, saying that "... the possibility of obtaining some gains from pursuing regionally discriminating policies which would be consistent with the Council's proposed strategies for stabilization deserves further examination."[36] But it has not hitherto been favoured except when the right of firms in certain centres in central and western Canada to claim capital consumption allowances was reduced by the 1969 federal budget below the level permitted elsewhere in Canada.

Opportunities for subsidizing capital investment in more indirect ways also exist. Some, like the federal tax laws which provide subsidies for scientific research, are payable wherever the firm operates and therefore do not influence location. But some organizations, largely government-supported, give assistance in research in Nova Scotia but not in Quebec-Ontario. The Maritimes Transportation Commission will do research into transportation problems without charge for firms in the Atlantic provinces; and research upon general economic matters, which presumably indirectly aids Atlantic provinces firms, has been undertaken by the Atlantic Provinces Research Board and the Atlantic Development Board. However, while they may well achieve useful results, as means of attracting new manufacturing plants to Nova Scotia they are indirect and expensive.

Again, building up the infrastructure is sometimes directly aimed at paying part of the capital outlays which industrial firms would otherwise have to meet themselves.[37] Sometimes, even, it is intended solely to assist one particular firm. Prominent in this activity for several years was the Atlantic Development Board. It assisted financially in the provision of water supplies and other services. In general, this may be a

36 *Fifth Annual Review*, p. 14.
37 The ADB had committed itself to grants amounting in total to $10 million for sewers and water development for resource processing industries up to Oct. 31, 1968. Department of Forestry and Rural Development press release.

worthwhile activity, and where it can be directed specifically towards a firm which should be lured to the province or it saves a desirable firm in the province from extinction, it may achieve the desired result and perhaps some worthwhile side-effects at not too high a cost. But usually it is an exceedingly expensive way of attracting new manufacturing industry to the province, if that is its main objective. In some instances, considerable outlay on improvement of water supplies and other infrastructures have been made merely to bolster a very minor and shaky firm in an isolated community.

MUNICIPAL TAXES

Remission of all or part of municipal taxes is not in essence different from the methods of subsidization already discussed. If municipal taxes are thought of as payment for use of civic services such as protection of property, refuse collection, and maintenance of highways, then tax remission is simply the provision of these services (which become factor inputs to a firm) at reduced prices.

Municipal taxes do not seem to be an important force in determining the location of manufacturing plants. As we saw in chapter 8, they constitute only about 2 per cent of total costs and not one firm included in the Site-Choice Study indicated that it had been influenced by them. Nevertheless, the granting of partial or total exemption from local taxes has been a fairly common practice in certain parts of Canada, and in Nova Scotia it is often done for IEL clients under special enabling legislation of the province. It is relatively easy to arrange administratively, but since it tends to cause ill-will amongst other ratepayers who feel that they are having to pay higher taxes to compensate for concessions granted to newcomers to the area, the practice often has adverse political repercussions. For this reason, such concessions are usually granted for a limited period (ten years in the case of IEL clients).

Since tax concessions are usually decided on an individual basis, they could be confined to new manufacturing industry and therefore their cost would be low. And apart from the political considerations already mentioned, there seem to be no undesirable side-effects – though there would similarly be no notable good side-effects either.

There seems to be no firm evidence that this method of input subsidization has been effective. This is perhaps not surprising since, even if local tax concessions could be freely given for indefinite periods, they would not result in a very large reduction in firms' costs. Total remission of municipal taxes would only reduce the overall costs on an average by about 2 per cent – less than half the goal we set. Also, concessions by one municipality invites retaliation by others and the whole exercise degenerates into an unseemly Dutch auction in which the effect upon the ultimate pattern of industrial distribution is small. Though most firms will accept any concessions offered to them, some firms deliberately refuse them believing that to accept creates a bad public image for themselves and puts them under an obligation to the local council; they may even be frightened away by offers of concessions since these indicate a willingness on the part of municipal governments to abandon equitable policies for the sake of short-term expediency, and create the expectation that districts with such local governments are unlikely to be well governed in other ways.[38]

ENTREPRENEURSHIP

All subsidies on factor inputs are indirectly subsidies on entrepreneurship, since they tend to increase the profitability of the firm. But there are a few measures which are not linked to the input of any other factor and are therefore directly aimed at entrepreneurship:

1 *Subsidy on output or cost*
As the value of output is within a few percentage points of the total costs of a firm, there does not seem much difference between a subsidy based upon the one or the other. There are plenty of instances in the Canadian economy of such subsidies though they are generally found in sectors other than manufacturing – in shipbuilding, transportation, farming, fishing, and mining. So it is already an accepted form of subsidy. However, general application to certain manufacturing industry in certain regions might raise political difficulties. Administration of such a scheme might also be difficult because there would be plenty of scope for firms to manipulate or misrepresent their revenue or costs in order to inflate the subsidies they received. Perhaps the way which would be politically and administratively easiest would be by remission of part of the federal sales tax chargeable upon goods manufactured in Nova Scotia, which is a negative output subsidy.

Subsidies of this type, however, do seem to have a number of attractive features. They can be set at any level and there is therefore no longer any need to worry whether the effect would be big enough. If a 5 per cent subsidy on costs were required, then grants of 5 per cent upon the total costs a firm incurred in Nova Scotia would be precisely

38 A firm interviewed in the Multiplant Firm Study indicated that it always refused tax concessions for these reasons.

what was needed;[39] or a reduction of the federal sales tax levied on goods manufactured in Nova Scotia to approximately half its present level would have much the same effect. Also, since the subsidy could be limited to new manufacturing industry, its cost would be low. And there would be no adverse side-effects (though there would not be any side-benefits either); in particular, the subsidies would be neutral in effect and would not tend to distort the pattern of production.

2 Corporation tax remission or abatement

Corporation income tax holidays would not be new to Canada. The area development legislation provided that they be extended to all new manufacturing firms setting up in "designated areas" up to 1967. They are therefore presumably a politically feasible instrument of regional development policy; and because they operate through the existing tax system, they are simple to administer. Also, they can be low cost because they can be directed accurately at new manufacturing firms; they would produce no side-effects, good or bad; and they would do nothing to distort the pattern of industry.

There is no indication that they were successful. Indeed, the federal government was apparently sufficiently convinced that they were ineffective that it replaced them with capital grants. Perhaps the main reason was the same one mentioned in connection with accelerated depreciation (p. 152) – that new manufacturing plants seldom make any profits for some years. Even if a new plant was normally profitable from the word "go," it would not be possible to achieve the required 5 per cent subsidy by corporation tax holidays. Net taxable income is only about 6 per cent of the value of output (see Table 10/1), and the present corporation tax is only in the region of 50 per cent for a very large company (it varies slightly from one province to another); so total remission of all corporation income tax would be only the equivalent of reducing costs by about 3 per cent.

3 Risk reduction

As risk is considered a deterrent by most firms, any action which reduces risk has the same effect as a subsidy on entrepreneurship. Al-

39 A subsidy based upon the value-added by manufacture in Nova Scotian plants would probably be better than one geared to their total costs or the value of their output, since it would benefit only Nova Scotian manufacturing activity and discourage the routing of goods manufactured outside the province through Nova Scotian plans for resale after little or no reprocessing. A 12.5 per cent subsidy on value-added would be approximately equivalent to a 5 per cent subsidy on total costs or output.

most certainly the most effective and practical method of achieving this
is by means of industrial estates. Much of the risk of the enterprise is
then assumed by the owner of the industrial estates. If the new plant is
successful, the entrepreneur keeps the profit; if it fails, he just hands
the plant back.

We found previously that industrial estates were probably a very
effective, cheap, and practicable means of subsidizing the capital inputs
of firms. To this quality we must now add the advantage they can
bestow upon new plants by shouldering some of the entrepreneurial
risk. Since risk is a product of ignorance, another possible way of reducing risk would be by improving the supply of information available
to entrepreneurs. Expansion of the existing economic research facilities
maintained by governments and the systematic feeding of information
thrown up by them to the business community would almost certainly
help.

4 Psychic income
We have observed that entrepreneurs probably considered psychic income as well as monetary profit. An entrepreneur, like any other man,
does not live by bread alone. The living conditions in the district in
which his business demands that he and his family must live – the facilities for education and cultural and recreational activities – will be a
consideration of some importance to firms' policy-makers. To any
benefits we attributed to improvement of the infrastructure and general
facilities of Nova Scotia when we discussed this matter as a means of
reducing capital costs we should now add any psychic income which
these facilities would bring to entrepreneurs.

While we should take psychic income into account, since everything
that makes Nova Scotia more attractive to an entrepreneur will help
towards the desired result, it should not be overstressed. In the Site-
Choice Study it did not appear as an important location-determining
factor and to try to subsidize industry by improving the region's facilities would be an indirect and high-cost approach, though the benefits
would also be enjoyed by other parts of the economy. Such an approach certainly could not be carried out on a scale which would produce psychic income which the average entrepreneur would be prepared to substitute for a 5 per cent reduction in costs (which would be
roughly equivalent to a doubling of money profits).

5 Developing the supply of entrepreneurs
Our study of the relatively slow growth of Nova Scotia's manufacturing
industry concluded with the strong indication that an inadequate sup-

ply of entrepreneurs in Nova Scotia was one of the major causes. Given the immobility of entrepreneurs, the easiest way out of this difficulty is to improve the home-produced supply. This is perhaps the most effective method of subsidizing factor inputs to the firm.

The forces and conditions which turn a man into an entrepreneur or turn an existing entrepreneur into a better one are not clearly understood; but some things can be done which undoubtedly help. Bringing together people in circumstances where information about new developments can be given, where ideas may be discussed, and minds can be stimulated by other minds, almost certainly helps to create an atmosphere in which enterprise flourishes. Consequently, the various conferences organized from time to time by governments and their agencies, and the various forms of business education provided by universities and other bodies, seem to be on the right track. But they are on a desperately small scale and much more might profitably be done. There seems to be no administrative obstacle to expanding in this sphere and, since education of any sort is nowadays accepted as a desirable thing, there should be no political difficulties. Since it cannot be limited to manufacturing and it is, in any event, an indirect way of achieving the results for which we are looking, the cost would be high. However, since the underlying sociological and psychological structure of a society is so crucial to the long-term health of the community, it would appear that any other measure taken should be supplemented by measures to develop entrepreneurship. It is also one way of improving Nova Scotia's position which should cause no distortion of the pattern of manufacturing industry in Canada; on the contrary, by dispelling ignorance and improving the supply of a factor of production, it can do nothing but good.

We have been talking of the value of education and training in respect of the development of the local pool of entrepreneurship. Since in the smaller firm the entrepreneur often also exercises a senior management role, this approach can at the same time improve management in Nova Scotia – the other principal reason which emerged from our discussion in Part Two for Nova Scotia's lag in development in the manufacturing sector.

Another essential precondition of a stimulated supply of vigorous entrepreneurship is the sweeping away of the various restrictions against competition and ease of entry into manufacturing industry. But, under pressure from vested interests, the state power has been used to reduce competition in Nova Scotia. While the professions and public utilities are the usual fields for such restrictions, manufacturing has not been completely free from them. The protection of milk producers in their present antiquated system of retail distribution is one example.[40] And the government policy of forbidding Industrial Estates Limited to try to attract to the province any firm which might compete with an existing firm is another.[41] The general tone in every sector is inactivity as old family businesses, connected by intermarriage, live together quietly and take no action which might rock the boat. Featherbedding only perpetuates this situation. The purifying wind of competition, if allowed to blow through without restriction, would do much to stimulate the spirit of enterprise and create a business outlook conducive to development. Due to political pressures, the more intense because of the connections between the old business families and the political parties, it will need a strong and determined government to give the lead.

Improvement of the supply of entrepreneurship from outside the province is also of vital importance. The Site-Choice Study laid bare the very minor extent to which Nova Scotia was ever considered as a possible site for new industry by Quebec-Ontario enterpreneurs. Our analysis in Part Two suggested that, on the average, firms with good management would be as well off in Nova Scotia as in Quebec-Ontario, but that they went straight to Quebec or Ontario without even considering the opportunities elsewhere. Only occasionally, it seems, and in unusual circumstances, do outside entrepreneurs seriously look at Nova Scotia. The experience of two firms will serve as illustration. Both were large foreign firms which were planning to set up manufacturing facilities in Canada for the first time. Each firm drew up a list of locations to be considered. Nova Scotia was included on these lists due to quite fortuitous circumstances. In one case, an executive of the company who was in a position to influence the choice of sites had been brought up in the Maritimes; in the other, the company president had the previous summer spent a very enjoyable vacation in Nova Scotia and had become aware of the advantages it offered to his corporation's particular type of operation. Had the person concerned in the first case been born in Ontario or the president in the second case gone to Florida for his vacation, Nova Scotia almost certainly would not have been considered by either firm. As it was, both examined the potentialities of Ontario, Quebec, and other provinces, Nova Scotia along with them. Nova Scotia won in both cases.

40 For some time, the Public Utilities Board refused permission for a dairy to sell milk in two-quart bottles – a common practice elsewhere – on the grounds that it might hurt the profits of the other companies.

41 Since IEL is prepared to help existing firms wishing to expand their output in their particular line of business, there seems no reason to deny help to a prospective newcomer which is prepared to do what existing firms refuse to do.

Nova Scotia is evidently not unique in this situation. Murray D. Bryce observed that "A final reason why the transfer process [the shift of activity from the industrialized country to the undeveloped ones] often fails to work as it should lies in the information gap between the potential opportunity in the underdeveloped country on the one hand and the availability of foreign industrial capital and know-how on the other."[42] He holds the view that "No matter how good the other parts of the program may be, the program is likely to fail if considerable emphasis is not given to a highly organized and hard-hitting promotion effort. There are many examples which support this conclusion. The industrial development of Puerto Rico, the most successful program so far in the world in attracting large numbers of outside investors, has been largely based on good promotion."[43] A little has been done about this in the past. The Nova Scotia Department of Trade and Industry maintains an organization, one of whose objects is to publicize the advantages of Nova Scotia to outside firms; and Industrial Estates Limited energetically pursues any firm which seems to be a prospect. But there are no signs that the message is getting through. Perhaps the methods have been wrong. The people who need to be persuaded – the businessmen who made the location decisions – must be very few in number. Occasional use of the ordinary blanket advertising media must be a very expensive and ineffective way of trying to reach them. Perhaps better results might be achieved by employing agents in the major centres (expatriate Maritime businessmen might be the best) to pick up information regarding new firms or branch plants which are under consideration. Perhaps one, great, well-publicized splurge in which irresistible bribes are offered to any firm undertaking to set up a plant during a short period would give the programme the shove it needed to start it moving, after which its own momentum might keep it going. This is a problem outside our field and one we must leave in the hands of the publicity man. Certainly, his job is not made easier by Nova Scotians' time-honoured practice of public self-debasement. While he is trying to present an image of Nova Scotia as an attractive and dynamic place in which to locate new industry, governments, Boards of Trade, and various other organizations, intent upon extracting more doles from the federal government, are painting the gloomiest possible picture of Nova Scotia as a depressed, isolated, and miserable area beset with insoluble problems.

42 *Policies and Methods for Industrial Development* (New York, 1965), p. 25.
43 *Ibid.*, p. 129.

13 Stimulating Demand
for Outputs

Up to now we have been considering only policies designed to reduce the cost of manufacturing in Nova Scotia. Another approach, and in principle just as appropriate, would be to stimulate the demand for Nova Scotian manufactured products. If prices of goods manufactured in Nova Scotia could be raised relative to the prices of similar goods produced in central Canada, then the comparative attraction of Nova Scotia as a location for manufacturing industry would be increased.

A start might be made by seeking to shift the preferences of local consumers towards Nova Scotian goods. Advertising is the obvious method to employ and from time to time attempts have been made to persuade consumers of the superiority of locally produced goods or to appeal to local patriotism. There is no evidence that they have had any appreciable effect. No doubt this is at least partly due to the short-lived and half-hearted nature of the campaigns. But the cost of doing an effective job in this respect would be colossal. Consumers have been conditioned by life-long advertising to buy branded goods produced mainly in central Canada or the United States, and long-term, large-scale advertising would be necessary to combat the now deeply ingrained belief, however irrational, that these national brands are superior. And local patriotism does not seem a potent force in the market place; consumers seldom seem prepared to buy a commodity they consider inferior merely because it was produced locally.[1]

1 The writer has encountered considerable bitterness on the part of manufacturers in Nova Scotia on this score. In particular, firms new to the region complain that the Nova Scotian consumer not only will give no preference to the products of a firm which has answered the call to come to the province, but seems to have a predisposition to believe that goods produced locally cannot be any good.

If trying to steer the preferences of local consumers to Nova Scotian manufactures is futile, attempts to influence consumers elsewhere in Canada or abroad is scarcely worth considering. However, a little might be done by designing the publicity being put out to promote Nova Scotian tourism so that some of the effect might brush off on manufacturing goods. For instance, if tourist promotion succeeded in familiarizing the public with a Nova Scotian emblem, this same emblem might be stuck or inscribed upon manufactured goods produced in the province. But we must leave the techniques of advertising to publicity experts. However, one thing needs stressing. What has just been said about the near futility of trying to bend consumers' preferences towards Nova Scotian manufactures in general was not intended to imply that products of individual firms should not be advertised. The facts of the market place, regrettable though they may be, dictate that most manufacturers must try to manipulate demand if they are to survive and prosper. Indeed, it is the neglect of modern marketing techniques which may well be at the root of the poor performance of many of Nova Scotia's manufacturers.

Instead of trying to promote Nova Scotian manufactures, the same effect might be achieved by damaging the competitive position of similar goods produced elsewhere. This would be an old game to play since "protection" of the home producer against the foreigner by means of tariffs, quotas, and other devices has been practised universally. Canada is already a high tariff country and the prices of imported goods which are competitive to Nova Scotian manufactures are made comparatively high; and so Canadian demand is pushed towards Nova Scotian manufactures. Where these import obstacles, however, produce the same benefit to manufactures of the Quebec-Ontario region, they are doing nothing to produce the effect for which we were searching. The protection would need to be directed against goods produced only or mainly in Nova Scotia. For instance, an increase in the tariff upon imports of the sorts of steel goods produced at the Sydney steel plant would tend to shift Canadian demand towards the Nova Scotian product.

The protection game, however, is not as simple to play as it once was. International agreements (particularly the General Agreement on Tariffs and Trade) make it difficult for Canada to increase tariffs and other barriers without inviting retribution. Anyway, protectionism is not an unmixed blessing and the fostering of high-cost industries behind tariff walls often has undesirable consequences in the long run.

One device to hamper the foreigner is sometimes used and could be extended: that is, for governments to give preference to home-produced goods in their purchasing. The federal government could (indeed it already does when it can) buy naval ships built by Canadian shipyards, even though they are more expensive than similar ships that could be bought abroad. And both federal and provincial governments could ensure that all the materials used in the construction of their buildings and roads, all the supplies used in the running of their offices, and so on, were produced in Canada. Where the goods involved are of the type that are mainly manufactured in Nova Scotia, then the prices of Nova Scotian goods would tend to rise and production in Nova Scotia would become more attractive relative to production elsewhere in Canada.

This device could be extended to give direct support to Nova Scotian manufacturers in their competition with their central Canadian competitors. If Nova Scotian municipalities requiring such things as central-heating equipment and furniture for their offices and schools would always buy those produced in Nova Scotia, if the Nova Scotian government would buy such things as cakes and chocolates for its office canteens only from local producers, and if the federal government would steer its contracts for shipbuilding and repairing to the Halifax shipyards, then the effect upon the demand for Nova Scotian manufactures would be considerable. This is indeed already done to some extent. The Nova Scotia Liquor Commission, for instance, imposes a higher mark-up on beer produced outside the province than it does on the locally produced brew.[2] But there are political barriers to extension of the practice. The federal government would be under pressure from local interests elsewhere in Canada to distribute its purchases more evenly and Nova Scotian provincial and municipal governments would be criticized by their tax-payers for spending more than necessary on the equipment and supplies they needed, and for buying goods of lower quality or poorer variety. And retaliation must be expected from other provinces. In the end, the only effect would be a balkanization of intra-Canadian trade, which could scarcely benefit any part of the country.

If improving the demand for Nova Scotian manufactures by making goods from elsewhere more expensive proves too difficult, might not something be done to stimulate the demand by securing a lowering of barriers to foreign markets? For instance, if a Canada–United States agreement similar to the 1965 Auto Agreement could be concluded to provide easy access to American markets for fish products with a

2 The governments in some provinces have a clearly enunciated policy of local preferences. For instance, the Quebec government only awards contracts to Canadian firms outside Quebec if their bids are at least 5 per cent below those put in by Quebec firms. Other provinces seem to give preference to local manufacturers without being so explicit or consistent about it.

higher manufacturing content (fishsticks, for instance), would not foreign demand for goods of which Nova Scotia is the main producer grow? The answer is undoubtedly "yes," but the prospects do not seem very good. When the same firms dominate an industry on both sides of the border, such agreements seem possible. In other circumstances, powerful entrenched interests would probably block extension of the idea.

Trying to stimulate the demand for products manufactured in Nova Scotia as a means of making that province at least as attractive as the Quebec-Ontario region in the minds of entrepreneurs and potential entrepreneurs does not seem to promise much success.

14 Breaking through the
Non-economic Barriers

Our discussion of possible policies to close the per capita gap between the Nova Scotian and Quebec-Ontario manufacturing industries has been concentrated upon economic measures. We should not, however, become so engrossed with economic policies that we lose sight of the fact that the continued retardation of Nova Scotia's manufacturing industry relative to that of Quebec-Ontario does not seem to be primarily the result of economic forces. Some firms now supplying the Quebec-Ontario market from plants located in that region would undoubtedly be worse off if their manufacturing activities were in Nova Scotia but, as our analysis of Part Two demonstrated, Nova Scotia does not seem to be a significantly inferior location for a large proportion of manufacturing activity. The different degrees of development of manufacturing industry in the two regions can only, it seems, be attributed to the relatively poor supply of entrepreneurship in Nova Scotia. And since the entrepreneur often supplies the senior management services to his firm, this inadequacy spills over into the labour supply.

While the supply of entrepreneurship, like the supply of any other factor of production, is properly classified as part of the economic conditions, an inquiry into why it should be relatively poor in any particular location draws us into fields which are the concern of sociologists and psychologists rather than of economists.[1] But observation of the local scene almost invariably seems to lead to the conclusion that the weak supply of business enterprise in Nova Scotia arises primarily from the nature of its social fabric which has been woven over many years of iso-

---

1 It seems to be one of the crosses that the economist must bear that just when a problem starts to become really interesting he has to hand it over to other social scientists, or else invade fields in which he is not particularly expert.

lation undisturbed by natural, military, political, or economic events; which has not been revitalized to any extent by immigration; and which has been impoverished by the continued exodus of its more qualified and virile offsprings. Within the province is an acceptance of the customary way of life and a reluctance to fight hard to achieve personal material advancement.[2] Coupled with this is a sense of dependency which convinces Nova Scotians of their inability to shape their own destinies. When disaster strikes in one part of the province, or the province as a whole drifts further from the economic level enjoyed elsewhere, the population and its leaders instinctively just cry out for aid from outside. They nearly always accept without examination that they cannot, and should not be expected to, find their own way out of their difficulties.[3]

The shortage of local entrepreneurs would not matter if outsiders were available to fill the void. But the horizon of most entrepreneurs and potential entrepreneurs seems to be small. They are usually unaware of, and seldom take steps to investigate, the circumstances and opportunities outside the area with which they are familiar. It takes a very special advantage, such as the supply of a natural resource not readily available locally, to coax them from their home ground.

If the obstacles to the development of Nova Scotia's manufacturing industry are really sociological or psychological, one's instinct is to make a frontal attack on them. There are certainly some ways of doing this. Outside entrepreneurs might be induced by publicity to examine business opportunities in the province. The minds of the young, and perhaps even of the older persons, of the province might be stimulated through education and training. Building up the infrastructure of the province might also help by ensuring that the population does not continue to live in, and be satisfied with, the old and inferior conditions. And governmental measures which contribute to the cosy, non-competitive conditions within the province could with benefit be swept away.

But direct attacks upon the sociological and psychological structure of the province are unlikely to produce results for a long time. Attitudes

2 Absence of the "rat-race" is no doubt one of the main reasons why visitors to the province are impressed with the relaxed friendliness of its population. If Nova Scotians deliberately choose this way of life, realizing and cheerfully accepting the lower standard of living which it almost inevitably implies, then there is no point in our concerning ourselves further, and there is no need for governmental action to close the economic gap with other parts of Canada. But they do not.

3 For an account of one such instance where economic disaster threatened a community in Cape Breton, see R. E. George, *Technological Redundancy in a Small Isolated Society* (Montreal, 1969).

are not built up overnight, nor can they be altered quickly. If we cannot wait ten or twenty years for results, we are forced back upon economic devices. Fortunately, if they are properly designed and provided with appropriate non-economic supports (good education and training, infrastructure improvements, and the like), they may be effective in undermining the social and psychological barriers to progress. It is therefore of great importance that economic measures should be chosen not just for the short-run relief they provide, but for the prospect they hold out for improving the underlying socio-psychological condition of the province. They must be capable of awakening the province from within and of stirring the imagination of outsiders. This is precisely what all previous regional development programmes have failed to do. Objectively, the ADIA grants and tax holidays, the MFRA transportation subsidies, the ADB grants for infrastructure improvement, the readiness of Industrial Estates Limited to build factories for rent and to make loans, municipal governments' willingness to grant relief from local taxation, and all the other baits dangled before firms considering setting up new manufacturing plants in Nova Scotia, make up an impressive package. But it is a complicated package which seems to have excited no one. Indeed, many businessmen appear to have been unaware of the details of the various schemes. What seems to be required is the gathering together of all these titbits into one big irresistible bait.

If there is to be just one big economic incentive, which should it be? In our previous discussion we found that the cheapest and most convenient methods would be capital grants or industrial estates. Each could be carefully directed with little administrative or political difficulty towards new manufacturing activity. But capital grants are now rather old hat and it would be difficult to stir the imagination of entrepreneurs and potential entrepreneurs with them. This leaves industrial estates, which have the special advantages that they reduce the entrepreneurial risk and waiting period between the time a firm decides to locate in Nova Scotia and the time it starts production, and they would have most beneficial effects upon the local construction industry and the producers of construction materials. They seem to be the obvious choice. If estates were built at appropriate centres of the province and offered rent free for a long period (say ten years), they might well produce the desired impact.

To achieve its maximum effect, the industrial estate-building must be done on a speculative basis.[4] Some decision has therefore to be made as to the type of firm which one is hoping to attract, since this will deter-

---

4 One of the principal advantages of this form of incentive is surrendered by IEL when it delays starting a building until a potential client declares his willingness to come to the province.

mine the general type of buildings to be erected. Here the criteria discussed in chapter 11 are relevant. Ideally, one should aim at firms which, from a cost point of view, are best suited to the province; so some research into the cost structures of various types of manufacturing industries should be undertaken. Industrial estates should also provide the greatest side-benefits at least cost; so some sort of public cost-benefit analysis of the various industries seems to be called for. No negative criteria should be established merely to safeguard existing firms from competition; existing Nova Scotian firms should have the same right as newcomers to move into industrial estates if they wish to extend their manufacturing capacity, but, if they choose not to do so, they should not be protected from other more enterprising firms.

Once the estates are built, some care would have to be taken to ensure that they were let to firms which promise some chance of success. Firms which have already shown by previous performance that they have good potential are to be preferred to those who were moving in as an attempt to escape impending disaster. But there is not too much to worry about on this count. Even with a rent-free building, an incoming firm has to make significant capital investment, which automatically keeps out those without serious intent and without substance; and even if a tenant fails, the only direct financial loss to the owner of the estate is the cost of maintaining the building while it is vacant and of preparing it for a new tenant. Since the annual cost of buildings seems to be about 5 per cent of manufacturing firms' costs,[5] the annual cost of new factories to house plants which would provide the required additional output would amount to about $50 million. Such a building programme could not, of course, be attempted in one year; spread over ten years, the cost in the first year would be less than $5 million and would rise to about $50 millions per annum at the end of the period.[6]

These may seem large figures, and are probably two or three times the cost of the MFRA subsidies, the ADIA grants, and the ADB projects. But that is simply because these programmes have been unsuccessful and Nova Scotia's manufacturing industry remains small.

This approach, in which all eggs are put in the one basket, will have a chance of succeeding only if entrepreneurs and potential entrepreneurs know about it. It is essential therefore that the programme be promoted by whatever techniques are necessary to achieve the desired impact.

No one can guarantee that this or any other approach would lead to

5 Firms in the Multiplant Firm Study indicated that the annual cost of buildings was rather more than half their total annual capital cost.
6 If based instead upon 1968 values, the scheme would eventually cost a little less than $80 million per annum.

Nova Scotia's manufacturing industry developing to a point at which its output per head of the province's population would be similar to that of the Quebec-Ontario region. Perhaps the socio-psychological barriers are so great that even a simple, highly attractive bait, such as the one just discussed, would not lead to a significant closing of the gap. If that should happen, it would be difficult to escape the conclusion that the case was hopeless, and that either the "natural" economic pressures be left eventually to erase the problem by emigration (with perhaps some government help to oil the wheels) or governments must reconcile themselves to some form of permanent dole system to maintain the province at its present relatively low level.

Appendixes

Appendix A

DESCRIPTION OF THE SURVEYS

THE MULTIPLANT FIRM STUDY

This study was carried out by the author to obtain from appropriate firms information on the production and distribution costs of factories in Nova Scotia compared with the corresponding costs of similar factories in the Quebec-Ontario region. It would have been ideal if identical factories run on similar lines could have been found, one of each pair being in Nova Scotia and the other being in Quebec or Ontario. But industry is not so conveniently organized as that. Factories nominally within the same industry are seldom of similar sizes, seldom use factors of production in the same proportions, seldom employ the same methods, and seldom operate plants of similar type and condition. And costing systems are so arbitrary that the analysis of costs figures of different firms is likely to be meaningless.

So the study resorted to the device of confining comparisons to factories controlled by the same firm, where roughly similar production methods, management policies, and costing systems might be expected. Also, because even factories of the same firm inevitably differ considerably, it relied upon the judgment of the firms' senior executives as to what costs would have been had the factories being compared been similar in every respect. The introductory letter sent to the presidents of the firms therefore contained the following explanation:

My wish is to be able to compare the actual costs of operation of your plant at [city or town in which Nova Scotian plant situated] with what they would be if it were located in a similar district in Quebec or Ontario within a radius of about 200 miles from Montreal or Toronto. If you actually have a factory operating within these radii in a district similar to [city or town in which Nova Scotian plant situated] and the scale and type of production and the type and condition of its plant make comparison possible, please use your actual costs as the basis of comparison. If, however, your factories are not similar, please compare the actual costs of your [city or town in which Nova Scotian plant situated] plant with what you might expect them to be if it were located in a similar district in Quebec or Ontario, within the radii mentioned.

Information so obtained was admittedly therefore largely subjective but, as senior executives are accustomed to making such judgments as part of their managerial duties, this method seemed to promise comparisons which were more meaningful than any based upon production or financial statistics related to dissimilar situations. In any event, it is what firms' senior executives believe to be true, rather than what is objectively true, which is important in policy-making. Further, the danger that the results might have been unduly influenced by estimates produced by one or two executives who were very wide of the mark was avoided by the use of medians instead of arithmetic means.

As far as could be discovered, twenty-seven firms maintained manufacturing plants in both Nova Scotia and Quebec or Ontario in 1962. In the latter part of that year, letters were sent to their presidents explaining the object of the study and asking them to provide the information sought by personal interview. The results were:

Firms whose president or other senior executive gave personal interviews and supplied all or most of the information required   12

Firms unable to arrange interviews at the appropriate time, but subsequently supplying, by written questionnaire (specimen attached at pp. 176–8), all or most of the information required   6

Firms unable or unwilling to supply information required   9

The eighteen firms that co-operated employed in their Nova Scotian plants 1,696 persons, of which 292 (18 per cent) were female. These plants had a combined output running at about $88 million in 1962 – that is, about 20 per cent of Nova Scotia's total production of manufactured goods. Eighty-seven per cent of this output stayed in the Atlantic provinces, 12 per cent was sent to Quebec or Ontario, the remaining one per cent going to the Prairies or to British Columbia. Eighty-six per cent of their raw materials came from abroad, 8 per cent from the Atlantic provinces, 6 per cent from Quebec and Ontario, and one per cent from western Canada.

The firms included in this study were selected solely because their first-hand experience of production in Nova Scotia and in either Ontario or Quebec appeared to make them uniquely suited to supply the information required. They were not chosen because they comprised a representative sample of all manufacturing industry. Consequently, there was always a danger that they might be special in some way. Perhaps they were firms to which labour costs were particularly important and so found the low wages in Nova Scotia attractive; perhaps their requirements of materials were modest so that the high cost of bringing them in mattered little; perhaps their materials were indigenous to Nova Scotia and expensive to carry to factories elsewhere; perhaps their materials could be imported from abroad into Nova Scotia more cheaply than into the more western parts of Canada; perhaps their product transportation costs were particularly high so that a factory in the Maritimes was needed to supply the local market; or perhaps their output was destined for export and so was better produced near a year-round port.

None of these dangers appeared to be real. Wages and salaries in these firms amounted to virtually the same proportion (22 per cent) of total costs as did wages and salaries for all Nova Scotian manufacturing firms; their material costs as a percentage of total costs (58 per cent) corresponded with the percentage applicable to firms in the two regions; only 8 per cent of their materials were obtained in the Maritimes; while most of their materials were imported, they were actually rather more expensive in Nova Scotia than they would have been in Quebec-Ontario; any special circumstances relating to transportation costs were negated by assuming that the Nova Scotian plants or their Quebec-Ontario counterparts would be supplying all the firms' existing markets; and only a small proportion of their output was sent abroad.

One further danger was present because information was to be obtained from a small sample of firms. It was known that while Nova Scotian units of production were on the average small relative to those elsewhere in Canada, there were a few which were giants by Nova Scotian standards. Had one such plant been included in the sample, there would have been the risk that all averages relating to the sample would in reality have been merely a repetition of that plant's characteristics. This was overcome by the use of medians (which were also necessary if the disclosure of confidential information was to be avoided). Medians did give rise to some statistical problems, but they overcame more than they created.

SPECIMEN OF MULTIPLANT FIRM QUESTIONNAIRE

COMPARATIVE COSTS OF OPERATION IN MANUFACTURING INDUSTRY,
NOVA SCOTIA AND ONTARIO OR QUEBEC

Part 1   *Details of Nova Scotia factory*

(a) *Address* ————————————————————————————————

(b) *Number of employees*

	Men	Women	Total
Factory			
Office			
Executives			
Total			

(c) *Products*

Product*	Annual value of sales
(i)———————	$
(ii)———————	$
(iii)———————	$
Total	$

*If range of products is large, please give details in broad groups only.

(d) *Destination of sales*

Percentage of total annual value of output

Maritimes	————————————%
Ontario and Quebec	————————————%
Prairies and BC	————————————%
Abroad	————————————%
Total	100%

Please mark by "x" those markets to which the products usually go **by** car load.

(e) *Sources of raw materials*

Percentage of total annual cost of raw materials

Maritimes	————————————%
Ontario and Quebec	————————————%
Prairies and BC	————————————%
Abroad	————————————%
Total	100%

Please mark by "x" those sources from which the materials usually **come** by car load.

(f) *Costs of operation*

Percentage of total costs

(i) Labour (including fringe benefits and training costs) ————————%
(ii) Executives (including fringe benefits and expenses) ————————%

(iii) Materials (cost at factory including freight charges,
    etc.)   ———————%
(iv) Electricity and water   ———————%
(v) Transportation of finished goods to customer   ———————%
(vi) Capital costs:
    (i) depreciation and obsolescence of buildings   ———————%
    (ii) depreciation and obsolescence of machinery, etc. ———————%
(vii) Taxes (municipal and provincial)   ———————%
(viii) Other costs (please specify) ——————— ———————%
               ———————— ———————%
               ———————— ———————%

(ix) Total   100%

Costs of training employees as percentage of labour
    costs   ———————%
Turnover of labour p.a. as percentage of labour force ———————%
Percentage of labour costs which results from em-
    ployee absences, whatever their cause   ———————%

Part 2   *Comparison of costs – Nova Scotia and Ontario or Quebec*
(Please see covering letter for explanation concerning basis for comparison.)
Have you a factory in Ontario or Quebec which is similar in size and type
of location, process, and plant to your Nova Scotia factory?————
If "yes," please give location—————————————————

(*a*) *Wage rate*
Average or representative rate per hour* in Nova Scotia as percentage of
rate for similar work in Ontario or Quebec
                    Factory personnel: ———————%
                    Office personnel: ———————%
(*If most of your employees are on piece-work, please use their average
earnings as basis for comparison.)

(*b*) *Labour productivity*
Output per hour of average Nova Scotia worker as percentage of output
per hour of his counterpart in Ontario or Quebec, assuming similar circumstances (e.g., similar machinery, similar type of operation, similar
management competency, etc.)
                    Factory personnel: ———————%
                    Office personnel: ———————%

(*c*) *Training costs*
(i) Training costs in Nova Scotia as percentage of
    training costs in Ontario or Quebec   ———————%
(ii) If not 100%, please indicate reasons for difference:

(*d*) *Absenteeism*
Costs arising from production dislocation and other
problems resulting from absenteeism (Nova Scotia as
percentage of Ontario or Quebec)   ———————%

(*e*) *Executive costs*
Level of salaries paid to executives in Nova Scotia as

percentage of salaries paid in Ontario and Quebec for
men of similar ability and responsibility   ————%
Is there any difficulty in obtaining executives of adequate ability for Nova Scotia factory?   ————

(f) *Materials costs*
Cost of materials in Nova Scotia as percentage of cost
of similar materials in Ontario or Quebec   ————%
How much of this difference is due to transportation
costs from your supplier to your factories?   ————%

(g) *Product transportation costs*
Supposing your Nova Scotia factory were called upon
to supply both its present market and also the customers who are now supplied from your Ontario or
Quebec factory (assuming it were capable of producing
sufficient output), how would costs of transportation
compare with those which would arise if it supplied
this same enlarged market but was located in Ontario
or Quebec? (Please answer by expressing the costs of
transportation from Nova Scotia as a percentage of
costs of transportation if located in Ontario or Quebec.)   ————%

(h) *Electricity and water costs*
Charges for electricity and water in Nova Scotia as
percentage of charges in Ontario or Quebec for similar
services.   ————%

(i) *Taxes*
Municipal and provincial taxes in Nova Scotia as percentage of those levied for similar operations in similar
location in Ontario or Quebec.   ————%

(j) *Capital costs*
(i) Costs of erecting factory in Nova Scotia as percentage of cost of similar factory in Ontario or
Quebec.   ————%
(ii) Cost of machinery and other factory equipment
in Nova Scotia as percentage of cost of similar equipment in Ontario or Quebec.   ————%

(k) *Other costs*
Are there any other costs not already dealt with above
which are greater or less in Nova Scotia *because of*
location (e.g., costs of holding larger inventories, costs
of maintaining local representatives, etc.). (Please express Nova Scotia costs as percentage of those of
Ontario or Quebec.)   ————%

THE SITE-CHOICE STUDY

In April and May 1965 the author obtained information by questionnaire from 360 firms which had set up new manufacturing plants in
Ontario or Quebec between 1959 and 1962. These firms were decided
upon by four selection processes:

(*a*) The first selection came by virtue of confining attention to the period 1959–62. The latest date might have been the end of 1964, this being the last issue of the DBS's *New Manufacturing Establishments in Canada*[1] (one of the two source documents) available when the study was begun. Included in the latest issues, however, would have been many firms which had not yet commenced production, and many which had been recorded in error; and most of the rest would have been tiny bakeries, dairies, dressmakers, and similar establishments which would have been unlikely to supply information of interest. So the line was drawn at the end of 1962. The period might have been started in 1956, the year to which the first issue of *New Manufacturing Establishments in Canada* referred, or perhaps even a little earlier. However, in order to cut down the magnitude of the task, the starting date was taken as the beginning of 1959.

There seems no reason for believing that the period 1959–62 was so unusual that what happened during those four years was different from normal experience. In Canada, 1959 was a year of partial recovery from the mild depression of 1957–8, 1960 produced a slight downturn, while 1961 saw a new revival which gained strength in 1962. None of the fluctuations was very pronounced and these four years comprised a fairly smooth plateau midway between the most prosperous and least prosperous post-war levels.

(*b*) The second selection came when the Canadian Manufacturers' Association compiled its *Canadian Trade Index* for 1964.[2] The publishers of the *Index* "... have access to and check various provincial directories and pamphlets, industrial commission notices and bulletins of various cities across Canada, commercial directories of all sorts, government publications covering the manufacturing industries and industrial development, D.B.S. reports, trade papers and magazines, newspapers, periodicals and publicity releases. In addition, their division and branch offices in all parts of Canada are always on the alert for new companies ..." so it does not seem likely that many new establishments escape their notice. They then select those which "... manufacture in Canada a product which has more than local distribution." This results in the elimination of such local establishments as "... small bakeries, dairies, milliners, dressmakers, some categories of small job printers and various small cottage industries." Also, as the *Index* has been developed primarily as a buyer's guide, its publishers have "... not been particularly interested in establishments whose sales are 'tied' to

1 Catalogue number 31-002.
2 The following quotations are from information obtained by letter from the editor of *Canadian Trade Index*.

one customer, as, for example, may be the case with a large number of smaller sawmills and the like." Firms which survive the publisher's test are invited to complete and return a questionnaire giving certain details, including the location of plants, types of products, size of labour force, and names of officers.

(c) The third selection was made when the firms receiving the *Canadian Trade Index* questionnaire chose to reply or not. Firms that do reply are, without charge or obligation, listed in the *Index*. This free publicity presumably acts as an incentive which encourages firms to respond. Yet only "... about 30% of firms reply when first sent a questionnaire ... There do not appear to be any special characteristics which stand out between those firms who do reply and those who do not. The distribution of those replying is similar as to size and variety to those who do not reply. If any conclusion could be drawn it may be that those who reply ... are most aware of the value of being listed in an industrial directory."

Eight per cent of the firms which were listed in *New Manufacturing Establishments in Canada* as having set up new plants in Quebec and Ontario between 1959 and 1962 had found their way into the 1964 *Index*. Bearing in mind the 30 per cent response the publishers receive from their questionnaires, it seems that they pick up and consider appropriate to their *Index* about 25 per cent of all new firms listed in *New Manufacturing Establishments in Canada*. Considering that they deliberately exclude nearly all small bakers' shops and sawmills along with other establishments of merely local importance, that there is known to be a high mortality among new firms, and that about 9 per cent of the firms listed by the DBS are subsequently found to have been entered in error,[3] it again seems to follow that they catch most.

What takes more explaining is that firms included in the *Index* which set up new plants in Ontario during 1959–62 outnumber by 2.5:1 those setting up new plants in Quebec during the same period. When asked about this, the editor said there was "... no intentional or other reason for having a special geographical emphasis in compiling the *Canadian Trade Index*" and that they were "... limited only by the number of sources available in each area of Canada from which relevant information can be gleaned." Part of the answer may be, however, that a higher proportion of Quebec's new establishments were in the clothing industry (17 per cent compared with Ontario's 5 per cent) which, judging from the response to the questionnaire used in this

---

3 In the 1959–62 issues of *New Manufacturing Establishments in Canada*, 9,104 new establishments were listed. During the same period 829 were removed because they were inappropriate to that publication and 1,367 were removed because they had gone out of business.

study, seems to contain a lot of reluctant form-fillers,[4] or in the wood industry (12 per cent compared with Ontario's 9 per cent) which probably contains many sawmills which would be ignored by the *Index* as being of only local interest or because they were producing for one buyer.

(*d*) The fourth selection occurred when the firms which were sent the questionnaire[5] used in this study (those listed in *New Manufacturing Establishments in Canada* as having set up new establishments between 1959 and 1962 and also listed in the 1964 edition of *Canadian Trade Index*), elected to reply or not. Details of the numbers and proportions of questionnaires which were returned by firms in various industries and of various sizes appear in Tables A/1 and A/2. Of the 634 questionnaires sent out, thirteen were returned by the Post Office as undeliverable (presumably because the firms concerned had gone out of business) and seventy-four were returned with a note to the effect that the firms had not set up new manufacturing establishments in the period under review. This left 547 firms which were, or may have been, appropriate to the study. Of these, 360 (66 per cent) returned the questionnaires completed with all or nearly all the information requested in a useable form. As there must have been a considerable number of firms which were not appropriate to the study among those which did not reply (one would expect firms to be disinclined to return blank forms), the actual response may well have been appreciably higher than 66 per cent.

The degree of response varied from 42 per cent in the case of clothing firms to 80 per cent in petroleum and coal. It also varied according to the size of the firm, the larger firms being more responsive than smaller ones; which is what one might expect since the larger firms are more accustomed to dealing with paper-work. There was little difference between the level of response from firms setting up new plants in Ontario (66 per cent) and in Quebec (60 per cent).

The four processes by which the firms for this study were selected, therefore, seem bound to have overweighted the sample with larger and more successful firms. We must expect, therefore, that the conclusions overstate the degree of consideration given to alternative locations. Firms in general are probably even more myopic than the study suggested.

A more difficult part of the study to interpret is that which deals with the reasons which prompted the choice of particular sites by those firms which considered sites in more than one province. The results were:

4 See Table A/1.
5 See pp. 187–8 for a specimen of the form used. Those questionnaires sent to firms in Quebec were printed in both English and French.

TABLE A/1

Response to the Site-Choice Study questionnaire: analysis by industries

Industry	Responses from[a] (number of firms)			Questionnaires returned		Not returned	Total sent out	Percentages	
	Quebec	Ontario	Total	"Not applicable"	"Undeliverable"			Of total sent out[b]	Of all new plants[c]
Food and beverages	6	18	24	6	—	8	38	75	3
Tobacco	1	1	1	—	—	1	2	50	17
Rubber	1	2	3	—	1	1	5	75	16
Leather	2	4	6	1	1	3	11	60	7
Textiles	1	8	9	1	—	8	18	53	6
Knitting	6	1	7	2	—	4	13	64	5
Clothing	5	3	8	3	1	11	23	42	1
Wood	3	11	14	2	—	4	20	78	2
Furniture	6	8	14	1	2	12	29	54	2
Paper	6	6	12	3	—	5	20	71	24
Printing	1	5	6	2	1	4	13	60	1
Primary metals	3	7	10	7	—	6	23	63	11
Metals fabricating	8	46	54	13	2	38	107	59	8
Machinery	5	39	44	4	—	12	60	79	23
Transportation	1	18	19	1	—	10	30	66	11
Electrical	16	22	38	4	—	10	52	79	28
Non-metallic mineral	3	8	11	8	1	12	32	48	4
Petroleum and coal	—	4	4	—	—	1	5	80	25
Chemicals	9	31	40	10	1	14	65	74	19
Miscellaneous	8	28	36	6	3	23	68	61	7
Total	90	270	360	74	13	187	634	66[d]	6[e]

a The first three columns refer to the number of new plants which wholly or partly completed the questionnaire; 78 per cent of the responses were wholly completed, and most of the rest were almost completed.

b Responses wholly or partly completed as percentage of total questionnaires sent out *minus* those returned "not applicable" or "undeliverable."

c Responses wholly or partly completed as percentage of all new plants set up 1959–62. Data on the new plants were taken from the starred entries in *New Manufacturing Establishments in Canada, June 1959–December 1962*, 31–002; adjustment of earlier data was necessary to bring them on to the 1961 industrial classification.

d Quebec = 60 per cent; Ontario = 68 per cent.

e Quebec = 3 per cent; Ontario = 9 per cent.

TABLE A/2

Response to the Site-Choice Study questionnaire: analysis by number of persons employed

Number of persons employed	Responses[a] from			Questionnaires returned			Total sent out	Percentages of total sent out[b]
	Quebec	Ontario	Total	"Not applicable"	"Undeliverable"	Not returned		
		(number of firms)						
Less than 25	37	139	176	33	9	116	334	60
25–49	19	48	67	13	1	25	106	73
50–99	12	27	39	8	—	8	55	83
100–199	4	20	24	1	2	6	33	80
200–499	8	8	16	4	—	3	23	84
500–999	—	6	6	1	—	—	7	100
1,000 and over	3	7	10	4	—	—	14	100
Not known[c]	7	15	22	10	1	29	62	43
Total	90	270	360	74	13	187	634	66[d]

a Wholly or partly completed responses; 78 per cent were wholly completed and most of the rest were almost completed.
b Responses wholly or partly completed as percentage of total questionnaires sent out *minus* "not applicable" and "undeliverable" responses.
c The number of persons employed was not given in *Canadian Trade Index* (Toronto, 1964).
d Quebec = 60 per cent; Ontario = 68 per cent.

Reason	Number of firms[6]
Availability of labour	20
Wage rates	5
Attitude and energy of labour	2
Availability of executives	3
Cost of materials	15
Local ancilliary firms	15
Cost of product transportation	24
Satisfying rush orders	7
Contact with customers	20
Availability of sites	14
Cost of sites	3
Municipal taxation	1
Combining management of more than one plant	10
Language barriers	4
Personal preferences	3
Location of competitors	1
Municipal publicity	1
Political considerations	1

This study was not, of course, the first of its kind and previous ones have produced such apparently contradictory results that they must be regarded with misgiving. In some, transportation costs turned out to be the most important locational force; in others they seemed very subsidiary. Some suggested that non-monetary considerations were paramount; others that they had little bearing on the matter.

These apparent conflicts seem to arise because, while empirical studies spotlight those factors which may sometimes be important in determining the choice of a site, they cannot eliminate other factors as irrelevant. For instance, G. E. McLaughlin and S. Robock examined firms belonging to industries which had moved from the northeastern United States to the south.[7] They found that the main factor influencing the firms' choice was product transportation costs. That product transportation costs are sometimes important is therefore established. But the availability of electric power, which was not mentioned by the firms studied, may also have been of importance. Had there been no supply of electricity in the areas where these firms eventually settled, it seems likely that most would have gone elsewhere. But the factor was not mentioned because all the sites seriously considered by the firms were presumably adequately supplied. Everything depends upon which sites the firms are comparing with the sites they actually chose. The com-

6 Each firm was invited to give the three most important reasons influencing its choice of site. Consequently, most firms appear in the table three times.
7 *Why Industry Moves South* (Washington, 1949).

parisons will normally be between the chosen sites and the other one or two that were near alternatives. So it seems likely that when the firms examined by McLaughlin and Robock gave the reasons "markets," "raw materials," or "labour," they were explaining why they chose one site in the south in preference to another in the south – not why they chose the south in preference to the northeast. It would be strange if they had left the thickly populated and highly industrialized northeast and gone several hundred miles to the south to reduce product transportation costs.

Similarly, W. F. Luttrell examined the experience of eighty-five manufacturers who had established branch plants away from the districts of their parent plants.[8] He found that one of the three main factors was the speed of getting products to their markets. But as the main home markets for shoes, hosiery, clothing, textiles, and most of the other products made by the firms examined would certainly be in the larger cities, it seems unlikely that they really meant what they seemed to mean. They were presumably comparing the advantages of the sites they had actually chosen with others which they had considered outside the main cities. But even if all possible sites had been considered, we are not much further on, for it seems likely that there were sites away from the main cities from which transportation might have been even quicker, but which were probably rejected because labour was not available locally. Transportation, combined with adequate labour, was therefore probably the important consideration – not transportation alone.

And again, M. L. Greenhut found that marketing considerations (product transportation costs and pattern of demand) were relevant to only one out of the eight firms he examined.[9] But this should not be taken to imply that these considerations are irrelevant to location. If asked to name a region from which product transportation costs would have been prohibitive, almost certainly each firm could have done so. What the firms presumably meant was that, in the particular (limited) region they considered as possible locations for their new plants, there was not very much to choose between alternative sites in respect of product transportation and demand pattern, and the eventual choice was therefore governed by other considerations.

Such then seems to be one of the limitations of empirical studies relating to the choosing of sites. There appears to be no prospect of overcoming it. Each time a firm has to decide about the location of a

8 *Factory Location and Industrial Movement* (London, 1962).
9 *Plant Location in Theory and Practise: The Economics of Space* (Chapel Hill, NC, 1956).

new plant, it has an almost infinite number of possibilities. The site eventually chosen will be the one which appears to the firm's policy-makers to be the best of those which seem worth considering – which will usually be a small number within a limited geographical area. But it is unlikely to be superior in all respects. Suppose three sites are considered, site A, site B, and site C. All are equally desirable as far as wage-rates and the availability of labour are concerned, but differ in other characteristics as follows:

	Product transportation	Raw materials transportation	Non-pecuniary advantages
	(Ranking in order of desirability[10])		
Site A	1	2	2
Site B	2	3	1
Site C	3	1	3

Because the firm sets great store by non-pecuniary advantages, it immediately rules out site C. Then, after pondering the relative advantages of site A and site B, it chooses the former. If it is then asked to explain why it chose site A, it will probably reply that it was because of product transportation and raw materials transportation. If, on the other hand, site A and site C had been the last two in the contest and the former had again won, then the firm's answers would have probably specified product transportation and non-pecuniary advantages. In either circumstances, the level of wage-rates and the availability of labour would probably not have been mentioned at all; yet they might well have been critical factors and site A would have been immediately ruled out had it not been satisfactory in these respects.

It seems impossible to compile a questionnaire which would allow one to disentangle all the respects in which the chosen site was superior or inferior to all other sites (and then it should logically be extended to find out in what respects all other sites were so inferior that they were not even considered). Personal interviews with firms might well produce more satisfactory results but, even then, in the end the results would be in the form of a great hodge-podge of comparisons which could not be aggregated.

The best that can be said of such empirical exercises is that, if enough of them are carried out and enough firms examined, a general impression of what is important and what is not may emerge. If some factors are mentioned consistently, then one would eventually be justi-

10 For instance, site A is the most satisfactory site in respect of product trans-portation, inferior to site C but superior to site B in respect of raw materials, transportation, and so on.

fied in thinking that they are the ones that most often influence site-choice. It is much more difficult, however, to rule out a factor as unimportant. If it is seldom mentioned, it may mean merely that it is of fairly uniform quality in the locations which, for other reasons, are worthy of consideration. The Site-Choice Study can no more escape the above criticism than can earlier studies, though its unusually large coverage makes its results perhaps just a little more acceptable.

SPECIMEN OF SITE-CHOICE STUDY QUESTIONNAIRE

Reference: ——————————

1 When you set up the new plant:

    (a) Was it the first time your firm had produced in Canada?
        (Please tick on   —————— Yes
        appropriate line) —————— No

    (b) If not, in which provinces or territories did you previously operate?
        (Please tick on   —————— Newfoundland
        appropriate line) —————— Nova Scotia
                        —————— Prince Edward Island
                        —————— New Brunswick
                        —————— Quebec
                        —————— Ontario
                        —————— Manitoba
                        —————— Saskatchewan
                        —————— Alberta
                        —————— British Columbia
                        —————— Yukon
                        —————— North West Territories

2 How did you decide upon the province in which to start up your new operation? Was it:
    (Please tick on   —————— Because the choice seemed obvious to you and
    appropriate line)   consideration of other provinces did not appear
                               justified?
                  —————— After considering in a general way the possibility
                           of locating in other provinces?
                  —————— After carrying out detailed estimates of probable
                           costs and revenue of locating in other provinces?
    (If you have ticked the first of these three, please omit questions 3 and 6.)

3 Which other provinces or territories did you consider?
    (Please tick on   —————— Newfoundland
    appropriate line) —————— Nova Scotia
                        —————— Prince Edward Island
                        —————— Quebec
                        —————— Ontario
                        —————— Manitoba
                        —————— Saskatchewan
                        —————— Alberta
                        —————— British Columbia
                        —————— Yukon
                        —————— North West Territories

4 Have you or any of your colleagues who were parties to the decision about where your new premises should be situated visited Nova Scotia during the last 10 years?
(Please tick on   ———— Yes
appropriate line)   ———— No

5 Did you retain consultants to advise you upon the best location for your new operations?
(Please tick on   ———— Yes
appropriate line)   ———— No

6 Which were the most important factors which made you decide to set up in your present location?
(Please place 1, 2, or 3 on the lines opposite the three principal factors, in order of importance)
————   The availability of the types of labour you required.
————   The level of wage-rates.
————   The attitude and energy of workers.
————   The availability of executives locally.
————   The cost of obtaining materials.
————   The cost of obtaining fuel.
————   The costs of electricity and other public utility service.
————   The availability of local firms to which you could easily put out work or which could quickly supply any special requirements you might have.
————   The cost of transporting your products to customers.
————   The ability to satisfy customers' rush orders.
————   The ability to maintain close personal contact with customers.
————   The tendency of provincial and municipal public authorities to favour local suppliers.
————   The cost of machinery and other equipment.
————   The availability of a suitable site or premises in your present location at the time you were planning your new operations.
————   The cost of suitable sites or premises.
————   The availability of investment capital.
————   The rate of interest at which investment capital was available.
————   The incentives offered by governments by way of corporation tax relief, assistance in obtaining funds for investment or provision of sites or premises.
————   The level of municipal taxation (after taking into account any tax concessions that municipalities might have granted).
————   The ease of combining the management of your new business with any other business you were already operating.
————   The absence of language barriers which might have created management difficulties.
————   The personal preferences of yourself and your colleagues concerning the area in which you wished to live.
————   Other reasons (please specify)————————————————————
        ——

(Note: If only one or two factors were important, please insert only '1', or '1' and '2', as the case may be.)

7 Approximately how many persons do you have on the payroll of your new premises?
———————— persons

THE SELECTED LOCAL AREAS STUDY

In 1961 the writer undertook a survey of manufacturing in the Colchester, Pictou, and Cape Breton counties of Nova Scotia for the Joint Federal-Provincial Committee on Seasonal Unemployment in Nova Scotia. Information was obtained by personal interviews from seventy-one firms, which was almost a complete coverage of manufacturing firms employing fifteen or more persons. The managers of the main Nova Scotian branches of three chartered banks, and the senior executives of two public utilities and a railway company were also interviewed. While most of the information obtained had no bearing on the subject matter of this book, its findings have been used in one or two places where they seemed relevant.

Because it confined its attention to firms employing fifteen or more persons, the study was concerned with only the largest 20 per cent of firms in the areas covered. Consequently, the proportion of firms surveyed that used consultants, experimented with product modification, and otherwise showed initiative may be expected to be higher than would be present in a random sample. Similarly, the absence of capital-raising difficulties among the firms surveyed does not rule out the possibility that smaller firms might have had problems in this connection.

It should also be noted that none of the firms was from the Halifax-Dartmouth area, the main industrial centre of Nova Scotia. There seems no reason, however, to suppose that this omission influenced the conclusions of which use has been made in this book.

Appendix B

BASIC STATISTICS RELATING TO
NOVA SCOTIA, QUEBEC, AND ONTARIO
USED IN COMPILATION OF TABLES IN
PARTS ONE, TWO, AND THREE

For notes, see pages 211–13.

TABLE B/1
Estimated mid-year populations, 1946–62

	Nova Scotia	Quebec (thousands)	Ontario
1946	608	3,629	4,093
1947	615	3,710	4,176
1948	625	3,788	4,275
1949	629	3,882	4,378
1950	638	3,969	4,471
1951	643	4,056	4,598
1952	653	4,174	4,788
1953	663	4,269	4,941
1954	673	4,388	5,115
1955	683	4,517	5,266
1956	695	4,628	5,405
1957	701	4,769	5,636
1958	709	4,904	5,821
1959	719	5,024	5,969
1960	727	5,142	6,111
1961	737	5,259	6,236
1962	746	5,366	6,342

SOURCE: DBS, *Population by Sex and Age, 1921–1966*, 91–511.
Tables 1/1, 1/3, 1/5, and 7/2 were derived in part from the above data.

TABLE B / 2

Ages of population, 1951 and 1961

Age	Nova Scotia		Quebec		Ontario	
	1951	1961	1951	1961	1951	1961
0–4	82,540	91,239	541,524	671,256	514,722	740,193
5–9	68,816	84,760	463,444	624,074	399,292	674,519
10–14	58,131	80,329	361,140	568,065	325,300	593,037
15–19	51,533	64,239	337,501	467,426	315,685	436,883
20–24	46,275	49,311	340,902	369,633	352,360	386,966
25–29	46,773	43,956	332,855	362,567	387,239	422,651
30–34	46,503	43,360	296,455	373,258	351,043	459,825
35–39	44,938	45,041	276,376	357,641	340,797	469,312
40–44	37,974	44,577	241,914	308,093	302,342	397,251
45–49	30,156	41,139	203,128	275,074	268,129	360,749
50–54	27,666	34,742	172,529	236,260	247,478	309,795
55–59	25,014	27,333	139,618	189,663	210,308	258,327
60–64	21,340	23,564	116,198	149,900	182,484	218,511
65–69	19,440	21,341	93,161	116,923	155,097	180,063
70 and over	35,485	42,076	138,936	189,378	245,266	328,010
Total	642,584	737,007	4,055,681	5,259,211	4,597,542	6,236,092

SOURCE: DBS, *Census of Canada, 1951*, vol. I, Table 19; *Census of Canada, 1961*, vol. VII, part 1, no. 4 (99–514).

Table 1/6 was derived from the above data.

TABLE B / 3

Destination of immigrants arriving from abroad, 1946–62

	Nova Scotia	Quebec	Ontario
1946	4,604	9,712	29,604
1947	2,294	8,272	35,543
1948	2,813	24,687	61,621
1949	1,626	18,005	48,607
1950	1,167	13,575	39,041
1951	2,035	46,033	104,842
1952	2,702	35,318	86,059
1953	2,206	34,294	90,120
1954	2,207	28,419	83,029
1955	1,841	22,117	57,563
1956	1,639	31,396	90,662
1957	2,789	55,073	147,097
1958	1,786	28,443	63,853
1959	1,087	24,816	55,976
1960	1,210	23,774	54,491
1961	901	16,920	36,518
1962	989	19,132	37,210

SOURCE: DBS, *Canada Year Book*, 11–202, appropriate years.
Table 1/5 was derived in part from the above data.

TABLE B / 4

Personal income, 1946–62

	Nova Scotia	Quebec (millions of dollars)	Ontario
1946	412	2,339	3,738
1947	421	2,606	4,017
1948	415	2,951	4,570
1949	438	3,062	4,904
1950	463	3,317	5,285
1951	499	3,763	6,093
1952	553	4,152	6,749
1953	591	4,469	7,209
1954	607	4,647	7,397
1955	627	4,847	7,918
1956	675	5,318	8,617
1957	721	5,742	9,399
1958	757	6,071	9,978
1959	804	6,353	10,566
1960	848	6,736	11,023
1961	882	7,272	11,490
1962	934	7,803	12,252

SOURCE: DBS, *National Accounts, Income and Expenditure, 1926–1956*,
13–502; DBS, *National Accounts, Income and Expenditure, 1960* and
1965, 13–201.
Table 1/1 was derived in part from the above data.

TABLE B / 5

Transfer payments, excluding interest on
government debt, 1946–62

	Nova Scotia	Quebec	Ontario
		(millions of dollars)	
1946	62	250	375
1947	49	205	269
1948	44	225	266
1949	47	246	280
1950	49	285	292
1951	48	274	306
1952	63	352	441
1953	65	389	464
1954	69	443	525
1955	72	467	541
1956	73	483	549
1957	85	555	655
1958	105	709	811
1959	115	681	956
1960	126	776	1,051
1961	135	966	1,132
1962	146	1,053	1,202

SOURCE: DBS, *National Accounts, Income and Expenditure*, appropriate
years.
Table 1/1 was derived in part from the above data.

TABLE B / 6

Labour force by industrial sectors, 1961

	Nova Scotia	Quebec	Ontario
Agriculture	12,038	131,197	168,775
Forestry	4,296	42,441	17,935
Fishing and trapping	7,493	3,029	2,185
Mines, quarries, and oil wells	10,105	25,854	42,660
Manufacturing	34,081	466,443	643,284
Construction	15,524	126,361	153,866
Transportation, communication, and other utilities	24,962	161,268	195,223
Trade	36,763	248,038	370,540
Finance, insurance, and real estate	5,652	62,163	98,454
Community, business, and personal service industries	44,953	350,864	467,127
Public administration and defence	36,816	99,194	181,263
Unspecified and undefined	4,136	51,267	51,703
Total	236,819	1,768,119	2,393,015

SOURCE: DBS, *Census of Canada 1961*, vol. III, part 2, no. 1 (94–518).
Table 1/2 was derived from the above data.

TABLE B / 7

Labour force in principal industries, 1961

Nova Scotia	
Fish products	5,275
Iron and steel mills	3,918
Saw mills	2,529
Shipbuilding and repairing	2,228
Pulp and paper mills	1,549
Dairy products	1,526
Printing and publishing	1,288
Aircraft and parts	1,191
Bakery products	1,077
Other food processors	973
Knitting mills	963
Sash and door and planing mills	934
Beverage manufacturing	797
Petroleum refining	531

Quebec and Ontario	Quebec	Ontario
Pulp and paper	28,974	21,900
Bakery products	15,633	17,409
Iron and steel mills	4,423	27,777
Truck bodies and trailers	408	31,161
Printing and publishing	9,653	20,815
Men's clothing	20,213	8,333
Women's clothing	22,038	6,401
Dairy products	10,310	16,790
Commercial printing	10,462	16,489
Aircraft and parts	16,209	9,755
Miscellaneous machinery and equipment	7,494	17,954
Communications equipment	12,510	10,421
Beverages	10,700	11,203
Shoe factories	11,985	8,599

SOURCE: DBS, *Census of Canada, 1961*, vol. III, part 2, no. 1 (94–518).

Table 1/4 was derived from the above data.

TABLE B / 8

Number of establishments, manufacturing industry, 1946–62

	Nova Scotia	Quebec	Ontario
1946	1,397	10,818	11,424
1947	1,480	11,223	11,860
1948	1,440	11,122	12,127
1949	1,480	11,579	12,951
1950	1,482	11,670	12,809
1951	1,474	11,861	13,025
1952	1,533	12,024	13,172
1953	1,591	12,132	13,114
1954	1,526	12,191	13,178
1955	1,524	12,194	13,276
1956	1,402	12,112	13,215
1957	1,356	12,250	13,580
1958	1,297	11,828	13,276
1959	1,314	11,584	13,081
1960[a] (a)	1,295	12,042	13,486
(o)	1,278	11,961	13,387
1961[a] (a)	1,249	11,892	13,476
(o)	1,002	10,955	12,081
1962[a] (a)	1,249	11,769	13,667
(o)	1,030	11,104	12,586

SOURCE: DBS, *General Review of the Manufacturing Industries of Canada*, 31–201 (data for 1946–8 appeared in *The Manufacturing Industries of Canada*).

Tables 1/3, 3/10, 10/2, 10/3, and 10/4 were derived in part from the above data. For Tables 10/2, 10/3, and 10/4, the original figures (o) were used for 1961 and 1962; Tables 1/3 and 3/10 were based upon adjusted figures (a) for those years.

TABLE B / 9

New establishments,[b] manufacturing industry, 1957–62

	Nova Scotia	Quebec	Ontario
1957[d]	59	1,053	967
1958	38	682	807
1959	65	760	803
1960	44	774	749
1961	72	679	758
1962	47	645	826

SOURCE: DBS, *New Manufacturing Establishments in Canada*, 31–002, appropriate years.

Table 10/3 was derived in part from the above data.

TABLE B / 10

Types of ownership, manufacturing industry, 1946–62

	Nova Scotia		Quebec		Ontario	
	Individual and partnership	Incorporated companies	Individual and partnership	Incorporated companies	Individual and partnership	Incorporated companies
			(number of establishments)			
1946	913	280	7,172	3,017	6,753	4,486
1947	1,095	353	7,363	3,308	6,885	4,781
1948	1,037	369	7,174	3,424	7,111	4,825
1949	1,009	395	7,080	3,606	7,176	5,072
1950	988	410	6,992	3,783	6,916	5,100
1951	970	425	7,017	3,959	6,915	5,328
1952	1,028	426	7,075	4,042	6,940	5,447
1953	1,076	438	7,010	4,223	6,682	5,662
1954	1,017	435	6,952	4,359	6,547	5,872
1955	981	446	6,782	4,479	6,374	6,057
1956	870	442	6,595	4,570	6,066	6,289
1957	822	452	6,555	4,747	6,072	6,674
1958	773	438	6,057	4,851	5,666	6,803
1959	780	449	5,816	4,857	5,419	6,895
1960ᶜ	775	475	6,167	5,333	5,686	7,509
1961ᶜ	538	441	5,360	5,189	4,726	7,203
1962ᶜ	533	471	5,273	5,441	4,898	7,538

SOURCE: DBS, *General Review of the Manufacturing Industries of Canada.*
Table 10/2 was derived in part from the above data.

TABLE B / 11

Number of persons employed, manufacturing industry, 1946–62

	Nova Scotia		Quebec		Ontario	
	Male	Female	Male	Female	Male	Female
1946	25,164	4,560	253,420	103,856	370,871	127,249
1947	25,547	4,738	273,284	106,165	406,878	130,703
1948	25,681	4,667	276,769	107,197	421,020	130,638
1949	24,819	4,492	279,416	110,859	425,881	131,309
1950	24,015	4,464	278,717	111,446	434,333	132,180
1951	26,108	4,404	303,091	114,091	464,295	135,138
1952	28,523	4,848	313,699	115,999	476,165	133,531
1953	27,438	4,602	322,432	119,123	491,388	143,166
1954	25,367	4,244	309,938	114,157	464,194	134,720
1955	25,766	4,452	312,799	116,776	476,955	136,917
1956	26,251	4,686	325,807	120,330	499,123	142,067
1957	26,581	4,949	328,903	120,480	502,608	141,637
1958	24,312	4,698	312,091	117,267	470,375	135,987
1959	23,512	4,656	313,919	117,318	478,414	137,332
1960ᵉ (a)	23,846	4,814	316,172	117,519	466,770	134,067
(o)	23,791	4,815	316,485	117,464	468,703	134,764
1961ᵉ (a)	22,558	4,903	310,109	117,808	461,932	135,982
(o)	22,009	4,792	306,918	116,811	457,373	134,042
1962ᵉ (a)	23,981	5,046	316,264	118,910	477,296	143,281
(o)	24,355	5,072	335,308	125,581	511,881	150,866

SOURCE: DBS, *General Review of the Manufacturing Industries of Canada.*
Tables 1/4, 3/2, 3/6, 3/8, and 3/10 were derived in part from the above data. In every case, adjusted figures (a) were used for 1961 and 1962.

TABLE B / 12

Number of employees in establishments employing fifteen or more persons, manufacturing industry, 1946-62

	Nova Scotia	Quebec	Ontario
1946	24,567	324,327	462,379
1947	24,729	344,297	499,550
1948	25,230	349,283	513,495
1949	24,101	354,847	518,071
1950	23,352	354,966	527,934
1951	25,265	380,372	559,525
1952	28,240	392,771	569,530
1953	26,749	403,939	594,314
1954	24,708	386,713	558,685
1955	25,332	392,434	573,227
1956	26,404	409,031	601,297
1957	27,090	411,452	602,449
1958	24,697	392,647	565,682
1959	23,836	395,077	576,500
1960c	24,499	396,707	562,759
1961c	23,353	389,577	553,403
1962c	26,598	432,887	630,544

SOURCE: DBS, *General Review of the Manufacturing Industries of Canada.*
Table 3/7, n. (b), was derived in part from the above data.

TABLE B / 13

Number of wage-earners in establishments employing fifteen or more persons, manufacturing industry, last pay weeks in October, 1946-63

	Nova Scotia		Quebec		Ontario	
	Male	Female	Male	Female	Male	Female
1946e	19,037	3,311	182,022	73,134	283,189	84,743
1947e	18,055	3,104	195,790	74,835	313,456	89,075
1948	17,850	2,963	196,187	76,187	318,039	85,928
1949	16,860	2,861	189,243	77,267	309,669	87,589
1950	17,300	2,973	198,571	80,221	334,065	90,380
1951	20,371	3,108	214,248	76,795	337,805	81,139
1952	21,900	3,333	219,608	82,884	350,704	86,905
1953	20,008	3,011	218,972	80,078	351,646	92,211
1954	19,000	3,028	206,149	77,543	326,799	83,752
1955	19,543	2,978	211,551	81,750	349,067	90,288
1956	20,537	3,392	222,959	83,134	360,103	93,202
1957	21,022	3,501	220,328	81,209	347,302	87,452
1958	19,122	3,304	201,215	78,803	328,820	85,066
1959	18,699	3,317	211,895	83,465	340,820	88,660
1960	19,249	3,512	216,022	82,965	327,433	85,490
1961f						
1962f						
1963	21,358	3,926	222,160	84,866	364,163	102,406

SOURCE: DBS, *Earnings and Hours of Work in Manufacturing,* 72-204, appropriate years.
Tables 3/3 and 3/5 were derived in part from the above data.

TABLE B / 14

Number of salaried employees in establishments employing fifteen or more persons, manufacturing industry, last pay weeks in October, 1946–63

	Nova Scotia		Quebec		Ontario	
	Male	Female	Male	Female	Male	Female
1946ᵉ	1,760	750	32,735	15,701	48,841	28,007
1947ᵉ	1,898	782	33,429	15,722	54,709	29,216
1948	1,918	733	35,396	16,622	57,889	30,123
1949	1,798	728	37,695	17,008	60,992	31,021
1950	2,003	742	41,600	17,609	72,206	33,526
1951	2,242	796	47,002	19,069	80,302	35,744
1952	2,640	852	52,098	20,267	88,489	37,856
1953	2,638	887	53,426	21,247	93,594	40,456
1954	2,395	856	53,613	20,961	95,693	40,339
1955	2,504	882	58,334	21,553	101,075	41,242
1956	2,648	965	62,029	22,866	108,757	44,280
1957	2,745	1,014	62,784	23,738	112,004	45,055
1958	2,728	959	63,467	22,612	108,855	42,379
1959	2,801	999	64,037	23,166	104,736	42,376
1960	3,074	1,127	66,781	24,176	107,556	42,841
1961ᶠ						
1962ᶠ						
1963	3,508	1,161	70,399	24,914	118,204	45,854

SOURCE: DBS, *Earnings and Hours of Work in Manufacturing.*
Tables 3/3 and 3/5 were derived in part from the above data.

TABLE B / 15

Wages and salaries, manufacturing industry, 1946–62

	Nova Scotia	Quebec	Ontario
		(thousands of dollars)	
1946	43,060	565,986	845,217
1947	46,113	662,838	1,037,977
1948	52,553	756,216	1,210,640
1949	54,687	809,579	1,305,544
1950	54,888	851,335	1,412,999
1951	63,976	1,005,602	1,669,387
1952	75,245	1,125,945	1,844,186
1953	76,391	1,225,573	2,017,982
1954	71,740	1,214,661	1,954,767
1955	76,556	1,271,078	2,088,906
1956	83,949	1,396,415	2,310,634
1957	90,635	1,477,828	2,430,676
11958	86,006	1,476,606	2,412,655
1959	87,694	1,546,933	2,564,684
960ᵃ (a)	92,318	1,616,817	2,577,502
(o)	92,280	1,620,314	2,585,677
1961ᵃ (a)	90,074	1,637,148	2,617,827
(o)	88,919	1,626,572	2,597,408
1962ᵃ (a)	98,491	1,736,086	2,818,754
(o)	103,123	1,887,095	3,078,766

SOURCE: DBS, *General Review of the Manufacturing Industries of Canada.*
Tables 3/1 and 3/2 were derived in part from the above data; in each case, adjusted figures (a) were used for 1961 and 1962.

TABLE B / 16

Wages and salaries paid by establishments employing fifteen or more persons, manufacturing industry, 1946–62

	Nova Scotia	Quebec	Ontario
		(thousands of dollars)	
1946	38,257	527,539	799,246
1947	40,467	617,942	984,006
1948	46,993	707,493	1,150,205
1949	48,853	758,453	1,240,352
1950	48,612	797,867	1,344,372
1951	57,003	944,899	1,593,176
1952	68,176	1,060,266	1,761,447
1953	68,708	1,153,887	1,928,435
1954	64,322	1,141,756	1,862,936
1955	68,922	1,194,868	1,992,432
1956	76,288	1,316,124	2,209,881
1957	82,657	1,390,792	2,318,387
1958	77,998	1,386,329	2,293,847
1959	79,323	1,454,324	2,445,575
1960^c	83,751	1,520,930	2,458,927
1961^c	81,363	1,531,228	2,473,541
1962^c	95,956	1,802,750	2,967,598

SOURCE: DBS, *General Review of the Manufacturing Industries of Canada.*
Table 3/7, n. (*b*), was derived in part from the above data.

TABLE B/17

Average weekly earnings of wage-earners in establishments employing fifteen or more persons, manufacturing industry, last pay weeks in October, 1946–63 (dollars)

	Nova Scotia			Quebec			Ontario		
	Male	Female	All wage-earners	Male	Female	All wage-earners	Male	Female	All wage-earners
1946[e]	33.90	17.18	31.44	34.95	19.49	30.51	37.09	20.53	33.26
1947[e]	37.47	17.62	34.58	39.66	22.02	34.82	42.70	24.13	38.57
1948	40.66	20.25	37.74	43.80	25.11	38.60	47.10	26.92	42.86
1949	42.87	19.94	39.56	45.19	25.93	39.61	48.88	28.45	44.34
1950	42.98	20.89	39.74	48.15	27.65	42.21	53.33	30.69	48.46
1951	48.30	22.14	44.77	53.58	29.37	47.26	58.60	33.66	53.87
1952	50.41	23.89	46.89	57.74	32.00	50.64	63.60	36.78	58.27
1953	53.15	23.45	49.27	59.72	32.67	52.48	65.00	37.74	59.34
1954	52.41	23.01	48.37	60.28	33.80	53.04	66.54	38.56	60.83
1955	55.62	24.70	51.53	63.69	35.53	55.84	69.25	40.06	63.25
1956	58.19	25.88	53.61	67.56	37.46	59.39	73.39	41.69	66.87
1957	61.70	25.24	56.50	68.24	37.38	59.93	75.38	42.25	68.71
1958	62.31	28.09	57.27	70.50	39.37	61.74	78.32	44.87	71.45
1959	67.49	29.35	61.74	74.55	40.74	64.99	82.58	46.35	75.10
1960	68.26	29.23	62.24	75.93	41.85	66.47	83.79	46.80	76.13
1961[f]									
1962[f]									
1963	73.34	33.36	67.13	84.33	47.35	74.11	95.03	52.25	85.64

SOURCE: DBS, *Earnings and Hours of Work in Manufacturing.*

Table 3/5 was derived in part from the above data.

TABLE B / 18

Average weekly earnings of salaried employees in establishments employing fifteen or more persons, manufacturing industry, last pay weeks in October, 1946–63 (dollars)

	Nova Scotia			Quebec			Ontario		
	Male	Female	All salaried employees	Male	Female	All salaried employees	Male	Female	All salaried employees
1946[e]	46.86	23.54	39.89	53.30	26.53	44.57	54.19	25.87	43.82
1947[e]	53.44	25.67	45.34	59.09	28.95	49.45	62.01	28.84	50.46
1948	56.49	27.29	48.42	62.20	31.52	52.39	65.20	31.40	53.63
1949	59.45	28.29	50.47	64.41	33.05	54.66	66.81	32.74	55.32
1950	61.20	29.18	52.55	68.13	34.41	58.10	71.40	34.84	59.81
1951	67.83	31.95	58.43	75.77	37.32	64.67	79.67	39.49	67.29
1952	68.54	34.74	60.30	79.92	40.52	68.88	85.77	42.24	72.73
1953	72.01	35.48	62.82	84.12	42.33	72.23	89.28	44.23	75.69
1954	76.73	35.64	65.91	88.64	44.83	76.32	93.91	45.88	79.67
1955	76.48	37.88	66.43	91.26	46.74	79.25	96.52	48.03	82.47
1956	82.64	39.06	71.00	96.89	49.40	84.10	102.19	50.18	87.14
1957	89.06	41.16	76.14	102.24	51.59	88.34	107.75	52.91	92.02
1958	92.58	42.67	79.60	106.18	53.83	92.43	111.44	55.16	95.67
1959	94.33	44.10	81.13	110.63	55.49	95.98	116.08	56.90	99.04
1960	97.69	45.29	83.63	114.21	57.62	99.17	119.71	59.45	102.55
1961[f]									
1962[f]									
1963	105.38	50.20	91.66	126.90	63.96	110.45	132.47	65.88	113.86

SOURCE: DBS, *Earnings and Hours of Work in Manufacturing.*
Table 3/5 was derived in part from the above data.

TABLE B/19

Weekly hours of work of wage-earners in establishments employing fifteen or more persons, manufacturing industry, last pay weeks in October, 1946–63

	Nova Scotia			Quebec			Ontario		
	Male	Female	All wage-earners	Male	Female	All wage-earners	Male	Female	All wage-earners
1946e	46.0	43.6	45.7	47.1	41.2	45.4	44.0	38.8	42.8
1947e	46.2	43.4	45.8	47.1	40.7	45.4	44.2	38.8	43.0
1948	46.0	44.5	45.8	46.8	40.9	45.2	43.9	38.9	42.9
1949	44.8	42.6	44.5	46.3	40.2	44.5	43.8	39.4	42.8
1950	45.0	43.7	44.8	46.7	40.6	44.9	44.0	39.5	43.0
1951	43.4	42.9	43.3	44.8	37.8	43.0	42.4	37.9	41.6
1952	42.4	42.5	42.4	45.5	40.1	44.0	42.8	39.3	42.1
1953	41.7	41.2	41.6	44.4	38.5	42.8	42.0	38.7	41.4
1954	41.4	39.3	41.1	43.7	38.7	42.3	41.8	38.6	41.2
1955	41.6	39.9	41.4	44.7	39.8	43.3	42.1	39.3	41.6
1956	41.3	41.0	41.3	44.5	39.7	43.2	41.9	39.1	41.3
1957	41.0	38.7	40.7	42.7	37.9	41.4	40.9	37.9	40.3
1958	40.5	40.9	40.5	42.9	38.8	41.8	41.6	39.0	41.0
1959	41.7	40.2	41.5	43.6	39.0	42.3	41.8	39.2	41.3
1960	41.2	37.8	40.7	43.0	38.8	41.8	41.5	38.6	40.9
1961f									
1962f									
1963	41.6	39.8	41.3	43.6	39.0	42.3	42.4	39.1	41.7

SOURCE: DBS, *Earnings and Hours of Work in Manufacturing*.
Tables 3/3 and 3/5 were derived in part from the above data.

TABLE B / 20

Weekly hours of work of salaried employees in establishments employing fifteen or more persons, manufacturing industry, last pay weeks in October, 1946–63

	Nova Scotia			Quebec			Ontario		
	Male	Female	All salaried employees	Male	Female	All salaried employees	Male	Female	All salaried employees
1946[e]	44.1	40.7	43.1	42.5	39.6	41.5	41.3	39.2	40.5
1947[e]	42.6	40.0	41.9	41.3	39.1	40.6	40.8	38.6	40.0
1948	42.4	39.9	41.7	41.4	39.0	40.6	40.6	38.4	39.8
1949	40.9	39.6	40.5	41.1	38.8	40.4	40.4	38.3	39.7
1950	41.0	40.1	40.8	40.5	38.4	39.8	39.8	38.1	39.3
1951	42.3	40.2	41.7	40.3	38.1	39.7	39.5	37.9	39.0
1952	43.2	39.8	42.3	40.0	38.2	39.5	39.6	37.7	39.0
1953	40.9	39.2	40.5	39.7	37.9	39.2	39.2	37.6	38.7
1954	41.6	38.6	40.8	39.4	37.8	39.0	39.2	37.7	38.8
1955	42.0	38.4	41.1	39.7	37.9	39.2	39.3	37.8	38.8
1956	41.3	38.3	40.5	39.4	37.8	39.0	39.1	37.7	38.7
1957	40.5	37.9	39.8	38.8	37.5	38.4	38.9	37.6	38.5
1958	39.3	37.4	38.8	38.7	36.9	38.2	38.7	37.4	38.4
1959	39.3	37.7	38.9	38.7	37.6	38.4	38.8	37.5	38.5
1960	39.3	37.3	38.8	38.7	37.5	38.4	38.7	37.5	38.4
1961[f]									
1962[f]									
1963	39.5	37.5	39.0	38.2	37.2	38.0	39.0	37.5	38.6

SOURCE: DBS, *Earnings and Hours of Work in Manufacturing.*
Tables 3/3 and 3/5 were derived in part from the above data.

TABLE B / 21

Cost of materials used,[e] manufacturing industry, 1946-62

	Nova Scotia	Quebec	Ontario
		(thousands of dollars)	
1946	100,354	1,297,009	2,001,901
1947	111,354	1,601,056	2,651,698
1948	140,762	1,954,112	3,118,084
1949	135,842	2,027,794	3,256,455
1950	147,131	2,225,476	3,598,821
1951	172,115	2,696,639	4,334,394
1952	183,141	2,745,618	4,387,431
1953	180,544	2,816,373	4,560,135
1954	161,295	2,806,248	4,412,537
1955	175,194	3,152,541	5,014,225
1956	214,779	3,605,522	5,683,753
1957	238,287	3,570,909	5,827,318
1958	217,264	3,597,785	5,704,319
1959	223,016	3,749,732	6,190,618
1960[a] (a)	224,959	3,846,030	6,129,671
(o)	220,293	3,881,173	6,126,027
1961[a] (a)	223,614	4,045,078	6,434,649
(o)	206,463	3,982,420	6,337,293
1962[a] (a)	256,825	4,409,664	7,232,223
(o)	242,585	4,353,341	7,176,221

SOURCE: DBS, General Review of the Manufacturing Industries of Canada.
Table 4/1 was derived in part from the above data; adjusted figures (a) were used for 1961 and 1962.

TABLE B / 22

Consumption of purchased electricity,
manufacturing industry, 1949-62

	Nova Scotia	Quebec	Ontario
		(millions of kilowatt-hours)	
1949[d]	231	15,777	6,951
1950	231	16,719	8,250
1951	288	18,711	9,748
1952	300	20,437	9,059
1953	312	21,679	9,249
1954	327	22,473	8,977
1955	334	22,721	10,084
1956	367	21,646	10,806
1957	350	21,403	11,555
1958	389	25,128	11,599
1959	397	24,987	13,107
1960	435	29,441	13,421
1961[h] (a)	383	19,020	13,715
(o)	358	18,811	13,334
1962[h] (a)	402	17,947	14,644
(o)	376	17,750	14,237

SOURCE: DBS, General Review of the Manufacturing Industries of Canada.
Table 5/2 was derived in part from the above data; adjusted figures (a) were used for 1961 and 1962.

TABLE B / 23

Cost of purchased electricity, manufacturing industry, 1946–62

	Nova Scotia	Quebec	Ontario
		(thousands of dollars)	
1946	1,498.3	39,657	28,692
1947	1,719.0	45,002	32,472
1948	1,843.8	46,817	33,604
1949	1,851.7	48,089	33,958
1950	1,916.6	51,882	39,095
1951	2,294.0	60,136	46,031
1952	2,388.4	66,135	49,659
1953	2,626.8	72,348	57,989
1954	2,553.4	73,450	59,987
1955	2,771.8	77,377	67,160
1956	3,078.3	80,757	73,077
1957	3,319.1	81,860	78,419
1958	3,089.9	90,606	78,228
1959	2,887.3	91,201	86,932
1960	3,175.7	94,104	91,156
1961[h] (a)	3,443.8	83,072	94,311
(o)	3,134.2	80,068	90,270
1962[h] (a)	3,217.2	85,132	100,812
(o)	2,928.0	82,054	96,492

SOURCE: DBS, *General Review of the Manufacturing Industries of Canada.*

Tables 5/1 and 5/2 were derived in part from the above data; in each case, adjusted figures (a) were used for 1961 and 1962.

TABLE B / 24

Consumption of electricity generated for own use, manufacturing industry, 1949–62

	Nova Scotia	Quebec	Ontario
		(millions of kilowatt-hours)	
1949[d]	137	819	1,799
1950	143	789	1,845
1951	157	835	1,952
1952	167	799	1,920
1953	186	775	2,073
1954	159	836	2,153
1955	163	898	1,907
1956	46	1,476	1,974
1957	179	1,600	1,862
1958	110	1,521	2,206
1959	111	1,758	1,903
1960	49	1,986	2,083
1961[c]	155	10,797	1,906
1962[c]	167	10,659	1,876

SOURCE: DBS, *General Review of the Manufacturing Industries of Canada.*

TABLE B/25

Monthly electricity bills for unrestricted twenty-four-hour power, 1962 (dollars; consumption, k.w.h. per month)

	Billed load 5 k.w.			Billed load 50 k.w.			Billed load 100 k.w.		
	500	1,000	1,500	5,000	10,000	15,000	10,000	20,000	30,000
Halifax	17.50	24.75	32.00	175.00	247.50	320.00	350.00	495.00	640.00
Montreal	12.72	15.37	16.96	127.20	153.70	169.60	241.68	292.03	322.24
Toronto	12.82	14.53	16.24	128.25	145.35	162.45	246.50	290.70	324.90

SOURCE: DBS, *Electricity Bills for Domestic, Commercial and Small Power Service, 1962*, 57–203.
Table 5/3 was derived from the above data.

TABLE B / 26

Cost of purchased fuel,[j] manufacturing industry, 1946–62

	Nova Scotia	Quebec	Ontario
		(thousands of dollars)	
1946	5,202	35,314	64,646
1947	6,211	46,594	83,289
1948	7,732	64,162	104,585
1949	7,604	60,984	104,837
1950	9,059	66,795	116,896
1951	9,723	75,449	124,905
1952	10,595	75,838	123,977
1953	8,925	73,417	128,255
1954	8,246	77,036	126,780
1955	7,890	82,079	135,770
1956	10,268	100,293	156,279
1957	12,737	105,321	168,407
1958	10,965	92,771	163,671
1959	11,152	88,520	175,178
1960	9,175	85,266	161,111
1961[l] (a)	6,460	73,240	142,236
(o)	6,154	69,496	137,044
1962[l] (a)	7,263	76,745	151,295
(o)	6,919	72,822	145,773

SOURCE: DBS, *General Review of the Manufacturing Industries of Canada.*
Table 4/2 was derived in part from the above data; adjusted figures (a) were used for 1961 and 1962.

TABLE B / 27

Value-added by manufacture,[k] 1946–62

	Nova Scotia	Quebec	Ontario
		(thousands of dollars)	
1946	71,739	1,125,992	1,659,285
1947	84,936	1,324,398	2,136,014
1948	95,774	1,534,215	2,486,868
1949	102,294	1,651,630	2,708,554
1950	97,781	1,798,320	3,068,142
1951	119,487	2,083,934	3,569,400
1952	130,715	2,288,643	3,811,107
1953	127,917	2,424,647	4,130,126
1954	129,778	2,448,028	3,930,730
1955	139,646	2,622,333	4,426,655
1956	159,820	2,888,149	4,868,570
1957	175,683	2,947,898	5,047,711
1958	176,998	2,970,775	4,914,074
1959	161,452	2,998,776	5,332,082
1960[a] (a)	178,952	3,175,748	5,317,213
(o)	174,808	3,172,770	5,319,684
1961[a] (a)	166,143	3,220,868	5,536,034
(o)	159,218	3,207,856	5,429,853
1962[a] (a)	179,869	3,481,327	6,110,540
(o)	174,613	3,465,633	6,006,765

SOURCE: DBS, *General Review of the Manufacturing Industries of Canada.*
Tables 1/3 and 3/8 were derived in part from the above data; in both cases, adjusted figures (a) were used for 1961 and 1962.

TABLE B / 28

Selling value of factory shipments,[1] 1946–62

	Nova Scotia	Quebec	Ontario
		(thousands of dollars)	
1946	178,793	2,497,972	3,754,524
1947	204,219	3,017,049	4,903,473
1948	246,112	3,599,306	5,743,141
1949	247,592	3,788,497	6,103,805
1950	255,887	4,142,473	6,822,954
1951	303,619	4,916,157	8,074,731
1952	326,840	5,176,235	8,372,174
1953	320,012	5,386,785	8,876,505
1954	300,073	5,395,787	8,533,167
1955	331,130	5,922,367	9,617,643
1956	384,398	6,622,503	10,655,099
1957	427,299	6,679,595	11,078,593
1958	411,929	6,754,798	10,864,028
1959	398,664	6,916,200	11,668,461
1960[a] (a)	416,849	7,194,063	11,710,373
(o)	406,182	7,206,096	11,685,676
1961[a] (a)	403,349	7,450,035	12,197,996
(o)	375,307	7,327,258	11,957,330
1962[a] (a)	450,944	8,069,813	13,544,866
(o)	426,677	7,936,346	13,342,557

SOURCE: DBS, *General Review of the Manufacturing Industries of Canada.*

Tables 3/1, 4/1, 4/2, 5/1, 6/1, 6/2, and 10/1 were derived in part from the above data; for Tables 5/1, 6/1, 6/2, and 10/1, the original figures (o) were used for 1961 and 1962; Tables 3/1, 4/1, and 4/2 were based upon adjusted figures (a) for those years.

TABLE B / 29

Capital investment, manufacturing industry, 1946–62

	Nova Scotia	Quebec	Ontario
		(millions of dollars)	
1946	8.1	106.7	197.9
1947	8.2	175.6	277.4
1948	12.6	188.1	293.3
1949	8.9	164.2	240.2
1950	7.6	152.5	217.9
1951	12.4	198.5	395.2
1952	16.9	230.9	477.2
1953	13.3	185.1	499.4
1954	9.9	203.9	416.3
1955	22.1	264.1	411.8
1956	25.2	336.7	630.1
1957	17.7	375.8	675.9
1958	12.5	300.6	503.2
1959	15.0	318.8	502.4
1960[c]	27.0	304.6	554.8
1961[c]	40.8	292.3	534.2
1962[c]	19.4	333.7	648.2

SOURCE: Department of Trade and Commerce, *Private and Public Investment Outlook*, appropriate years.

Table 6/1 was derived in part from the above data.

TABLE B / 30

Inventories held at year end, manufacturing industry, 1954–62[m]

	Nova Scotia		Quebec		Ontario	
	Raw materials	Finished goods	Raw materials	Finished goods	Raw materials	Finished goods
			(millions of dollars)			
1954[d]	27.5	17.3	556.0	266.7	753.0	538.8
1955	27.2	15.5	574.9	281.1	783.9	536.1
1956	29.5	21.0	625.5	324.8	892.9	614.7
1957	37.7	16.5	644.5	326.5	872.7	611.9
1958	32.7	16.8	600.0	337.3	830.4	610.3
1959	30.6	14.0	609.7	336.6	891.5	661.8
1960[e]	33.6	15.4	574.0	352.5	802.6	661.5
1961[e]	33.7	23.8	602.5	437.5	842.6	845.4
1962[e]	30.8	23.3	624.4	444.8	948.3	900.4

SOURCE: DBS, *General Review of the Manufacturing Industries in Canada.*
Table 6/2 was derived in part from the above data.

TABLE B / 31

Taxable corporation income, manufacturing industry,
1957–62

	Nova Scotia	Quebec	Ontario
		(millions of dollars)	
1957[a]	26.3	464.3	758.4
1958	20.0	429.7	712.7
1959	22.3	464.7	845.5
1960	25.2	447.3	768.1
1961	24.7	440.8	773.1
1962	26.5	482.4	897.5

SOURCE: Department of National Revenue, *Taxation Statistics,*
appropriate years.
Table 10/1 was derived in part from the above data.

TABLE B / 32

Business failures reported under Bankruptcy and Winding
Up acts, manufacturing industry, 1955–62

	Nova Scotia	Quebec	Ontario
1955	1	207	51
1956	1	234	81
1957	2	247	99
1958	3	255	72
1959	1	251	99
1960	2	188	104
1961	1	164	98
1962	—	189	111

SOURCE: Data supplied by DBS.
Table 10/4 was derived in part from the above data.

TABLE B / 33

Truck traffic, net ton-miles and revenue, by for-hire trucks,[a] 1957–62

	Nova Scotia		Quebec		Ontario	
	Net ton-miles (millions)	Revenue (thousands)	Net ton-miles (millions)	Revenue (thousands)	Net ton-miles (millions)	Revenue (thousands)
1957[a]	113.0	$11,412	1,687	$135,170	2,547	$174,229
1958	65.7	6,734	2,007	157,791	4,114	268,155
1959	49.2	6,832	2,101	157,996	4,504	287,439
1960	64.6	7,733	1,880	154,350	3,938	271,089
1961	74.8	7,450	1,875	157,006	4,677	292,802
1962	74.1	7,803	2,071	169,654	4,447	284,344

SOURCE: DBS, *Motor Transport Traffic: Atlantic Provinces*, 53–208; *Quebec*, 53–209; *Ontario*, 53–210. Table 7/3 was derived from the above data.

TABLE B / 34

Mileage of paved highways and rural roads and expenditure on their construction, 1946–62

	Nova Scotia		Quebec		Ontario	
	Mileage	Expenditure (thousands)	Mileage	Expenditure (thousands)	Mileage	Expenditure (thousands)
1946	959	$3,561	4,638	$22,181	8,054	$22,713
1947	949	8,947	4,949	26,489	8,509	26,687
1948	1,084	12,592	5,521	46,087	8,908	25,556
1949	1,084	12,977	6,109	31,341	9,461	28,654
1950	1,215	14,113	6,433	26,253	10,102	34,347
1951	1,301	8,234	6,843	50,630	10,304	50,583
1952	1,395	4,961	7,581	65,577	10,882	64,842
1953	1,544	6,318	7,962	49,758	11,398	58,353
1954	1,679	4,832	8,345	48,179	12,189	46,583
1955	1,860	7,088	8,995	64,963	11,515	69,085
1956	2,038	10,432	9,361	70,436	12,192	95,694
1957	2,242	15,509	10,285	87,249	12,181	120,256
1958	2,561	17,527	10,938	121,934	14,108	172,480
1959	2,842	21,661	12,098	117,985	14,436	181,722
1960	3,189	22,308	12,804	90,256	16,171	180,983
1961	3,358	18,010	13,119	80,869	19,931	167,907
1962	3,518	15,885	13,266	110,507	20,315	166,718

SOURCE: DBS, *Road and Street Mileage and Expenditure*, 53–201 (prior to 1958 entitled *Highway Statistics*).

Table 7/2 was derived in part from the above data.

NOTES TO TABLES IN APPENDIX B

a (*o*) denotes data contained in publication for years indicated; (*a*) denotes data adjusted to make them comparable with previous years. The statistical changes which made adjustments necessary in order to restore the comparability were as follows:

In 1960 a new standard industrial classification was introduced. This resulted in the exclusion of some establishments (such as publishers of non-commercial magazines) and the inclusion for the first time of some establishments (such as poultry processors, dental laboratories, book publishers, and electroplaters). Also, coke produced in integrated steel mills, which had previously been counted in both the selling value of factory shipments and in materials used, was omitted from both.

In 1961 a new "establishment" concept was introduced. Many plants which had previously been treated as two or more separate establishments belonging to different industries were henceforth considered as a single establishment belonging to the industry to which the major part of its production was proper. Also, further reshuffling of industries took place (for instance, poultry processors were again excluded, as were many sawmills); and the basis for valuation of the production of sawmills was changed.

In 1962 data relating to the numbers of workers and the salaries and wages paid to them were split into "manufacturing activity" (which excluded many working proprietors and others included as employees or workers in previous years) and "total activity" (which included some salesmen and others previously excluded from manufacturing statistics). Original figures (*o*) relating to employees, wages, and salaries listed in the tables refer to "total activity."

The method of adjustment was as follows:

if

     1959 (*o*) = value given for 1959 in 1959 issue of source document;

     1959 (*r*) = value given for 1959 in 1961 issue of source document;

     1960 (*o*) = value given for 1960 in 1960 issue of source document;

     1960 (*r*) = value given for 1960 in 1961 issue of source document;

     1960 (*a*) = adjusted value for 1960;

     1961 (*o*) = value given for 1961 in 1961 issue of source document;

     1961 (*r*) = value given for 1961 in 1962 issue of source document;

1961 (a) = adjusted value for 1961;

1962 (o) = value given for 1962 in 1962 issue of source document;

1962 (a) = adjusted value for 1962;

then

1960 (a) = 1960 (r) × 1959 (o)/1959 (r);

1961 (a) = 1961 (o) × 1959 (o)/1959 (r);

1962 (a) = 1962 (o) × 1959 (o)/1959 (r) × 1961 (o)/1961 (r).

b Figures are inflated by about 10 per cent because some entries in the source document were included in error. Some referred to old establishments which merely changed their names in the years indicated, some to establishments which were not proper to manufacturing industry, and others were inappropriate for other reasons.

c Data for 1960, 1961, and 1962 are not strictly comparable with those for previous years (see n. (a)), but information is not available to permit their adjustment.

d Data for earlier years are not available.

e Data for 1946 and 1947 refer to the last pay weeks in November.

f Surveys were not undertaken in 1961 and 1962.

g Materials actually used during the year, priced at laid-down cost at plant. Work done by outside establishments is included.

h In 1961 published data (o) excluded electricity purchased by firms with factory shipments valued at less than $500,000. Figures in the table have therefore been adjusted (a) to include an estimate of the electricity used by these smaller firms, by the following method:
If 1960 (o), 1961 (o), and 1962 (o) = cost of electricity used by establishments with shipments of $500,000 or more in 1960, 1961, and 1962 respectively, and 1960 (a), 1961 (a), and 1962 (a) = estimated cost of electricity used by all establishments in 1960, 1961, and 1962, then 1961 (a) = 1961 (o) × 1960 (a)/1960 (o), and 1962 (a) = 1962 (o) × 1960 (a)/1960 (o). Data for 1961 and 1962 are not strictly comparable with those for preceding years due to changes in the concept of the establishment. Data were not available, however, to permit adjustment for these changes.

i Data relating to fuel are subject to the same qualifications as n. (h) describes for electricity. In addition, after 1959, fuel produced in the petroleum industry for its own use was excluded.

j Fuel actually used during year, priced at laid-down cost at plant.

k Up to 1951 value-added was gross value of production minus the cost of fuel, electricity, and materials. For 1952 and 1953 it was based upon the selling value of factory shipments less the same deductions. In 1954 and subsequent years the value of any decrease in inventories of goods finished or in process was also deducted, or the value of any increase was added.

l Before 1952 data refer to value of goods produced however disposed of, including any put to stock. In 1952 and subsequent years they refer to the value of shipments from the factories even if not produced in the year indicated.

m Includes only inventories held at plant or plant warehouses. Goods purchased for resale without further processing are excluded.

n Before 1957 profit was counted in the province where the return was filed, which was normally where the head office of the firm was situated. Since the majority of interprovincial firms had their head offices in Quebec or Ontario, the figures for those two provinces were inflated by profits attributable to plants elsewhere. After 1957 the profits of such firms were allocated in proportion to the numbers of persons employed in each province.

o Carried in trucks registered in the province indicated.

Index

This book

was designed by

ANTJE LINGNER

under the direction of

ALLAN FLEMING

and was printed by

University of

Toronto

Press